KILLERS, KIDNAPPERS, GANGSTERS AND GRASSES

Killers, Kidnappers, Gangsters and Grasses

On the Frontline with the Metropolitan Police

DICK KIRBY

PEN & SWORD TRUE CRIME

First published in Great Britain in 2022 by
Pen & Sword True Crime
An imprint of
Pen & Sword Books Ltd
Yorkshire – Philadelphia

ISBN 978 1 39907 432 2

Printed in the UK by CPI Group (UK) Ltd, Croydon, CR0 4YY.

Pen & Sword Books Limited incorporates the imprints of Atlas,
Archaeology, Aviation, Discovery, Family History, Fiction, History,
Maritime, Military, Military Classics, Politics, Select, Transport, True
Crime, Air World, Frontline Publishing, Leo Cooper, Remember
When, Seaforth Publishing, The Praetorian Press, Wharncliffe Local
History, Wharncliffe Transport, Wharncliffe True Crime, White Owl
and After the Battle.

For a complete list of Pen & Sword titles please contact

PEN & SWORD BOOKS LIMITED
47 Church Street, Barnsley, South Yorkshire, S70 2AS, England
E-mail: enquiries@pen-and-sword.co.uk
Website: www.pen-and-sword.co.uk
or
PEN AND SWORD BOOKS
1950 Lawrence Rd, Havertown, PA 19083, USA
E-mail: Uspen-and-sword@casematepublishers.com
Website: www.penandswordbooks.com

'The Golden Rule is, there are no Golden Rules'
   George Bernard Shaw, *Maxims for Revolutionaries*

To the ReCIDivists and all retired police officers of
the Golden Era:
   This – as you'll recall – is the way it was.

★　★　★

To all serving members of the Metropolitan Police:
This – as you may be disappointed to learn – is the way it
never will be again.

★　★　★

And to Ann:
'I would not wish any companion in the world, but you'
   The Tempest, Act III, Scene I

Praise for Dick Kirby's Books

Contents

About the Author

Dick Kirby was born in 1943 in the East End of London and joined the Metropolitan Police in 1967. Half of his twenty-six years' service was spent as a detective with the Yard's Serious Crime Squad and the Flying Squad.

Before being discharged with an injury award and pension in 1993, Kirby was commended by Commissioners, Judges and Magistrates on forty occasions for displaying 'courage, determination and detective ability'.

Married, with four children and five grandchildren, Kirby lives in a Suffolk village with his wife. He appears on television and radio and can be relied upon to provide forthright views on spineless, supine senior police officers (and other politicians) with their insipid, uninformed, absurd and mendacious claims on how they intend to defeat serious crime and reclaim the streets.

He contributes regularly to newspapers and magazines, reviews books, films and music and is employed by television companies as a consultant and researcher. He also writes memoirs, biographies and true crime books which are widely quoted – this is his twenty-fifth.

Kirby can be visited on his website: www.dickkirby.com

Acknowledgements

There are three important people whom I immediately wish to thank. The first is Jeff Edwards, my chum for over half a century, to whom I am much indebted for his thoughtful and very kind foreword to this book. Before he became a nationally acclaimed crime correspondent, I knew him as a young, intrepid crime reporter for an East End newspaper. He pursued his enquiries amongst members of the local underworld with a fearlessness that many a young cop would have envied.

Next, the American author Joseph Wambaugh. Joe and I have been friends for over forty years, and I regard him as being the greatest living crime writer. Not only has he been an inspiration to me, we've shared common ground, apart from being authors. Both of us were very active detective sergeants, albeit on different sides of the pond, and both of us have been sharply critical of the command structure of our respective former police forces.

Last – and by no means least – there is Brigadier Henry Wilson, the commissioning editor of Pen & Sword Books. Over the past ten years he has provided wise counsel and encouragement, and when my waters have become particularly troubled, he has been on hand to pour calming oil upon them. I am most grateful to him.

Then there are the staff at Pen & Sword Books, including Matt Jones and Tara Moran for their enthusiasm, George Chamier for his ruthless, lynx-eyed editing and Jon Wilkinson for his tremendously imaginative designs. Always very helpful to me are Bob Fenton, QGM of the Ex-CID Officers' Association, and Susi Rogol, editor of the London Police Pensioner, and I'm much obliged to both of them.

Whenever I write a book, a great many people come to my assistance, for which I'm truly grateful, although in this particular instance there are a number of contributors who, for one reason or another, have had their identities cloaked.

Those who have not are: Russ Allen; John Beadle; the late Terry Brown GM; Mike Bucknole FNAVA, BA (Hons), PgC; Robert Cook; Jim Dickie QPM; Mick Carter; Gordon Cawthorne MBE; Ian Chiverton; Gerry Gallagher; Paul Galpin; the late Hilda Harris; Julie Hillman; Maurice Marshall; Jan Northam;

Albert Patrick, Julia Pearce; the late 'Nipper' Read QPM; Bert Richens; Allan Rowlands; Graham Seaby MPhil, LLB; Keith Taylor; Derek Webster; Steve Wheatley; the late Ray Wood OBE; John Woodhouse; Tony Yeoman; and Peter Young MBE. I'm most grateful to all of them.

Photographs were supplied by: Mike Bucknole; Mick Carter; Ian Chiverton; the late Terry Crawley; Gerry Gallagher; Bill Gladstone; Julie Hillman; Barbara Jerreat; Ann Kirby; Julia Pearce; Graham Seaby; Ann Taylor; Derek Webster; Ray Wood; John Woodhouse; and Daisy Yeoman. Other photographs come from the author's collection, and while every effort has been made to trace the copyright holders of all photographs, Pen & Sword and I apologise for any inadvertent omissions.

My thanks go to my family for their love and support: my daughter Sue Cowper and her husband Steve (for directing me through the minefield of cyber-space), their children, Emma Cowper B Mus, Jessica Cowper B Mus and Harry Cowper M Theatre; my daughter Barbara Ann Jerreat and her husband Rich: their children, Sam and Annie Grace Jerreat; and my sons Mark and Robert.

Most of all, my thanks go to my wife Ann, who guided me before, during and after the Golden Years of Policing with tact and loving kindness.

Dick Kirby
Suffolk 2022

Foreword

JEFF EDWARDS

*Former Chief Crime Correspondent of the
Daily Mirror and President of the Crime
Reporters' Association*

I have known and been friends with Dick Kirby for about fifty years. We first met in the 1970s, at a time he calls 'The Golden Age of Policing'. I doubt he would argue with my preferred description of both of our professions then as 'When Dinosaurs Ruled the Earth'.

He was a Detective Constable in the Metropolitan Police based at Forest Gate police station in East London. I was an aspiring young reporter on the *Newham Recorder*, one of two then thriving weekly newspapers competing to serve the district.

I like to think that in a small way we helped each other achieve our ambitions.

In my case it was to become a nationally known crime journalist, in his case to become first a top drawer detective, and then an outstanding author on police matters. Allow me to explain.

Part of my job, twice a week, was to go into the five police stations which served the London Borough of Newham and try to find out as much as possible about the recent crimes, the arrests and the upcoming court cases.

And believe me, there was plenty of it.

If memory serves me correctly, Forest Gate and the neighbouring West Ham police station at that time had the highest recorded crime figures, not just in the Metropolitan Police area but in the country as a whole. Murder, armed robbery, rape, burglary, gangland shootings, stabbings, lorry hijackings, arson, fraud: you name it, the police in Newham had to deal with it, every day. And there was much more besides.

For a young news hound like me it was hog heaven. Of course, in 1970 I didn't know I was to go on to become a Fleet Street crime reporter. My real ambition up to that point, aged just twenty-one, was to be a top-flight sports reporter. Football, boxing, cricket, rugby – they were the things I really wanted to write about. But as part of my career development I had first to learn the art of news reporting, and those weekly visits to the police stations were to change my life. I became fascinated by the action and the intrigue of police matters.

Looking back, the way people like us did our jobs was antiquated. It certainly wouldn't be permitted now. I would roll up at the front desk and ask to see the duty sergeant or inspector who had been designated to 'deal with the press'. We would usually adjourn to an interview room, and they would lug with them enormous leather-bound log books. These would be the Major Crimes Book, the Minor Crimes Book, the Motor Vehicle Crime Book and the 'OB' – the Occurrence Book – which could sometimes be the most interesting of all. It contained everything from reported UFO sightings to officers injured on duty when bitten by a mouse they were trying to remove from a terrified woman's bath.

The officer tasked with this role had received no training for it whatsoever. No press officer or civil service wonk to chaperone them and tell them what they must not reveal. So out it tumbled; the outlines of terrible crimes, sums of money and details of personal property stolen. How the crimes had been committed. Full names and home addresses of victims and witnesses. Even the full details, names, addresses and occupations of women alleging rape or indecent assault, although out of common decency we edited those out of any published story.

Gory details of injuries inflicted with kitchen knives, broken bottles, fists and sawn-off snooker cues were all read out. The names and other details of those arrested and what they were charged with were also freely disseminated. My notebook bulged with information.

Data protection ? 'Never heard of it.'
Privacy of the individual ? 'So what?'
Duty of Care? 'You're having a laugh.'

But being a well brought-up young man, I did think it was a matter of courtesy, particularly if the crime was a serious one and thus a CID matter, to find out who the officer in the case was and to contact them. I also quickly learned that what was in those log books was usually just a sketch, the tip of the proverbial iceberg. You needed to speak to the CID officers who had hands-on control of the investigation. They always knew much more interesting detail than was contained in those heavy leather ledgers. So I would go back to my office in East Ham, call the CID and ask to speak to the officer dealing.

And that is how I first met Detective Constable Dick Kirby.

Now, it is worth saying that in those days, when it came to 'the Press', police detectives tended to fall into one of two groups. One group usually wouldn't give you the time of day. The others were more affable, usually inviting you to come in to the nick and have a chat; or much more likely, they would say, 'I'll be round The Spotted Dog (The Duke of Fife, The Baker's Arms, The Two Puddings) later. Why don't you come down and have a pint?'

Fortunately, Dick Kirby was one of the approachable ones. I don't remember what the job was I called to discuss, or which pub we met in. But I found myself in the company, along with some of his colleagues, of a lively individual with a nice line in mimicry, a healthily jaundiced view of the world and a sharp, self-deprecating sense of humour. Above all, Dick was a great spinner of yarns with an eagle eye for detail and a thespian's ability to speak the part of every character in the episode he was describing. And it was about that time that I stopped wanting to be a sports reporter and set my sights on being a specialist crime reporter. It was so much more interesting.

Dick, along with some of his colleagues, was also a wise counsel from whom I learned a lot about the world very quickly. It was from him, late at night in a saloon bar somewhere, that I received the advice, 'Keep in mind, in this world things rarely turn out to be what they seem to be at first.' I can't put my finger on it, but I know what he meant, and for me it became one of those useful guide rules for life which I have never forgotten.

Of course, way back then, neither of us had an inkling that after a great career in the police, Dick would go on to have a second great career as an author. But as he helped change the direction of my life, I like to think I was able, albeit unintentionally, to put a small touch on the steering wheel of his life, too.

In 1975 I moved on to my first Fleet Street posting on the long defunct London *Evening News*. Around that time, every cop I knew was raving about a book by the American writer Joseph Wambaugh, called *The Choirboys*. It was a fictional story about a group of young Los Angeles police officers, set in the 1960s. The book was a fast-paced and extremely funny account of cop life, filled with an astutely observed mix of action, reflection, elation, depression, wry humour and pathos. It was a spot-on-target account of police life in any big city, because Joe Wambaugh was the real deal. Before becoming an author he had served many years as a patrol officer in the LAPD. His characters were all based on people he knew and had worked alongside. At the time he was a prolific author, penning other police classics including *The Blue Knight* and the sad and riveting documentary *The Onion Field*, which was made into an excellent feature film. Shortly before this movie was due to open in London in 1979, a woman I knew was working for the publicity department of a film distribution company. She called me and said Joe Wambaugh was coming to London. Would I like to meet him? And while he's here he'd like to meet some London cops; could I arrange that?

You bet I could. And that's how I introduced Dick Kirby to Joseph Wambaugh.

Joe had asked to be taken out to an Indian restaurant, because there weren't any in Los Angeles in those days, so we went to London's swankiest curry emporium, Veeraswamy in Swallow Street in the West End. I like to think that after that meeting the clock on the ignition sequence of Dick's career as an author started running.

Over the last twenty years, Dick has published over twenty books, an astonishing total. Many of you will be familiar with his previous works.

Many former police officers have written their memoirs over the years. It has to be said, in my view, most of them are not very good. They tend to be one-dimensional, often ego-driven and very similar in content.

Dick's books are nothing like these. His stories are always rich in the detail of events and the vast cast of characters on both sides of the law. Best of all, Dick has the rare ability to translate hilarious events from the saloon bar to the page, seamlessly. I often think he actually missed his later-life vocation. He should have been up there script-writing with the great British comedy creators like Jimmy Perry, David Croft and Johnny Speight.

In this latest work we encounter the full panoply of characters inhabiting Dick's world: dodgy solicitors, dangerous robbers, thieves, burglars, con men, artful dodgers, wily old codgers and bad people of every shade. The cops do not all come out looking like Gary Cooper, either.

Through Dick's eyes we do meet many fine, dedicated and stalwart examples of the best people ever to serve in British policing. We understand the 'fieldcraft' needed by lively CID officers of that period to get the job done. 'Guile and Low Cunning' is one of the more colourful ways Dick describes it. I'll say no more. But as well as the many hard-grafting, decent and upstanding officers he recalls, we also meet more than a handful of incompetent, lazy, ineffectual and downright bent cops.

That's what's so appealing about Dick Kirby's books. Police work is an abrasive business, on both sides of the divide. When Dick Kirby writes, there is no sugar coating, and no holds are barred. Nothing is off limits.

It's just the unvarnished truth.

Prologue

As my wife and I strolled along the Railway Walk that bisects Park Road and Lavenham High Street, in a sudden burst of nostalgia I said, 'You know, during the time I was in the Job, it really was a golden age of policing.'

★ ★ ★

It was true. Free accommodation was allotted to those who, like us, couldn't afford their own property, and rent aid was provided for those who could. Medical and dental bills were paid. The pay was not a fortune but it was adequate and a decent pension was paid after thirty years' service.

It was not all plain sailing, and it would be fatuous for me to suggest that the Metropolitan Police of the 1960s was some sort of Utopian law-enforcement paradise. It wasn't. Of course it wasn't perfect. But there was a genuine feeling of camaraderie amongst the rank and file, who were guided and inspired by the senior officers who had come up through the ranks, having learned by experience. At police stations, no one was allowed to patrol the area by car until all the beats had been filled – because in those days, uniformed police officers did indeed patrol the streets, and detectives who worked incredibly long hours detected. The CID officers did so for a niggardly allowance; it was not until 1975, which was ninety-seven years after the Criminal Investigation Department was formed, that they were paid overtime. Prior to that, we CID officers worked those 70–80–90+ hour weeks for the love of the job, for the satisfaction of 'getting things done', for putting the bad guys away.

I have been retired for almost thirty years from the police force which once had the admiration – and was the flagship of crime-busting – of the western world. When Scotland Yard was on the case, the public perceived that the days of the criminals were numbered; and they were usually right.

However, something went badly wrong.

In recent years there has been one monumental cock-up after another in the Metropolitan Police: the bungled Stephen

Lawrence murder enquiry; the shooting of an innocent man, Jean Charles de Menezes; Operation Midland, when a bunch of gullible so-called detectives were taken in by a fantasist, resulting in well-known public figures being pilloried after it was illogically (and untruthfully) alleged that they were part of a group of murderous paedophiles; the decades-long investigation into the murder of private investigator Daniel Morgan, in which police corruption was alleged.

Recently, two black sisters were reported missing. There was an inadequate response from the Met, and when the sisters were found murdered, the crime scene was guarded by two police officers. They promptly took photos of the two bodies and posted them on social media, together with appalling comments. As in the Stephen Lawrence enquiry, there were allegations of racism and, following an investigation, the two officers were sentenced to long terms of imprisonment. Nevertheless, there were those amongst their contemporaries who thought the officers were hard done-by.

If that were not enough, there was the case of Stephen Port, who in the space of fifteen months raped and murdered four gay men. The last three bodies were found in the same location. Police said the deaths were drug-related and were not linked. Forensic tests were not carried out. It was a chapter of utter incompetence, underlined by the inquest jury, who said that there were 'fundamental failings in these investigations from the beginning'.

Allegations were made that it was homophobia on the part of the investigating officers which resulted in this tragic mess, although the Coroner dismissed this suggestion and, for what it's worth, so do I. I believe that it was a combination of inexperience, lack of leadership, ignorance of the criminal law, slovenly working practices and, in all probability, bone-idleness.

Seventeen officers were investigated, but although none faced misconduct proceedings, it was felt that the actions of nine of them 'fell below the standard required'. Just like some of the officers who featured in the previously mentioned debacles, seven of these officers were promoted.

The sisters of one of Port's victims were furious, saying they would not accept these findings. They were quite right. They shouldn't.

It can be no crumb of comfort for those sisters, or for any of the sorrowing loved ones of those victims, to hear the simpering words of the Assistant Commissioner for Professionalism, who wants the public to believe that 'we are trustworthy, that we care, that we have changed and that we are learning.'

'Learning'? Learning what? How to arrest a depraved serial killer when the evidence was staring the so-called detectives in the face?

★ ★ ★

At the time of writing, the most publicized of these recent jaw-dropping gaffes was the murder of a young woman named Sarah Everard. Walking home one night, she was stopped on the streets of South London, handcuffed, bundled into a car, raped and murdered; her body was then set on fire. The person responsible? A serving Metropolitan Police Constable, Wayne Couzens, who pleaded guilty to those offences and on 30 September 2021 was sentenced to a whole life term of imprisonment.

Bad though it was to have had a murderous, predatory, drooling pervert in their midst, could the Metropolitan Police be held in any way culpable for Couzens' actions? Well – yes, they could.

Prior to his acceptance by the Met, Couzens had been seen in Kent in 2015 driving his car naked from the waist down. This was reported, but for whatever reason, no action was taken; and with the tragic, pathetic system of vetting checks carried out by the Met, this was not picked up.

Obviously, something of the kind *was* picked up by his colleagues, because Couzens was referred to as 'The Rapist'. This stemmed from his reputation for drug abuse and viewing extreme pornography; following his acceptance into the Met in 2018, between March and October 2019 he shared his views on social media – and as a result, five serving and one former police officer later came under investigation.

Then between February and July 2020 Couzens was posted to the Parliamentary and Diplomatic Protection Command. He patrolled Parliament – an armed police officer with debauched tendencies.

Anything else? Actually, there was. Just 72 hours prior to Ms Everard's savage murder, Couzens was seen, in a vehicle registered to him, once more naked from the waist down. This was reported to the Metropolitan Police. It was decided that this really was something that should be investigated. But it wasn't. And three days later, Sarah Everard's terrifying ordeal commenced, ending in her death.

So as well as being branded 'institutionally racist and homophobic', the Metropolitan Police was now described as being 'misogynistic' as well. This was certainly the view held by a female former Chief Constable of Nottinghamshire. The then Commissioner wanted 50 per cent of the Met's officers to be women; at the time of writing, women in all ranks account for approximately 30 per cent of the workforce. So is that the answer? Well, not according to the direct action group 'Sisters Uncut', which believes, 'Any female officer who puts on a uniform this morning . . . is compliant in that violence and is no sister of ours.' Looks like a no-win situation, doesn't it?

So how did this calamitous state of affairs come about? At whose door can the blame be laid? I'll tell you.

*   *   *

For many years past, the Metropolitan Police has been a rudderless ship, adrift in murky waters.

The captains who have never before been to sea have been completely unaware of the undertow and, even if the rudder was functional, there have been no charts to steer the craft by. The crew (also landlubbers), who have been promoted way beyond their experience or capabilities, comprises every possible type of ethnicity, every kind of gender fluidity, and possesses impressive university degrees, but is bereft of one iota of common sense, determination or purpose. And with the ship careering towards some very jagged rocks, there is nothing to save it from being smashed into smithereens.

But don't worry. The captain and the crew will be quite all right. Washed up on a convenient beach, having faced disaster, very much like Fred Astaire and Ginger Rogers, they will pick themselves up, brush themselves down and start all over again as though nothing had happened, to secure fresh laurels and look forward to the medals, dame- and knighthoods and peerages sure to come their way. And when they've moved on, there are plenty more just like them to fill the spaces left.

So who suffers? Only the general public, who've paid their wages and have received little or nothing in return. Burglaries are given lip service; car thefts are not investigated.

Stabbings and shootings – mainly black on black – occur on the streets of London literally on a daily basis, but they could be stopped. Resolute police officers led by senior officers who possess leadership, knowledge and experience could infiltrate those gangs and with guile and cunning turn gang members against each other. They could smash the gangs, render them so bewildered and disorientated – and fearful of the police – that they would not want to venture out of doors, let alone strut around the streets casually stabbing or shooting anyone whom they perceive to be 'disrespecting' them or who are residents of a different postcode.

But it doesn't happen. Senior officers and other politicians are terrified of the voices which grow louder and louder from Marxist-inspired groups, of the disapprobation they would receive if they were to come down hard on the criminal scum who now effectively run the streets of London. And therefore senior (and not so senior) police officers 'take the knee' – one did so in Downing Street – and that's why, with a chronic lack of leadership, police officers stand by, watch and do nothing while serious offences are committed. Sometimes they go further and run away from confrontation.

When environmental protesters blocked Waterloo Bridge, a uniformed police officer was seen skateboarding across it. Incredibly, during those demonstrations, officers (also in uniform) were seen dancing and fist-pumping the air to show solidarity with the demonstrators – the ones that police were supposed to be dispersing – who chanted to the officers, 'We love you.' Mind you, a police commander did admit to being 'disappointed'.

When protesters blocked junctions of the M25 motorway by simply sitting down across the carriageway, causing queues of traffic miles long, one police officer was heard to whimper to a protestor, 'Can I facilitate you?' A senior officer was said to be attempting a 'Dynamic Risk Assessment' – which I suppose means whatever the speaker wants it to mean. It is possible that it's university-generated police-speak meaning to vanish up one's own arsehole.

Priorities have become utterly muddled. Instead of promoting the idea of ridding the streets of murderous thugs, a deputy chief constable suggested painting the livery of police cars in rainbow colours, in order to win the trust of the LGBT+ community and encourage them to come forward and report hate crimes to the police. So with stabbings, shootings and all kinds of orchestrated mayhem being perpetrated on London's streets, would the multi-hued police cars drift by, oblivious to the chaos and anarchy all around them but keenly on the lookout for distressed gay personnel whose feelings have been hurt?

Not necessarily. They might be on the hunt for wolf-whistlers. This would be at the behest of an Assistant Commissioner, who recently admitted that whilst wolf-whistling might not necessarily be a crime, 'Nevertheless, *we want to know about it!*'

Let's get real, shall we? Women must be kept safe on the streets. The statistics are appalling. In the six months between Sarah Everard's murder and her killer being sentenced, no fewer than seventy-nine women, the youngest fifteen, the oldest eighty-five, were killed. But to shield them from intimidation and harm, banning wolf-whistling is the 'sticking plaster' approach favoured as a quick fix by the senior numbskulls, completely out of touch with reality, who inhabit Scotland Yard.

Following Couzens' sentencing and the ensuing furore which demanded the Commissioner's immediate sacking, 650 officers were hysterically drafted on to the streets of London in the hope that they would prevent a further murder. What a pity that they were not there in the first place. And headless chickens were beginning to look eminently sensible when compared to the stammered-out, knee-jerk advice dished out by the Yard. What was a woman to do if she were stopped by a police officer whom she didn't trust? 'Er . . . rush out on the road and stop a bus!' Jesus Christ!

There's a cadre of young police officers who carry out tasks of enormous bravery on the streets of London, but they're at a premium. There could be a lot more, but they're hamstrung by a chronic lack of leadership and a great deal of demoralization.

★ ★ ★

Well, that's enough of that. Much more and you'll be urgently seeking sharp objects to apply to your wrists as the present tragic state of law and disorder sinks in, so I'm going to tell you about some of the things that occurred to my contemporaries and me in former days. Some of the characters featured in this book have had their names and descriptions, as well as the times and locations associated with them, changed for obvious reasons. By today's standards, you might feel the language to be unacceptable, but that was the vernacular of the times. People knew that and accepted it. The late Sir Stirling Moss had an expression that encapsulated our motivation – 'Ten-tenths motoring' – although it could also be described as 'seat-of-your-pants policing'.

Some of you might find that what happened was incomprehensible, maybe even alarming, and perhaps it was, but we had a lot of fun, coupled with thrills and spills; and most importantly, we got things done and the public was looked after.

That's what we did. That's what we got paid for. And *that*, I assure you, was what it was all about.

Come on – it's time to take a stroll down felony lane.

Introduction

Some people are 'naturals' – you know, 'a natural athlete', 'a natural scholar' or 'a natural speaker' – and a few are 'natural police officers'. Alas, I possessed none of those attributes. If I achieved anything in my life, be it in education, athletics, police-work, oratory or writing, it was through the application of a lot of hard work; I made a lot of mistakes but I also received a liberal helping of good fortune and the support of some of the best people in the world.

And when one does well, it's nice to be complimented, although it was my experience that the Metropolitan Police was usually agonisingly slow when it came to praising good work; mind you, if one's conduct was complained about, greased lightning looked positively sluggish compared to the speed with which the complaints mechanism was set going.

I can't complain about the number of commendations I received – although I should have been grateful for a few more – but there were many times when I thought that a particular piece of police-work which I'd carried out merited recognition, and it wasn't. That annoyed me, especially in one case which was a series of separate trials in which fourteen armed robbers were later sentenced to a total of 161 years' imprisonment. I thought I'd done rather well with my contribution, and so did the trial judge, who gave me an outstanding commendation at the conclusion of the particular trial in which I featured, as did the clerk of the court, the ushers, the prosecuting counsel (who also took me out to lunch) and the foreman and every member of the jury who queued up to shake my hand. However, when the final trial was finished, the judge – whose memory was becoming more than a little wobbly – praised another officer whom he'd confused with me, so that officer was commended by the commissioner and I ended up with nothing. However, that's the way of the world, and I've no doubt there are many other former officers who can tell a similar story.

But I do remember my first bit of official recognition. It was an incident which occurred at 11.10pm on 15 July 1968, and I recall it for a number of different reasons; first, that framed piece of paper congratulating me for my actions on that date and signed by 'J' Division's most senior officer now hangs on my study wall. And secondly, no matter what information that officer had received about my conduct that night, it was wrong. I had done nothing worthy of commendation whatsoever.

But the third reason was that I benefitted from that incident because I saw how real police-work should be carried out; and it was a turning point in my career.

★　★　★

On that evening, as Police Constable 757 'J', I was just about to walk out of Ilford police station's yard to commence patrolling my night-duty beat, when the Duty Officer in his unmarked Austin Cambridge pulled up beside me. He was wearing on the back of his head a battered cap which had seen better days, and he had, as usual, a pipe in his mouth. It was seldom removed, and when the Duty Officer spoke, pipe between his clenched teeth, it was in a kind of staccato shorthand.

'Right – Kirby – in.'

As I got into the passenger seat, he added by way of explanation, 'Get a couple of shopbreakers.'

He drove around the area, seldom communicating with me; we stopped and questioned a couple of pedestrians for whom shopbreaking was the last thing on their guiltless minds, and then, around 11 o'clock, we drove into Queen's Road. This was a narrow cul-de-sac by the side of the Palais dancehall, and as we slowly drove down this road full of parked cars, he suddenly stopped by an unattended Vauxhall Velox. He peered at it, grunted, then reversed the Austin Cambridge out into Ilford High Road.

'Palais,' he muttered. 'Out soon.'

He scratched his forehead. 'Kirby – call the van,' and he gestured towards the R/T set.

I had received no instruction on how to use R/T communications[1] and I simply picked up the heavy metal microphone and stared at it.

'Button,' growled the Duty Officer.

So I pressed the button and said something inane, such as, 'Er – hallo, Scotland Yard.'

---

1 In fact, I never did receive any official instruction on how to transmit and receive R/T communications, or how to take fingerprints or how to use the teleprinter; like many other officers, I simply picked it up as I went along.

'Oh Christ, give it here,' he sighed, snatched the microphone from me, jammed his thumb on the transmit button and snapped, 'Juliet India Two from Juliet India One – High Street, junction with Queen's Road – now.'

The van duly pulled up opposite to us at the junction, and as it arrived, so the clientele of the Palais spilled out into the High Road and started to disperse. Included in the exodus were four black youths, who turned into Queen's Road.

'That's them,' muttered the Duty Officer to me, and into the microphone he said, 'Juliet India Two, stand by.'

As you'll appreciate, I had not the faintest idea what was going on. When the Vauxhall Velox slowly drove out of Queen's Road containing the four youths and the Duty Officer barked an order into the microphone, the van pulled across the junction and blocked the Vauxhall's exit. The Duty Officer and I jumped out of the car, as did the occupants of the Vauxhall. I was told, 'Kirby – driver', and I caught hold of him. As he volubly protested his innocence, I shepherded him, together with his companions, into the van.

Now I was in a dilemma. As far as I was aware – and in the absence of any other information – I had been party to an illegal arrest, and I knew all about illegal arrests from what had been drummed into me at training school and the monthly District Training classes; this was something for which I could be sued (and quite possibly fired), and therefore it was in my best interests to assuage the feelings of this obviously innocent party. It didn't help that he and his companions were black, either; the training school had also been responsible for pounding racial awareness into me. So I quickly made up my mind; if these four quite obviously innocent members of the public were going to remember any police officer who had been kind, patient and helpful to them this evening, it was going to be me.

Taken into the station's charge room, they were lined up and gave their details. Then the Duty Officer, hands on hips, addressed the driver in his usual clipped, telegraphic style, his pipe jerking up and down as he spoke. 'You. Car. Where'd you get it?'

It was clear that if he was going to offer any explanation at all, the driver would address it to me, the policeman who had been so charitable and respectful to him, and he did. Looking directly into my pleading spaniel's eyes, which wanted so desperately to believe him, he replied, 'Right. Now I tell yah. I got it from Shead's at Brixton. I paid six hundred quid for it, right?'

I expelled a noisy sigh of relief. The driver had been asked for an explanation, he had provided one that appeared completely creditable, and now he could be released.

'Turn your pockets out,' ordered the Duty Officer.

One of the items that he produced was a driver's licence. The Duty Officer looked at it and glanced sharply at the driver. 'This ain't the name you gave me.'

'I find it on the floor of the bog in the Palais,' explained the driver patiently. 'In fac', when you stop me, I was just on the way here, to hand it in.'

He had not even paused before offering this explanation; this, too, was entirely plausible.

The Duty Officer grunted. 'Lock 'em up. Night-duty CID.'

I groaned inwardly. Lock them up? This could only inflame the situation! So I gently ushered them into the cells and waited, my forehead damp with perspiration whilst the Night-duty CID were summoned.

★   ★   ★

Now, there's something which requires clarification. Those of you who are reading this and who know me, who've worked with me or who've read any of my books, will be somewhat flummoxed by my craven behaviour on this occasion, but the explanation is this.

On the date of this incident I had been a police constable at Ilford for exactly nine months; and I was utterly useless. My first arrest had been for drunk and incapable of a man very much smaller than me, and it was difficult to say which of us had been the more apprehensive. I had already been acquitted of assault occasioning actual bodily harm and I had unwisely led a charge into a disturbance at a public house which had swiftly accelerated into a real wild west-style saloon punch-up in which I and another officer had been injured. During my testimony in a shoplifting case – in which I had provided no incriminating evidence whatsoever; I had simply accepted custody of the shoplifter from a store detective – I had been unnecessarily savaged by a spiteful little solicitor. The solicitor's barracking was done purely to humiliate me before the magistrates, and he succeeded. In the normal course of my duties I received little or no assistance from the majority of the police constables on my relief, who were bone-idle, column-dodging piss-takers, and it was generally accepted – with, I should add, some justification – that any task I was faced with I would cock up. The confidence which I had accrued in the years between leaving school and the real world of the Metropolitan Police had been eroded. Probably the most crushing incident was when it was decided to raid a nightclub suspected of infringing the licensing laws. Every member of my relief was to participate in the raid – except me. I was conspicuously left out. In addition, I had yet to sit my intermediate probationer's examination at Hendon – I'd only just scraped through my final exam at Peel House Training School with the required pass-mark of 75 per cent – and at a time when during the probationary period officers could be summarily dismissed for 'failing to be a good and efficient constable' it appeared highly likely that I was soon to become one of their number.

Quite frankly, had I been a single man I would have saved them the trouble. I'd had a couple of abrasive interviews with the chief inspector and I'd just about had enough; in those circumstances, I'd have resigned. But I *wasn't* single; I was married with two small children and we'd moved into police married quarters – how *could* I resign? If I had put my papers in – or more than likely, been kicked out – what would I do? Where would we live? What would become of us? Apart from that, I wasn't lazy – certainly I was useless but I was as keen as mustard and I really, desperately wanted to succeed as a police officer. But I couldn't; with little or no guidance or support, I blundered from one nonsensical situation to another.

And now this. I honestly believed that I was faced with the prospect of being sued for a wrongful arrest, and it really knocked the stuffing out of me. I was completely demoralized, which explains my supine behaviour. But – as you're about to discover – there was no need for it.

★   ★   ★

The job of the Night-duty CID was to patrol the whole of 'J' Division from 10.00pm to 6.00am, to deal with any allegation of crime, whether prisoners were involved or not. In either case, their brief was to deal with the matter as fully as possible and, if they were unable to complete their enquiries, to turn it over to the Day-duty CID of the station concerned. With such a huge area as 'J' Division to cover, whatever action needed to be taken had to be quick and decisive. This particular evening, the Night-duty CID consisted of a second-class detective sergeant with two aids to CID, and eventually they turned up.

The detective sergeant was short, affable and smartly dressed; the two aids were very big and rather belligerent-looking. None of them appeared to be strictly sober.

'Wotcher, Sarge,' said the DS to the Duty Officer, who held the rank of station sergeant. 'What've we got here, then?'

I was ignored as the four officers went into a huddle, and I could only make out the odd word or two from the Duty Officer: 'Four of 'em . . . ringer . . . gave me a load of bollocks.'

The DS nodded, sagely. 'Let's get 'em out, then.'

The prisoners were duly led out and the DS addressed the driver. 'Right, you. Where'd you get the car?'

The driver smiled ingratiatingly. 'Well, it like I tell the officer here,' gesticulating towards me. I nodded eagerly as he said, 'I bought it from Shead's at Brixton a week ago. I pay six hundred quid for it and then . . .'

'I'm not listening to this shit,' interrupted the DS. To the beefier of the two aids he said, 'We can't afford to fuck about with this all night. Have a word, will you?' and strolled off, chatting with the duty officer.

Fixing the driver with a deeply unfriendly stare, the aid said, 'Right. Come 'ere, you', and took him into a waiting room.

It seemed to me that just seconds later I heard the driver exclaim, 'Orl right! I nick the motor and plate it!'

Then I heard a growl from the aid, which produced a further admission: 'Yeah, the licence. I nick that an' all!'

There was some more muttered conversation and then the aid emerged from the room.

'Which one of you lot's Neville?'

One of the remaining three stepped forward.

'Me,' he said, fearfully.

'Right, I wanna word with you, son,' said the aid, but Neville quickly (and perhaps wisely) replied, 'I was wiv 'im when 'e nick thuh wheels!'

And so it went on, with passengers number three and four similarly making incriminating statements whilst I stood there like a fool, my mouth hanging open at this display of proactive police-work.

What eventually happened to them I don't know, except that they were all variously charged with the larceny of and/or receiving a motor car. Wherever it was that they appeared at court, they must have pleaded guilty, because I certainly didn't make a statement or give evidence. As to who the DS was, or who the aids were, I've no idea; I never saw them again.

* * *

As I later discovered, when the Duty Officer saw the 1963 model Vauxhall Velox in Queen's Road and looked at the registration plate he knew immediately that this number had been allocated to a Triumph Mayflower during the first few months of 1951 – and the reason he knew this was because he was an absolutely brilliant authority on the registration of motor vehicles. But he hadn't told me. It would certainly have helped matters if he'd exercised a little man-management, but in fairness to him, perhaps he felt he didn't need to; he was in charge, and all I had to do was to follow his instructions.

However, from that moment things started to look up. A couple of weeks later, I attended Hendon Police College, and having sat the intermediate exam I came second in my class. On the same day I celebrated my twenty-fifth birthday and also received the letter of appreciation from the chief superintendent of 'J' Division. By the end of the year I had made thirty arrests, including one of a known thief, made off-duty, for larceny from a motor car; this would result in a further letter of appreciation from 'J' Division's chief superintendent.

The following year, I was one of a two-man rowdyism patrol in plain clothes; in one week we accounted for twenty-one arrests, including twelve made simultaneously. I sat my final probationer's exam at Hendon, scoring 194 marks out of 240, and was confirmed as a police constable; moreover, my arrest total for the year now numbered sixty-seven.

I was now far more confident making arrests and giving evidence at court, but I looked with awe at the 'J' Division 'Q'-Car crews in their anonymous, sleek Jaguars; little did I realize that within two years I would commence the first of five triumphant 'Q' Car tours, each lasting thirteen weeks.

And all that happened because my confidence had been restored by a pat on the back which I certainly didn't deserve.

I applied to join the CID, and my career really took off. I passed the examination for sergeant and obtained a pass-mark of 90 per cent at the Detective Training School. I was stationed on 'K' Division, which was so big it was split into two, with a detective chief superintendent for each half. Thanks to the 150 arrests accrued on the 'Q'-Car tours added to my other arrests, I achieved the highest number on both halves of 'K' Division and was appointed detective constable.

And eight years after that encounter in Queen's Road, I was working in Switzerland, conducting enquiries in a town named Winterthur.

By now I was attached to the Serious Crime Squad and I was deeply immersed in an investigation into the activities of a gang of international forgers and swindlers known as 'The Hungarian Circle'.[2] I had just finished making a telephone call when a member of the *Kantonspolizei* walked into the office.

'Oh, Herr Kirby,' he said. 'There's one of your countrymen next door, another police officer. Would you like to meet him?'

Who should be in the next office but that Duty Officer from eight years previously; what an amazing coincidence it was, meeting him in the same building in a small town with a population of 100,000 – half that of Ilford – 480 miles away from where we'd first met. Now a chief inspector, he told me he was there having received a bursary to research Sir Arthur Conan Doyle and his famous fictional detective. I raised my eyebrows in feigned interest and made muted noises of admiration, but really this was as far removed from police-work as Winterthur was from 221b Baker Street; I thought it was nothing more than a 'jolly' and something he was being paid to do into the bargain. In answer to his query as to what I was doing in that northern Swiss town, I modestly told him I was now a detective sergeant at the Yard investigating a world-wide conspiracy which, if unchecked, would have netted the gang something in the region of £500 million.

He sniffed. 'Huh! Haven't progressed very far, have you?'

I was glad to see that none of his man-management skills had deserted him!

---

2 For further information regarding this investigation, see *You're Nicked!* Robinson Books, 2007

CHAPTER 1

Coppers' Idiosyncrasies

Police officers often get bees in their bonnets about different types of offence. One of the oddest of these quirks was possessed by a Police Constable named Bert, who was pretty well prehistoric when I joined the Job.

Bert's father was one of 1,056 police officers who were summarily dismissed in 1919 when the Metropolitan Police went on strike for the third and final time. Bert, on the other hand, was determined to show that he was an indispensable member of the force, and his particular idiosyncrasy was to ensure that every motorist should have his car taxed and show a road fund licence.

'I tax my car, so there's no reason why they shouldn't tax theirs,' he sternly informed me, and after he paraded for duty he would obtain a clutch of Process Books in which to enter details of recalcitrant motorists who were flouting that particular law.

For younger readers, I should point out that whilst most vehicles still have to be taxed, up to a few years ago proof of this was required in the shape of a three-inch-diameter paper tax disc, which was then affixed to the inside of the car's windscreen.

On one occasion Bert's zealous eye spotted a car being driven towards him with no road fund licence displayed and, stepping into the roadway, he held up an imperious hand, and the car braked to a halt.

'Are you aware it's an offence to drive a car without a valid road fund licence, sir?' demanded Bert.

'I *have* got a road fund licence, officer,' protested the driver and then looked towards the nearside corner of the car's windscreen. 'Good heavens! I *did* have one there – it must have slipped down!'

'You'd better find it then, hadn't you?' said Bert, and it took all of half an hour, working assiduously with a screwdriver, for the car's owner to dismantle the dashboard.

Finally, he withdrew the road fund licence from the dashboard's dusty interior.

'There!' he cried, flourishing the tax disc, which was fully valid. 'I *told* you I had one!'

Bert was not dismayed in the least; telling the driver to reassemble his dashboard, he nevertheless reported him for failing to display his road fund licence! Bert's zeal couldn't be questioned, but then again, such despotic actions are not the sort of stuff which promotes cohesive community relations.

★　★　★

Other coppers' idiosyncrasies were rather more understandable. The mother of one such officer had her house broken into, so quite naturally he had a down on burglars; another's daughter was the victim of indecent exposure, and in consequence, shifty-looking coves who insisted on unnecessarily wearing long, stained raincoats on swelteringly hot summer days attracted his interest.

My own particular quirk was seeing people being frightened. When I was a police constable, carrying out rowdyism duties in plain clothes, it infuriated me to see decent citizens being jeered at and shoved off the pavement – looking thoroughly frightened – by gangs of boozy, out-of-control yobs, and I discharged my duties with considerable vigour.

Later in my career, it was armed robbers who claimed my attention; they were masters of subjecting ordinary people to fear. Although I arrested a great many of the perpetrators, I dealt with far more victims of robbery; some of them took months to recover and some never recovered at all. I will never forget one particular middle-aged woman who was in a queue in a building society when an armed robber burst in. The raid was over in seconds – they normally are – and the woman was not hurt, physically, that is. But the shock to her was tremendous. She was not hysterical, nor did she cry, but I can still see her pale, drawn face now, when very quietly, almost in a whisper, she said, 'I thought I would never see my grandchildren, again.'

I had to nick that robber as a matter of honour; well, in circumstances like that you've got to, haven't you?

It's not surprising that about half of my commendations were for the arrest of robbers and other violent individuals. The arrest of this particular blagger was carried out in a spectacularly amusing ambush, details of which you may guess at but need not enquire after.

★　★　★

So that was my particular bête noire – seeing people frightened and abused who were unable to defend themselves. What brought this about? There's a reason for all things, and this was mine.

I can't say I was a naughty child, because I was not. In fact, I was quite irritatingly obedient. I grew up in a mid-terraced house, cocooned by strict but loving parents; a solitary child, I was dreamy (perhaps drippy) and quite happy with my own company, playing with my toys and reading my books.

I remember the day when things changed for me. It was on Wednesday, 6 February 1952. I was eight years of age.

As we were trooping into junior school, all the pupils and teachers were suddenly herded into the main hall; the headmaster wished to address the whole school. In sepulchral tones, he informed us that His Majesty, King George VI had died that morning and that we would now all bow our heads, to pray for his soul.

All of the children dutifully inclined their heads and closed their eyes, this being a necessary adjunct for successful prayer – except me. I don't know why. It wasn't done in a spirit of rebellion. I'd attended Sunday School on a regular basis so I knew what was what when it came to invoking effective prayer; all I can suggest in my defence is that it was a sudden, inexplicable 8-year-old's aberration.

But my disobedience did not go unnoticed. A beefy schoolmaster was standing a few feet away; he took three quick steps towards me, hissed, 'Shut your bloody eyes!' and with that, punched me with stunning force in my stomach.

I doubled over in agony, wheezing, trying to suck some air back into my lungs and tears streaming down my face; the other children crowded round me, having decided that my plight was far more interesting than consigning the late King-Emperor's soul to Providence.

A few years later, I went to secondary modern school, where my fellow pupils and I came under the care of a vicious, sadistic headmaster, who in my opinion was a borderline psychotic; in addition, many of the teachers appeared to be bullying, shell-shocked veterans of El Alamein. That was bad enough; but it was that incident on the day of the old King's death that left its indelible mark on me.

It's slightly surprising that I'm a committed monarchist. It's completely unsurprising that I left school when I was fourteen.

And of course, there's one other matter. Since he noticed that I hadn't closed my eyes, that sadistic schoolmaster obviously hadn't closed his, either. So as well as acquiring a bee in my bonnet about bullying and abuse, I added double standards and sanctimoniousness to my hit-list.

I daresay it explains a lot about my general persona. It was probably responsible for some of my successes in the Metropolitan

Police. It quite possibly accounted for a few of my indiscretions as well.

★   ★   ★

Men knocking their wives about is something that has happened since time immemorial; a few years ago, of course, families were rather more cohesive, so that if a daughter, sister or niece was being ill-used by her husband, partner or boyfriend she usually had some male relative handy who could be relied upon to sort out the malefactor, without the intervention of the police. Actually, this worked quite well. Bullies who enjoy bashing up someone unable to fight back (or defend herself) don't enjoy being on the receiving end of a good hiding.

Nowadays, things are a bit different, aren't they? Marriage has fallen into disfavour, people drift from one partner to another, families are fragmented; and in the unlikely event that such an abusive piece of dreg were to get his come-uppance, he'd be the one who'd go crying to the police.

And it's the police who are in the middle. 'The police didn't do nothing!' is the oft-heard cry from battered women; but inevitably, whilst the police have tried to do something, time and again and for one reason or another, abused women refuse to go to court to provide a little something called 'evidence'.

All very disturbing. And when something goes horribly, tragically wrong (and it often does), and senior police officers and other politicians are stirred into action, they come up with the most nonsensical, knee-jerk ideas that pass for solutions to this age-old problem. '*Make* them give evidence!' Really? And how does one do that? Another brilliant idea was, 'If they won't prosecute, cut their benefits!' – that, I thought, was an absolute corker.

So – what's the solution? If you come up with a feasible answer, let me know. I'd be fascinated to hear it; so would the unfortunate victims. In the meantime, let's go back 50-plus years, to – remember? – the golden age of policing.

★   ★   ★

I'd finished my two years' probationary period in uniform and I was in rather a quandary as to how my career should progress. I felt I was neither fish nor fowl. Really, because I'd enjoyed working two-man rowdyism patrols in plain clothes, I wouldn't have minded spending the rest (as I then thought it would be) of my twenty-eight years service doing just that – but the regulations were such that uniformed officers were only permitted to spend a certain number of days each year in plain clothes. Going for promotion in the uniform branch didn't attract me. Something that did was the Special Patrol Group; I still have my application to join the Group, which was never sent because shortly afterwards, and very much like Darth Vader, I was 'seduced by the Dark Side' and joined the CID.

But before that happened – and in what I can only describe as a moment of madness – my senior officers decided to entrust me with the care of a green-as-grass, wet-behind-the-ears, straight-out-of-training-school probationary police constable.

I discharged this delightful duty by endeavouring to instruct my charge in the ways of working the streets; it was hard going, I can tell you.

I received a call to go to a council estate, where one of the inhabitants had complained that she had been beaten up by her husband. Upon our arrival, there was the lady in question, bearing all the hallmarks of having received a pasting and requesting police assistance. Now (and because I had the kid with me) I gave the lady what was then thought to be the solution to her problem. It was certainly not its most satisfactory resolution but it was (at that time) the norm, and it had been instilled in us at Peel House.

It was to instruct the injured party to go to the local Magistrates' Court, see the Clerk of the Court and explain what had happened. He would then issue a summons, police would serve it on the errant husband, and the wife would then have to go to court to give evidence.

The lady digested this information in silence and then turned to me and said plaintively, 'Please, mister, I can't be doing all this shit. Can't you just come round and beat him up, like you did last time?'

My young apprentice's mouth fell open to such an extent that he began to give a creditable impersonation of a guppy, and I hastily had to tell the lady that this was a case of mistaken identity and that she had confused me with some other uniformed police constable.

As I led my trembling charge away I turned to bid adieu to the lady; and she solemnly winked at me with one battered eye.

Ah, things were so much simpler during the golden age of policing!

CHAPTER 2

Tales from the Sally Ann

The opportunity to look over the other side of the fence rarely occurs.

But once upon a time, it *did* sometimes happen; when a criminal pushed open the doors of delinquency, and a cop was permitted to peer inside. It happened, most especially, in the days when an officer was allowed to handle a supergrass. However, it also occurred when a detective had the opportunity to sit down with a criminal, especially an old-time villain, and listen to what they had to say about crimes of yesteryear.

I remember being thoroughly amused, whilst having a glass with an old-time blagger who recounted a trick that he and his wife had devised years before when he appeared at the Magistrates' Court and was in danger of being remanded in custody.

At a propitious moment, his wife would burst into court holding a shrieking infant in her arms.

'Oh, Yer Honour, give 'im bail!' she'd howl. 'Can't yer see baby's missing 'is Daddy already?'

It usually worked; and as the old rogue explained to me, the reason for the child's unhappiness was because, prior to entering the courtroom, its tender buttocks had been savagely pinched by his wife!

These encounters don't, of course, happen nowadays; but if, in years to come, someone in the Metropolitan Police has the innovative idea that conversations between criminals and detectives should be encouraged, take a tip from one who knows. Listen to the crim. Don't interrupt to show how clever you are. Nod, to encourage him. Replenish his glass. You never know, you might learn something.

I did, on a warm summer's day in 1981. I had just joined the Flying Squad and had yet to make my first arrest.

* * *

I stood facing a day room for the homeless in London's East End. Invariably, these hostels (whatever their correct title might be) were usually known as 'The Sally Ann' – standing for the Salvation Army. My eyes roamed over the inhabitants in the sagging armchairs – the unloved, the uncared-for, the unwanted and, let's face it, the just plain unlucky – some of them reading newspapers and others with newspapers over their faces who appeared to be dozing. An unpleasant odour permeated the place; a mixture of sweat, urine and antiseptic.

I was feeling distinctly uncomfortable; not arresting criminals was something I was unused to. But I soon hoped to rectify matters; I was looking for just one face – that of Paul Christopher Goddard, who was over the wall from prison. Goddard was a dangerous individual who had been serving a four-year sentence – to my mind, a mercifully short one – for robbery. Even so, he had come to the conclusion that this term of incarceration was far too severe and had decided to award himself a little unofficial parole. He industriously sawed his way through the bars of his prison cell in the North of England and made his way to London. And the information that I had received was that he was staying here at the refuge and was booked in under his mother's maiden name of Milner. I had a copy of the photograph published in *Police Gazette*, together with his description – aged twenty-seven, five feet eight, stocky build, dark brown wavy hair, a tattoo of an eagle on his right forearm – but as I looked round the room, I could see no one who resembled him. I was just about to start wandering round, pulling off the newspapers which obscured some of the faces, when one of the attendant nuns walked by. I stopped her, introduced myself, showed her the photograph and quietly enquired as to the whereabouts of Paul Milner aka Goddard.

'Sure, ye've just missed him, son,' she replied, in a soft Irish brogue. 'He went out just fifteen minutes ago, so he did.'

'Any indication as to where he was going or when he'd be coming back, sister?' I asked, but she shook her head.

'No idea, son.'

She smiled at me, her cheerful face a mass of wrinkles from a lifetime's vocation of caring for the flotsam and jetsam of society, before hurrying away.

I walked out into the reception area, sighed and scratched my head. Bugger! What to do now? Take a run round the streets, see if I could pick him up if he hadn't gone too far? Come back later? I sighed again. Just missed him by fifteen minutes; bloody nuisance! And just then, a grubby little man I hadn't noticed before and who had followed me out of the day room tugged at the sleeve of my jacket.

With a jerk of his head, he muttered, 'Mark the 'ot cross bun, Guv'nor!'

I looked back into the day room and saw the nun who had been so irreverently referred to, the same one with whom I had been speaking, talking urgently to one of the residents who was sprawling in an armchair and who had just lowered the newspaper from his face. As the nun whispered fervently and volubly to Paul Goddard, for it was he, so he turned his head, looked straight at me, leapt out of his chair and headed off at a rate of knots to the rear of the day room.

''E's going for the fire escape,' said my mysterious informant. 'Step lively, Guv'nor – out the front door and round to yer right!'

I needed no further bidding; I flew out of the hostel and turned right, just in time to meet Paul Goddard running flat-out towards me. There was a fairly ugly little altercation, I'm afraid, which culminated with both of us descending to the sidewalk with a thump, where punches were exchanged. The difference of opinion continued for several seconds, until Goddard's forehead came into smart contact with the pavement, and having applied handcuffs I lodged him in the back of a Flying Squad car.

'Look after him, Tone,' I said to Tony Freeman, my Flying Squad driver. 'Be back in a moment.'

I strolled back to the refuge, where I again made the acquaintance of the nun, who was completely unfazed by the turn of events.

'Sure,' she said, 'he must have crept back in when I wasn't looking.'

I looked at her guiltless face for some time before I came to the irrevocable conclusion that nicking a sister of mercy for harbouring an escaped convict was not really the sort of publicity sought by the Flying Squad, so I contented myself with saying, 'Well, if ever I'm in need of an alibi, I'll know where to come, won't I?'

A ghost of a smile crossed her face.

'Bless you, son.'

As I headed for the front door, my adviser was still in the reception area, which was otherwise deserted. A small man, he stood no more than five feet four or five, with a wiry build and grey, close-cropped hair. His face was so deeply lined that I put his age at about seventy, although he was, in fact, approximately ten years younger.

'Thanks for that, mate,' I said, quietly, and then on an impulse I added, 'Meet me in The Black Swan at midday and I'll buy you a drink.'

* * *

'Joe Knight' was how he introduced himself, and that day I bought him several drinks. As we sat down at a table in the pub, bitter for him, lager for me, I gave Joe a rather closer inspection. Grubby he certainly was, with stubble on his chin and a lined face with the weather-beaten complexion of somebody used to walking the streets and sleeping rough. If I were to say that his jacket had seen better days I would be stretching my tactfulness to its limits; any self-respecting tramp would have haughtily refused the offer of such a garment. From the jacket – or perhaps from Joe, or even a combination of the two – came an odour of mild decay. And then I looked at his wrists; they were chunky and muscular, and his fingers were thick and square-looking – workmanlike-hands. In the years that followed I discovered that many Special Forces personnel possessed such hands, probably as a result of climbing cliffs and throttling enemy sentries. My most enduring memory of Joe was his cough. I had never heard anything like it; it sounded like an assortment of nails being shaken vigorously in a metal box.

Joe interrupted my reverie as he raised his glass.

''Ere's to yer, Guv'nor. You're Mr Kirby, ain't yer? No, we ain't never met, but you nicked my brother Tommy, years ago, for receiving some dodgy gear. Think you was an aid at the time. Barking Magistrates' Court, it was. We both thought Tom was going to draw a carpet [this expression is explained in Chapter 16], but you spoke up for 'im and he walked away with a fine.'

I smiled and nodded, as though the whole memory of the case was flooding back to me, but really I should have shaken my head. Tommy Knight? I couldn't remember anybody by that name. If the arrest of Joe's brother had been carried out when I had been an aid to CID, my usual Magistrates' Court was Havering. If I'd gone to Barking Magistrates' Court, it would have been because of an arrest I'd made on CID night-duty or on a 'Q'-Car, but unlike nowadays, it would have been a quick 'in-and-out' – probably someone I'd arrested, charged and got weighed-off at court, all in the space of a few hours – a type of prisoner who was one of many in those days!

But there you are; a kind deed, and years later it paid off when Tommy Knight's brother, now down on his luck, had spotted me in the refuge and repaid me for a favour which I couldn't even recall bestowing. I slipped him a tenner (which I really couldn't afford) under the table and said, 'Thanks for that, Joe. If you hear anything else, let me know.'

Joe made sure that he'd pocketed the note before he burst out laughing.

'Leave it out, Guv'nor! Who's going to trust anything worthwhile to an old piss-head like me?' He laughed again and shook his head. 'No, today was a fluke, that's all. I don't move in the right circles nowadays. Not like just after the war. Cor, things were happening then, all right!'

I had been on the point of getting on with a little police work, but I can spot when there's a good story in the offing. In any case, I had broken my spell of inactivity and carried out an arrest, so I bought a fresh round of drinks and settled down to listen to a yarn.

* * *

Coincidentally, the story which Joe told me I'd heard years before, so I knew it was true; however, before I recount it, a little about Joe's background.

Joe had been born in 1920, in Bethnal Green, one of the most deprived areas of London. As he grew up he stole to supplement the family's meagre standard of living, boxed in fairground booths and was in and out of trouble with the law. When he was caught red-handed moving a large consignment of stolen cigarettes in 1940, it appeared prison was inevitable once more, but war intervened. He joined the Suffolk Regiment, but after training in Wales, boredom soon set in, and when in Regimental Orders there was a request for volunteers for 'duties of a hazardous nature', Joe put in his application; this was how he came to be accepted as a member of the newly-formed No. 6 Commando.

Over the next five years Joe's unit was in some of the toughest fighting of the war. He saw action in Floss, Norway, and in France and North Africa; and it was in the latter that Joe became one of forty-three casualties after the train in which they were travelling was attacked by enemy aircraft. He rejoined his unit in Tunisia, and in the ferocious fighting which followed, the unit's original strength of 250 was reduced to just 100 officers and men.

Following the Normandy landings, 6 Commando pressed on towards the Siegfried Line, and in April 1945 Joe took part in storming the road bridge across the River Aller. The commandos, with fixed bayonets, charged across the 400 yards of the bridge and killed every German whom they encountered. Joe was wounded once more, hospitalized, Mentioned in Dispatches and demobbed from the army the following year.

* * *

Joe had lost his wartime gratuity in a couple of days, spending most of it wildly and losing the rest in what he maintained was a crooked game of poker. So he – who had never done an honest day's work in his life – started looking for some of his lawless pre-war colleagues. The project he had in mind needed the participation of two other individuals, both of whom needed to be as unscrupulous as himself.

Here Joe checked himself; he gave very little away about his two companions, the venue or the offence for which they – and not he – were arrested. But from what I could pick up, it was a robbery in which luck played a significant part: sheer good luck for the crew of the wireless car which latched on to the gang following a well-executed robbery; and even more luck for Joe, who tumbled out of the getaway car and rolled right underneath a nearby parked lorry before the pursuing police car rounded a corner and missed him completely; but unfortunately, complete and utter bad luck for the two remaining robbers after a tyre burst on their vehicle, delivering them, plus the £900 payroll they had stolen, right into the arms of the pursuing law and consequently into terms of penal servitude.

Over the next few years Joe had staged enough successful coups to maintain a decent standard of living, but now we come to the tale that I've mentioned previously. Joe received information about Morris Sharman, a jeweller who was in the habit of taking large amounts of his stock home with him at night to his house in Ilford. Joe got to work, lining up a receiver and forming a plan. He decided that Thursday night would be the night of the burglary. However, matters – and not for the first time in Joe's criminal career – were about to go staggeringly wrong.

Yet everything started off so well. Thursday night was moonless, and the light in Sharman's bedroom was extinguished just before eleven. To be on the safe side, Joe gave it another hour and a half before silently making his way to the rear of the premises and then making good use of his Commando training by scaling a drainpipe, as silently as a cat. The catch on the spare bedroom window was as defective as Joe's informant had said it would be; so with a barely audible 'click' it surrendered to a little pressure and Joe slid into the room. He stayed immobile for five minutes; during that time he could hear the beating of his heart and his slow, regular breathing, but nothing else.

Joe padded into the study. There on the desk was an assortment of jewellery, masses of it! Sharman had thought it was so safe he hadn't even bothered to put it away. Joe started to scoop it into a small bag, when a heavy bracelet slipped off the desk and fell to the floor. If the study had been carpeted, it might not have made so much noise, but the floor was covered in very thin linoleum and it landed with a crack. Joe hurriedly swept the rest of the jewellery into the bag, anxious now to get away, but suddenly the study was flooded with light. There in the doorway, one hand on the light-switch, the other holding a poker, stood Morris Sharman. His eyes bulged at the sight of Joe.

'Bastard!' he shouted and flung the poker; it missed Joe but shattered the study window with a tremendous crash. That alone caused the lights of a few neighbouring houses to come on.

'HELP! POLICE!' roared Sharman, and as Joe launched himself at him, so several more people's lights were switched on.

Joe grabbed hold of one of the lapels of Sharman's dressing gown with his right hand, the bony edge of his wrist against the jeweller's throat and then took hold of the other lapel with his left hand, in order to pull it down and effectively choke Sharman into unconsciousness. But the garment was so cheap and so old that as Joe yanked downwards, so the material tore and partially disintegrated.

'HELP!' shrieked Sharman, struggling furiously. 'MURDER!'

By now, not only were most of the lights of the houses in the street blazing, but people had started to come out into the roadway. Pushing Sharman away, and neglecting the bag of jewellery, Joe decided that self-preservation was the order of the day, and quick. For years to come, residents still spoke of the astonishing apparition which, with a splintering crash of the remaining glass from Mr Sharman's first-floor study window, emerged head-first, performed a complete mid-air front somersault, landed in the front garden, bounced right over the privet hedge and set off down the street as fast as an express train.

So despite a bungled burglary and a complete lack of recompense for his endeavours, at least Joe had escaped with his freedom; or rather, he would have done, had not the local wireless car, which happened to be passing, turned the corner at that moment. Their arrival coincided with the message from Scotland Yard's Information Room of the extraordinary events which had occurred not two hundred yards away.

'I don't know nothing abaht it,' said an indignant Joe, who was also rather out of breath. 'Diving aht of windows? What's the matter with yer?'

'I reckon you're our best bet, chum,' replied the wireless operator, who was shining his torch at Joe.

'Why?' demanded Joe, belligerently. 'Where's yer proof?'

By now the van had turned up, and the crew heard Joe's last remarks. As they and the other police officers started to chuckle, the wireless operator laconically replied, 'You'd know if you were standing where I am!'

The beam of his torch had caught the myriad fragments of glass, courtesy of the remains of Morris Sharman's first-floor window, which had caught in Joe's jumper and now lit him up like a Christmas tree. And just when Joe thought matters really couldn't get any worse, lo and behold, they did.

★ ★ ★

Robbery with violence was, in the post-war years, a reasonably rare crime, and because the penalties were so severe, it was an offence which was triable only at a Court of Assize; in Joe's case, it was the Old Bailey. It was also Joe's misfortune to be arraigned before probably one of the most spiteful Judges ever to sit at the Bailey since the notorious Judge Jeffreys had been appointed the Common Serjeant there in 1671, one who took every opportunity to impose swingeing sentences, not because the offenders necessarily deserved them but because of the exquisite pleasure he derived from seeing the palpable shock on defendants' faces.

Joe pleaded guilty, and his defence counsel made much of his war record in mitigation; it produced nothing but a sneer on the Judge's face. He had not served in the armed services and was intensely jealous of people who had, especially those with proven fighting ability and courage; people like Joe, in fact. The dislike was mutual; Joe sat there, never once taking his eyes off the Judge's face and simmering with rage.

In passing sentence, the Judge concluded with the contemptuous words, 'I thoroughly dislike this type of offence and I cannot in all conscience say that I like the look of you, either. Seven years. Take him down.'

And with that, Joe exploded. Before the dock officers could get close to him, he had leapt to his feet, grabbed hold of his chair and swung it aloft.

'Look out, My Lord!' cried the Clerk of the Assize, and with that, Joe's chair went flying across the court room and, as the Judge ducked, splintered just above his chair, narrowly missing the Old Bailey sword of 1563 and sending the spineless Judge, squeaking with fear, out of the court room. The dock officers had, by now, pounced on Joe and dragged him off to the cells, without administering the sort of punishment normally dished out to recalcitrant prisoners. They didn't like the Judge, either. Nobody did.

★ ★ ★

I burst out laughing. 'I heard that story years ago, when I was a PC at Ilford. So that was you, was it?'

Joe chuckled and nodded. 'That was me. I got another twelve months on top for chucking the chair at that old bastard.'

He laughed again, which turned into a bout of frenzied coughing until he recovered sufficiently to add, 'It was worth every bleedin' day of it!'

In fact, it wasn't. Joe had never received such a heavy sentence before, and I think those long hours in Dartmoor broke him. When he was released, Joe drifted, getting involved in far pettier crime than previously; and as the years went by, drink had laid a heavy hand on his shoulder. I suppose I was lucky that Joe had been sufficiently sober to remember that I had uttered a few kind words to help his brother out at court, but now time had taken its toll and had brought him to the portals of the refuge for the homeless.

'Why don't you get in touch with the Commando Association?' I asked Joe. 'Perhaps they could help you out.'

Joe had no knowledge of the association, but I told him, 'I'll get the address for you. I'll stay in touch.'

Joe nodded, and we shook hands, but although I did get the address of the association I never did see him again. I was involved with a tremendous surge of Flying Squad work and when I should have popped in to see him, I'm afraid I didn't. In fact, I forgot all about him until three or four years later, when I was working on a murder investigation at King's Cross. The victim, the murderer and practically every prosecution witness was a vagrant, and I was making enquiries at all kinds of hostels all over North and East London when, once again, I found myself at the hostel where I had first met Joe. I went inside and, lo and behold, there was the self-same sister of mercy who had so thoroughly disillusioned me about the probity of nuns several years previously. I made desultory enquiries regarding the murderer and the missing witnesses, all without success.

'Is Joe about?' I asked her. 'You remember. Joe Knight?'

She shook her head. 'No, he left, son. Heard he died, so I did. Lung cancer, I heard. God rest him, poor wee man.'

She crossed herself piously.

'Died?' I echoed. I recalled that hacking cough so I guess that did make sense. But still . . . 'When did he die, sister?' I asked casually.

'Couldn't say, son,' she replied, just as carelessly. 'That's what I heard, that's all.'

I gave her an incredulous look with, I think, some justification. 'Are you sure?'

A frosty look crossed the countenance of this elderly sister of mercy. 'Surely yer not doubtin' me word, son?'

I sighed and shook my head. 'Oh, I believe you, sister,' I replied and then added with black humour, which I feel sure Joe would have relished, 'but I'm afraid that Joe never did!'

CHAPTER 3

Top 'Tec

Before I go any further I need to introduce you to Mick Carter, for a couple of reasons.

First, Mick was the best detective I never worked with. I don't know why; we both served on 'J', 'K' and 'N' divisions at the same time; I can only assume that we were bound up with our own investigations. Mick was a sergeant for twenty-seven years of his thirty-five-year career, and during that time he amassed a crop of commendations for courage, determination, tenacity and detective ability that would cause any present-day fledgling cop to experience a sexual disturbance.

Mick spent a total of six years with SO1(6) Department – the Stolen Car Squad to you – plus another three with his own 'mini' car squad, which he raised on the Met's No. 1 Area. Pursuing his enquiries all over the United Kingdom and much of Europe, Mick was commended for this work on no fewer than ten occasions, to add to his already impressive total.

He worked on a variety of 'Q'-Cars and ran five crime squads, in the latter doubling the arrests for burglary and tripling the number of arrests over all. So was he awarded a thoroughly well-deserved Queen's Police Medal for distinguished service? Well, no – wrong colour, wrong gender, wrong sexual orientation. Sorry, Mick, you're a white male heterosexual and you were too much of a proper hands-on copper!

The second reason for Mick's introduction is because – oh, it must be twenty-five to thirty years ago now – he was one of the founding members of the ReCIDivists' Luncheon Club. The others were the late Dave 'Sandy' Sanderson and former Detective Chief Superintendent Maurice Marshall, who later handed over the presidency of the club to Julie Hillman (you'll be hearing more later of both the latter two). A chance meeting between a few retired cops blossomed into thrice-yearly meetings attended by anything between forty and ninety old-timers. The food and drink are of the finest; and the stories that unfold are the stuff of legend – and not a few have found their way into this book.

* * *

It was at one of those meetings that Mick and I were having a quiet drink prior to being called in to luncheon.

'There wasn't too many commissioners I cared for,' said Mick, 'but Peter Imbert was an exception.'

I nodded. 'Well, he presented me with my long service and never-been-caught medal, so he must have been a good bloke!'

Mick laughed at that, and I added, 'But I know what you mean; when he was commissioner he had the guts to criticize the Police and Criminal Evidence Act, saying that it would stop detectives using their initiative and working on hunches. He also condemned the fact that criminals could refuse to answer questions without any adverse comment being made.'

'I bet that made the civil libertarians hit the roof!' laughed Mick and then he added, 'But he did drop a bit of a clanger with the rape interview.'

Mick had a point. He was referring to a fly-on-the-wall television programme which had been made, with Peter Imbert's agreement, when he was Chief Constable of the Thames Valley Police. Entitled 'A Complaint of Rape', it featured a woman with a history of psychiatric illness who alleged that she had been raped by three men. Although her face was never shown, she was interviewed – 'bullied' would be a more accurate term – by three male officers. It was appalling. Showboating for the cameras, they suggested to the woman that the sex she had experienced was consensual, that she was 'on the game', that nobody would believe her; and the wretched woman agreed to drop her complaint after she was told, 'This is the biggest bollocks I've ever heard.'

The programme caused a public outcry. Maggie Thatcher was given a rough ride in the Commons during Prime Minister's Question Time, and several months later, a rape squad was formed at Reading police station comprised of five women officers.

'Yes, and there were some good women officers who handled rape enquiries,' mused Mick. After a pause, he added, 'Although there was a rape case I dealt with where of necessity all of the investigating team were male.'

I glanced at the clock; luncheon wouldn't be served for at least a quarter of an hour.

'What happened?' I asked.

This was the tale that Mick recounted to me.

* * *

Janet Blake was a 41-year-old divorcee with two teenage children. Like many women in that position, she was starved of affection and thought she had found it with Dan, some thirteen years her junior, whom she had known for several months. After an evening spent drinking with Dan, his brother Jim and other assorted flotsam and jetsam in the King's Cross area, she decided to accompany Dan back to his gruesome dump of a flat in that area.

Love's dream faded rapidly when, over a period of hours, she was stripped naked, repeatedly criminally and indecently assaulted, and raped and buggered by Dan; then Jim joined in the fun and urinated over her head. She was detained in the flat and when she attempted to leave she was dragged downstairs for the next episode of appalling treatment to be meted out to her.

Have you ever seen a Spanish Porrón red wine decanter? I expect you have, and if you've visited the Costa del Crime, it could be you've drunk from one. The decanter is lifted up to above head height, the red wine flows into the thin glass spout and the lucky recipient hopefully catches it in their mouth – many people think it's tremendous fun.

But young Dan had another use for one such decanter. He thrust the glass spout into Janet's vagina, then into her anus, where she received a severe cut; the shock and pain of this assault was such that she defecated on the spout.

Well, that heralded the end of the evening's entertainment for the brothers. Janet was told to get dressed and leave. As she left the flat she collapsed in front of a cab driver, who took her straight to City Road police station.

There she was interviewed by two male Night-duty CID officers; treating her with the greatest sympathy, they arranged for her to be medically examined. Fortunately, the examination was carried out by Dr Hannah Hedwig Striesow (the name is pronounced 'Stry-sow' rather than 'Stree-sow'). Hannah – as she was universally known – fled Nazi persecution in Germany in 1936 and, arriving in England, worked as a nurse before starting her practice as a GP at Forest Gate, East London in 1949. She worked as a police examiner for thirty-six years and was adored by police and patients alike, especially by victims of rape, whom she treated with the greatest compassion.

It took very little time for Hannah to come to the conclusion that Janet's account of what had happened was an accurate one; and it said much for Janet's courage that she insisted pointing out to the officers the address where she had been taken.

A search made at the local collator's office revealed that not only were the two brothers well and truly known to the police, so were other members of their family, several of whom possessed reputations for violence.

The Divisional Support Unit was a successor to the now disbanded Special Patrol Group and was used in situations where civil unrest was likely to occur. Since the word 'No' did not feature in their vocabulary, they were the ideal unit to accompany the night-duty officers to Dan and Jim's flat and to smash the front door off its hinges.

Expecting such a visit, Dan and Jim had prudently vacated the flat, but two other brothers were present; believing they may have had some complicity in the evening's proceedings, an invitation was extended to them to accompany the officers to King's Cross Road police station. The interior of the flat revealed that a violent struggle had taken place and it contained a huge variety of forensic evidence; the flat was sealed until such time as a detailed examination could be carried out.

So when Mick Carter arrived at work that August morning, this was the investigation that was handed to him.

'Hang on, Mick,' I said, interrupting his discourse. 'Surely this was a job for someone of DI's rank?'

'You're right, it was,' replied Mick. 'But this was bang in the middle of the annual leave season, so there were very few officers about. There were two murder enquiries being conducted, and Jack Renwick, the DI, had to perform the duties of the chief inspector. And apart from all that, I was already involved in a major credit card enquiry involving sixteen prisoners – I was the most senior officer available!'

The fraud investigation had, of course, to be put to one side. But Mick had two uniformed police constables assisting him on that enquiry, so they were quickly conscripted on to the rape investigation. Mick sent Mark Sully (who had a university degree but less than two years' service) to the flat to obtain and catalogue the exhibits and to have the scene photographed, a task he performed with a professionalism far beyond his years.

Meanwhile, Mick and the other constable, Brian Ward, set to work interviewing the two brothers in an effort to trace their absent siblings, as well as other witnesses. Friends and relatives of the two wanted men were also visited, but the brothers kept on the move. Nor were they idle during this time; alibis were attempted to be fabricated, an offer of £100 was made to Janet to drop the proceedings and, when that failed, over a period of two weeks violent threats were made against her.

As is quite often the case in matters such as this, others were drawn in to intimidate the victim. Janet should have been able to fall back on her 17-year-old daughter for support; unfortunately, it was not forthcoming, because her daughter's then fiancé was one of those closely involved in the attempts to get Janet to drop the charges.

'The daughter's behaviour was absolutely incredible,' Mick told me. 'She seemed oblivious to the very harrowing and frightening experiences that her mother had sustained; she appeared more concerned that her fiancé would break off their engagement.'

It was an intolerable situation and one that Mick refused to put up with. He and his two police constables identified ten people who had been issuing the threats to Janet and arrested them for attempting to pervert the course of justice.

'I made it quite clear to all of them that if they didn't desist in their behaviour, I'd arrest them all over again, and this time they'd be kept in custody,' said Mick.

In the end, Mick had put so much pressure on the friends and relatives of those two sub-human deviants that they gave themselves up. Janet picked them out on an identification parade and, after an eight-hour interview in the presence of their solicitor, Mick charged the brothers with rape, buggery and other serious offences and ensured they were kept in custody.

But Janet still needed a great deal of moral support and she got it from Mick and the other two officers, who spent a considerable amount of time with her, visiting her sometimes twice a day up to and after the trial.

No woman officer was available to assist, but Janet was completely satisfied that the officers were looking after her welfare. In fact, the only female to have any input was a volunteer from the local Victim's Support Group; however, she upset Janet to such an extent that her services were abruptly dispensed with.

'You know, Mick,' I said, 'bearing in mind that bloody television programme, it's a pity that the public couldn't be made aware of an investigation like this, carried out solely by male officers.'

Mick smiled. 'That's the way it goes.'

'What happened at the trial?' I asked.

'That was your usual no-holds-barred sort of trial at the Bailey,' he replied. 'The defence was run along the lines that the victim consented to the rape and all the other despicable acts carried out against her.'

'How was Janet giving evidence?' I asked.

'Oh, she was brilliant,' replied Mick. 'Wouldn't budge an inch during cross-examination. Of course, the jury clearly thought that no woman would consent to that degrading behaviour and they were just out for a couple of hours before finding both brothers guilty. That bastard Dan copped eight years and his brother, sixteen months.'

'Not enough, really, was it?' I commented.

Mick smiled again. 'It never is. I hoped Dan would get twelve years and I thought his brother deserved five years. Mind you, Janet was very pleased with the outcome, and we continued visiting her for about three months after the trial to let her know we cared for her safety, but no more approaches to her were made.'

Commissioner's commendations were handed out to the three officers for their professional conduct and their detective ability; and what's more, Mick resurrected the complicated fraud case he'd been forced to defer. The sixteen defendants were convicted at Southwark Crown Court, where Mick was commended by the Judge and collected yet another commissioner's commendation. No stopping him, was there?

'Ladies and gentlemen, luncheon is served', called the club's manager, Colin Pridige, and Mick and I got to our feet.

'Funny coincidence, Mick, but round about the same time I was investigating a rape over at Holloway,' I said. 'I'd nicked this little shit and got him remanded at Highbury Corner Magistrates' Court. The gaoler was nowhere to be seen, so I brought him out of court to take him down to the cells. Know what? He slipped and went down three flights of cast-iron stairs.'

'Bad luck, that,' commented Mick.

'I blame myself,' I told him. 'If I could have reacted sooner and moved quicker, I think I could have saved him.'

I sighed, regretfully.

'But there you are; I couldn't and I didn't, and down he went.'

Mick gave me a sideways look as we strolled over to our table. 'I bet you were sorry about that.'

'Well, I was,' I replied. 'But I'll tell you something odd, Mick – did you know that when a rapist accidentally falls down three flights of stairs, he bounces when he reaches the bottom? Honest – I saw it happen!'

* * *

One more story before we leave Mick Carter; it features two thoroughly disagreeable pieces of work. One was black and violent, the other was white and a chief superintendent – and neither of them was particularly keen on the CID.

'That's what comes from keeping doubtful company on the Sabbath,' said the Sheriff-Substitute to Richard Hannay, in Hitchcock's film of John Buchan's *The Thirty-Nine Steps*, and the same applied to Laura Reynolds, who had had a tempestuous and often violent relationship with Mr Black over a considerable period of time.

In fairness to Miss Reynolds, she had been attempting to rid herself of Black's attentions for some little while, with good reason; Black had a number of previous convictions for violence, including stabbing one man and beating another with an iron bar.

Going to Miss Reynolds' workplace in Lewisham, and by a series of threats and intimidation over a period of eight hours, Black took her back to his bedsit in Leytonstone. There he bound and gagged her, tying her to the springs of his bed and robbing her of two gold rings; he also released her long enough to force her to write an authorization permitting him to collect her wages from her place of employment.

Having written it she was tied up once more, while Black left to collect her money; but now, in his absence, after two days' imprisonment, she managed to get free and ran all the way to the nearest police station where, in a very distressed and emotional state, she blurted out her story.

The late Detective Inspector Norman Willcock immediately led a team of officers to the flat; but by pure bad luck, Black had arrived home ten minutes previously; finding Miss Reynolds gone and not being a complete fool, he thought it reasonable in the circumstances that he might be about to receive a visit from the police and had therefore made himself scarce.

His whereabouts were sought without success, but one week after the offence had occurred, Willcock, together with Mick Carter and a uniform PC, paid another visit to the flat. Willcock looked up at the bedroom window; on his previous visit, he had pulled the curtains back – now they were drawn.

Shouting that they were police officers, they hammered on the door but without eliciting a response. Eventually, the door was kicked in, whereupon Black suddenly leapt out at them from behind a partition, holding a machete in one hand and a large wooden mallet in the other, and screamed at the officers to get out or he'd kill them. Telling the PC to go outside and summon assistance, Willcock grabbed a collapsible camp bed and Mick, a wooden chair.

'We felt like lion tamers, keeping the lion at bay with the chair and camp bed,' Mick told me. 'I remember thinking, "Fucking hell, if he throws that machete at one of us, it'll split our head open." I must say, this incident was one of the most frightening of my police career, and I thought one or more of us would end up dead or seriously injured.'

Although Black continually lashed out at them with the weapons, they managed to contain him for five or six minutes ('It felt like an eternity,' said Mick) until he eventually put the weapons down. It was only slightly amazing that nobody – including Black – had been injured.

'Did he get his come-uppance at the Bailey?' I asked.

'Not really!' laughed Mick. 'He claimed that he didn't know we were Old Bill; said that the girl had sent some thugs along to beat him up! The soppy jury accepted this, but at least he went down for two years on the false imprisonment charge. John Barber was the DCI and he put us up for a commendation, but it went to the uniform chief superintendent, White – do you remember him? – and we just got a DAC's commendation.'

'Yes, I remember White all right', I replied. 'What a horrible bastard he was. I remember once putting in a special bill for expenses for an out-of-town murder enquiry and he tried to dispute it, in front of his clerk so that he had an audience to witness my humiliation. But of course, I'd been on the Serious Crime Squad and for years I'd been submitting special bills for going all over the country and abroad besides, so I knew that whatever I submitted on those lines was absolutely spot-on and I took great enjoyment in telling him so. He never forgave me for that, and I wasn't surprised about your commendation. Do you remember Jim Griffiths?'

Mick nodded.

'Well, Jim got a DAC's commendation on one of my jobs, and White called him up to inform him of it. What happened then was typical of the man. Jim told me that White was in a towering rage when he went into his office and he shouted, "Griffiths, you've been on the division for four years and this is the seventh time I've had to inform you that you've been commended – *and it's got to stop!*"'

CHAPTER 4

The Female of the Species

I got up off the sofa to answer a ring at the front door. I was on sick leave and, to my delight, my visitor was Allison, a woman police officer with whom I'd previously worked; kiss-kiss. I noticed a bruise swelling underneath her eye.

'Hello!' I exclaimed. 'What happened to you?'

Allison pulled a face and explained that the previous evening, she and her male police partner, both in full uniform, had been patrolling in a marked police car. They had spotted a car whose driving suggested that the occupants might well be up to no good. They followed it, forced it to stop and Allison ran over and pulled open the driver's door, whereupon he punched her in the face.

'Yes, so I see,' I said, examining the bruise. 'Are you OK?'

Allison smiled and shrugged. 'Oh, I'm all right.'

'Tell me which hospital he's in, and I'll send him some flowers,' I said, trying a little black humour.

There was a pause. 'He wasn't nicked.'

'Not nicked?' I echoed. 'Why ever not?'

'My partner said he never saw anything,' replied Allison, 'so what was the point of going to court if he was going to follow me into the witness box and say it hadn't happened?'

I don't think I said anything; I was stunned. I knew only too well what the result would have been if someone had punched me or any of my male contemporaries in the face – but punching a woman colleague? I don't think I'd ever encountered such an occurrence. If it had happened on the Flying Squad to one of our women colleagues, well . . .

There was nothing wrong with Allison; she was bright, intelligent and a keen officer. There was everything wrong with her partner who whimpered that he 'hadn't seen anything'. Difficult to see how he could have missed seeing it. I shook my head. Times had changed. Although I wasn't to know it, at the end of this period of sick leave I'd be discharged from the police with an injury pension. Just as well. With behaviour like that in the ranks of the police, it was time to go.

*　*　*

My mood did not improve when the following tale reached my ears. I had been retired and a professional writer and author for several years when I was told of the situation at a particular East London police station. The CID office was open-plan. At one end of the room sat the detective chief inspector; at the other end sat the detective inspector.

Both were women. They were of different ethnicities, neither had a clue about investigative police-work, both had been promoted way beyond their capabilities, and each hated the other's guts.

Much of the working day was spent with these two senior officers shrieking insults at each other over the heads of the rank and file who sat between them. None of those detectives dared complain about this appalling situation, for fear of being labelled as 'racist' or 'sexist'.

I knew things were bad in the Met, but as bad as this? I mentioned this account to a contemporary, who nodded.

'Yes,' he said. 'I heard that story, too.'

Well, that couldn't be counted on as verification; he'd simply heard the story in the same way that I had. But when I spoke to someone else, a serving officer, he was able to throw a little more light on the matter.

'Oh, yes, it's true all right,' he told me. 'I've been there, I've seen it and heard what's going on. Those two get the DCs and DSs in the office to take sides with them, one against the other. It's bloody dreadful.'

This, I thought, is something the public should know about. At that time I was writing columns and comments for the national press and I suggested to a comments editor that it was a piece of information that would made really interesting copy.

'No, we can't use that,' replied the editor. 'It doesn't sound believable and, apart from that, it could be construed as being sexist.'

It's a bit late in the day, but I'm happy to share it with you now.

★   ★   ★

Needless to say, those two so-called senior detectives bore no resemblance to other women officers I'd worked with. Thelma Wagstaff, for example, when she was a woman detective inspector at East Ham, had her work cut out with a sometimes rebellious staff and a shit for a senior officer. But she rose to the rank of commander and did so much to set up training programmes for women officers investigating rape cases. Joyce Cashmore was a brilliant officer who was snapped up by Bert Wickstead when he first formed the Serious Crime Squad and who rose to the rank of chief inspector, as did 'Ilda 'Arris, who was so well respected as an investigator that her male subordinates did not refer to her as 'Ma'am' – they called her 'Guv'.

But they were 'old school'. Women officers then worked 7½-hour shifts, one week's nights and were paid 10 per cent less than their male counterparts. In 1973 that changed and they were fully integrated into the workforce; well, almost. At that time, women officers were still wearing tailored uniforms with skirts and black tights, and carrying handbags – but without truncheons.

Julia Pearce was the first female to be posted on 'B' relief at Holloway police station, where on night duty she was partnered with a very protective male officer. Every incident that they were called to elicited the same response from him: 'You stay in the car while I deal with this; it'll be safer for you.'

But as Julia told me, 'I was getting a little peed off with this; I didn't join to sit in a car and be safe.'

So when, on the fourth night, a call was received to a 'suspects on premises' at a department store and the entire relief, plus the dog van, turned out, Julia disregarded her partner's usual cautionary advice. As her colleagues rushed off to surround the building, she strolled over to the store's fire escape door, which was also an area used for containing refuse and which now held dustbins overflowing with their evil-smelling contents.

As she checked the door, it suddenly burst open and 'the suspect on premises' rushed out, knocking Julia into the dustbins and covering her in their noisome slime. Nevertheless, she reached out and grabbed the suspect's ankle, which brought him crashing face-first to the ground. The commotion brought the rest of the officers to the scene to behold a gruesome sight: Julia with her ripped tights, bloody knees and new, well-pressed uniform reeking of unidentified filth. The suspect was in a worse state: similarly covered in gunge but also with blood spurting from his nose, broken as the result of his fall. Largely unsympathetic to the suspect's plight, Julia's colleagues gave her a standing ovation, and she was never again advised to stay in the car.

But the suspect was a sore loser; he made a number of damaging assertions against the police and pleaded not guilty at court. However, after Julia had given her evidence, the defence lawyer requested a short adjournment; when he returned, the prisoner changed his plea to one of guilty and dropped all the allegations.

As Julia told me, 'I think it had something to do with my five foot three, against his five foot eleven!'

Julia was a wonderful asset to the Flying Squad, which was where I first met her in 1981. She served on the Squad for years and had a tremendous input to the 1983 Security Express robbery investigation, which featured such luminaries as Ronnie Knight and Freddie Foreman. I was appalled when I heard that her nickname was 'Treacle' – a diminutive of 'Treacle Tart'.

'It was Tony Yeoman who started calling me that,' Julia told me. 'I don't think I was ever offended by the name; in fact, being a female in a very male-dominated job, having a nickname gave me a sense of belonging. At training school I was given the nickname 'Mousey', probably because I was small, shy and squeaky. Did it bother me? No! I felt protected by my male colleagues, who always had my back, especially with the anti-female staff at Hendon. My male colleagues always stood my corner.'

Tony Yeoman, who Julia said was responsible for giving her the nickname, was referred to as 'Tarquin' or 'Tarq'; not that Julia believed her Squad nickname was conferred with any malice.

'After Tarquin started calling me Treacle it stayed with me my entire service. When I arrived at the Detective Training School to lecture on forensics, on my desk was a nameplate: "Treacle". It now sits proudly on my desk at home.'

But as I pointed out to Julia, if any of her present-day counterparts had such a nickname given to them, I have no doubt that, following long-lasting bouts of PTSD, mortification and hurt feelings, the payout they would receive would be enormous!

Julie Hillman was a terrific member of the 'N' Division Crime Squad. Utterly loyal ('Don't you fucking talk to my sergeant like that!'), she was forthright in dealing with the scum of Holloway, including 'Mad Max' who, without any provocation whatsoever, could be transformed from a placid individual to a raving lunatic in a split second.

'Don't get lippy with me!' warned Julie, and he didn't.

In the witness box at the Bailey, she was unshakeable and unflappable.

'Your colleagues have referred to my client's premises as "dirty",' said a defence barrister and sneered, 'I assume you'd agree with them?'

'No, I wouldn't,' replied Julie. Giving him a withering look (and after a significant pause), she told the court, 'They were – gruesome!'

Julie refers to me as 'My Sweet Man'; Julia, from her West Country domain, addresses me as 'Me 'andsome'; but 'Ilda 'Arris referred to me by a rather earthier epithet.

'Ilda and I were carrying out a blackmail enquiry in a constabulary on the south coast and I became quite friendly with the CID typist at the local police station.

One day (in my absence), the typist was in a rather gushing mood and said, 'Oh, Miss Harris, isn't Mr Kirby charming? He speaks so beautifully, he has such wonderful manners . . . ' but that was as far as she got.

'Who, 'im?' interrupted 'Ilda. ''E's just a filthy little rat!'

She later informed me of this conversation, and I was quite annoyed at my innocent little flirtation being upended.

'Hilda, you want to mind your own bloody business!' I told her, to which she replied primly, 'I was only looking after Ann's interests!'

'And anyway,' she added crushingly, 'you *are* a filthy little rat!'

CHAPTER 5

Brief Encounter

To those of you who are familiar with my scribblings it will come as no surprise whatsoever to learn that I detested briefs: defence solicitors and lawyers. All right, so that's a rather sweeping generalization. There are exceptions to every rule, and I certainly had no objection to a lawyer robustly defending a client when he was utterly convinced that the client was wrongly accused.

What I did object to was when it was patently obvious to the lawyer that their client was guilty of the offence with which he or she was charged, but the barrister then deliberately misled a jury, demanded every scrap of paper accumulated by the police during the investigation of the case, whether or not it had any bearing on the offence charged (this, of course, was before the days of 'disclosure') and bellowed at and humiliated witnesses. I disliked it when it was blatantly obvious that the defence team had been coaching their client on what to say. And what I abhorred more than anything else was when lawyers championed the cause of those anti-social members of society who were so out of control, so irredeemably worthless, that they represented a social worker's wet dream and sheer unadulterated misery to everybody else. And when the lawyers had finally finished bamboozling a half-witted jury (never a difficult task), and their grinning client swaggered out of the dock, free to continue spraying graffiti, spitting at passers-by and casually stabbing anybody who 'disrespected' them, I liked that least of all.

Let's look at matters from a different perspective. Say, for example, a man has been arrested for robbery. This man has no previous convictions, is gainfully employed, faithful to his wife, kind to his children and scrupulously accurate, down to the last penny, when submitting his income tax return. In fact, he has never done anything wrong in his entire life, and the fact that he has now been arrested for robbery is nothing more than an awful, gasp-producing mistake. But instead of dusting him down, pouring a conciliatory cup of tea down his throat, offering him the most abject, profuse apologies and a lift home, suppose you were told, 'No. We've got a robbery on our books and we want to clear it up. Let's fit him up – let's plant some incriminating evidence to wrongly convict him, that'll send him away for seven or eight years and pretty well ruin his life.'

Would you do that? *Could* you do that? No, and neither could I, but that's just what my Flying Squad contemporaries and I were accused of doing on an almost daily basis by blustering, bellicose barristers at the Bailey – and, apart from a smart bit of alliteration, that's not all. What was so infuriating was that these barristers knew full well that their clients were as guilty as sin. With or without the protection of the court, this was attempting to pervert the course of public justice on a grand scale.

How did we contend with these allegations? Protest too much and you were accused of histrionics; confine yourself to muttering 'no' or 'that's not true' and you ran the risk of appearing shifty to the jury.

One way in which I dealt with these matters was to issue a stock denial to the first half-dozen allegations before stating quite calmly (but in a penetrating voice), 'These allegations are utterly untrue. Not only does your client know that they are untrue and completely malicious, I suggest that you know it, too.'

This could lead to red faces and ten seconds-worth of stammering, and it could turn the tide. Sometimes. One barrister (who had probably heard of my ripostes in chambers) tried to turn matters round by roaring, 'Oh! Apart from being a liar and a perjurer, you're a mind reader as well, are you?'

Well, be that as it may, the one thing to avoid was the sort of astonishing outburst that emanated from one particular officer who was undergoing hostile cross-examination.

'I'm sick and tired of this!' he cried. 'Every time I step into the witness box it's always the same – I'm accused of fitting up a prisoner, beating him up, planting drugs on him – I'm fed up with it! I've had it up to here! These are the sort of scurrilous accusations I've been getting all the way through my service!'

'Really?' drawled the defence barrister. 'And how much service is that?'

'Er – well, eighteen months, actually!' was the flustered reply.

I bit my lip so hard I nearly drew blood. After the miscreant in the dock had been acquitted in about five seconds flat, I had a quiet word with the much-maligned officer. I had encountered him before; his inspector had no control over him whatsoever (in fact, he appeared terrified of him), and in consequence he was cocky, rude, lazy and disobedient. As a result of our little chat, he (plus everybody else who had had dealings with him) came to the conclusion that it would be best if his eighteen-month tenure with the Metropolitan Police progressed not one day further; and it didn't.

During my twenty-six years of policing I met quite a few of the dregs of society and their lawyers, and it was sometimes just a university degree which separated one from the other. Sometimes I was able to dish out a proportionate amount of justice, as I did in the first case I shall mention, but in the second I couldn't. In the first two cases the same solicitor appeared, and he made a token appearance in the third.

⋆ ⋆ ⋆

Tyrone Wilson was an exceedingly arrogant young man who made a living out of robbing women of their handbags. I was put on to his activities by Gerry, who was a superlative informant and who had worked as an agent for the British Army. I didn't get as much out of Gerry as I did, say, from Sammy the Snout (or perhaps, Rosie the Grass), but the difference was that whilst the two latter informants might or might not come up with the goods, Gerry's input was invariably 100 per cent accurate.

Gerry pointed him out one night to me, when both of us were sitting in the back of a police observation van. (Yes, I appreciate Gerry shouldn't have been there, but in those days that was one of the many ways in which criminals were caught.)

'That's him,' said Gerry, quietly. 'Tall skinny fucker.'

We were parked up in that particular spot because this was Wilson's favoured hunting ground, where several robberies had occurred and been attributed to him. In fact, it looked as though I was going to strike lucky, because Wilson was just hanging about and continued to do so for about five minutes.

'Heads up!' said Gerry, suddenly. 'Looks like a target for him!'

I peered through the blacked-out window. A woman aged about forty and carrying a handbag was walking straight towards Wilson. Nobody else was in the vicinity. This, I thought, was it.

'Gerry,' I said, urgently. 'When he makes his move, you hop it, quick.'

'Leave off, Dick,' replied Gerry, indignantly. 'You grab him and I'll give the bastard a good kicking – dirty fucker, that's what he . . . '

'Gerry!' I snapped, seeing all sort of difficulties suddenly arising. 'Just do as I bloody say! Right, now mind out . . .'

I had one hand on the door handle, ready to jump out of the van, when Wilson suddenly turned his back on the woman and lit a cigarette, while she passed by completely unmolested. A few moments later, he discarded his half-smoked cigarette and strolled off in the opposite direction.

'Fuck it!' I muttered. 'I could have sworn . . . get after him, Gerry. See where he goes and phone me later at the office.'

Gerry nodded and slipped out of the van. I was quite happy for him to tail the suspect; it mattered not whether it was on the streets of North London or in the back alleys of Londonderry, following a suspect undetected was something at which Gerry was superb.

The phone was ringing as I entered the office.

'Dick, it's me,' said Gerry. 'I followed him home; he went indoors and twenty minutes later turned the light out. Want me to hang on?'

I thought for a moment. 'No, you get off home, Gerry; that's what I'm going to do. I'll catch up with you later.'

The following morning, I arrived in the office to discover that half an hour after I'd booked off duty the previous night there'd been a mugging right in the area where Gerry and I had been keeping observation. The middle-aged woman victim had been badly shaken up; all that she could say about her attacker was that he was black and tall; apart from that, she would be unable to recognize him.

My mood was not improved when I received a phone call from Gerry.

'Our man was out and about last night, wasn't he?' he commented dryly.

I wasn't particularly surprised that Gerry knew; when he was on a case with me, sparrows couldn't fart without Gerry hearing them.

'Yeah. I was in a caff this morning. I heard a couple of tarts talking about it,' he continued. 'The bastard got rid of the woman's credit card last night to one of his girls. These two in the caff weren't involved; they'd just heard about it, that's all. But don't worry – we'll nab the bastard, for sure.'

Gerry had ended our conversation on an optimistic note, but for once he was wrong. We didn't – but somebody else did. It happened quite by chance. Another officer had arrested a young black girl for credit card fraud; she was on a suspended sentence for an exactly similar offence. Seeing a hefty lump of porridge heading her way, and hoping to mitigate her present trouble, she blurted out that in fifteen minutes time Wilson would be meeting her sister in a café to exchange stolen credit cards for a little cash. I wasn't around – pity! – but the other officer grabbed some aids, rushed down to the café and caught the repellent Wilson right in the act of handing over to a girl cards which had been obtained by means of a street mugging.

It got better than that, actually. Upon entry to the café, the police officer leading the raid, a heavily built three-quarter from the Metropolitan Police Three Area Rugby team, launched himself into the air and brought Wilson crashing to the ground. The girl, who had never been so frightened in her life, screamed the place down, before one of the aids exercised commendable tact and conciliation, telling her to 'SHUT THE FUCK UP!'

But no – eager as her sister had been to distance herself from wrongdoing, the girl pointed an accusing finger at Wilson and screeched, "IM TOLE ME 'IM NICK 'EM OFF SOME WHITE BITCH!'

'FUCKIN' GRASS!' roared Wilson as he lunged at the girl, but he was dissuaded from this unfriendly course of action when his head came into sharp contact with a table top. Both of them were brought in; the trembling girl was charged with handling stolen goods but also made a damning statement completely incriminating Wilson, after it was pointed out to her that charges might well be dropped, should she repeat her statement in court. The 'white bitch' later identified her attacker with absolute certainty on an identification parade, and the officer also obtained a startling confession from Wilson, which he had neglected to sign.

The confession was swiftly repudiated at the instigation of Fergus McFarlan. This was Wilson's solicitor, a member of a thoroughly poisonous practice in North London. McFarlan himself was quite dreadful; tall and thin, he had the appearance of a cadaverous spider, his shifty eyes peering from behind smeared National Health spectacles. His few remaining strands of his hair stuck to his skull, and his mouth was set in a permanent leer, displaying a yellowing set of protruding teeth. I imagine that mothers spotting McFarlan in the street would have hurriedly whisked their offspring out of harm's way, lest they fall prey to such an obvious deviant.

Wilson was charged and locked up. And several weeks later, this was where I came into the picture.

'Dick!' called out the rugby-playing officer. 'I'm in a bit of a jam – can you help?'

It transpired that McFarlan, whose applications for bail for his client at the Magistrates' Court had been summarily dismissed, was intending to make an application for bail to a Judge in Chambers at Snaresbrook Crown Court the following day. This, in his written notification, was because he stated that his client had no convictions for violence; that, plus the fact that he was plainly not guilty.

'Now I've just been warned for a trial that's starting tomorrow at the Old Bailey,' groaned the officer. 'You couldn't help out, by going to Snaresbrook for me, could you?'

I could and I would. It was essential for the safety of women walking along the streets that this piece of dreg continued to be locked up. I picked up the bundle of prosecution papers and read through them. Then I looked at Wilson's Form 609, on which his previous convictions were listed. The solicitor was quite right; according to this form, a copy of which had been handed to him, there were a number of convictions, but none were for violence.

It just didn't ring true. I went into the collator's office and picked out Wilson's card. As I looked through it – it was pretty bulky – I noticed that three years previously, he had been arrested for punching a bus conductor; however, there was no result shown. Back in the CID office I picked up Wilson's microfiche from the Criminal Records Office. Putting it into the viewer, I found the entry – he had been charged and had appeared at court but no result had been recorded. This, unfortunately was quite common; officers had got into the habit of not recording the results and sending them off to CRO; it was laziness which had become endemic, and an officer on light duties had been instructed to complete all these results and send them to CRO. There were so many of them that the backlog was taking between twelve and eighteen months to clear. I had been brought up in the CID to type in the result portion on the day the prisoner was dealt with at court or, at the very latest, the following day; and the fact that this slovenly type of behaviour had been allowed to fester, due to lack of supervision, was appalling.

So now I telephoned the court at which Wilson had appeared on the assault charge; a helpful clerk sorted through the records and gave me the date when he had been convicted of assault occasioning actual bodily harm, plus the fact that he had been fined a paltry twenty quid. It wasn't much, but at least he now had a conviction for violence. And then I asked the clerk one further question, and she supplied an answer which brought a smile to my lips . . .

Now for the game plan. I would give the objections to bail, not some pasty-faced little twerp of a junior barrister who would wander along to pick up an easily earned fifty quid. And because legislation had recently been introduced which allowed solicitors, rather than barristers, to apply for bail at a judge in chambers hearing, I hoped that McFarlan himself would be appearing; because if he did, that would truly be the cherry on the cake.

'What are you grinning at?' enquired the rugby player as I roughed out my objections.

'Tell you later,' I smiled.

*   *   *

'I'll give the objections to bail, if you don't mind,' I told the spotty junior barrister the following morning.

He was only too glad to get an easy ride – that, and copping a fee of fifty quid, of course.

'Has the defence received a copy of the prisoner's antecedents?' he asked.

I nodded. Of course, McFarlan hadn't an up-to-date copy, but that wasn't what I'd been asked, was it?

It was just coming up to ten o'clock when McFarlan bustled into court.

'Here's a copy of your client's antecedents,' I said, passing the forms over.

'I've already got a copy,' replied McFarlan rudely, tossing them to one side without a second glance.

'Well, now you've got another one, haven't you?' I commented, and with that, the usher called out, 'All rise!' as the judge entered the court.

After the briefest of preliminaries, the barrister said, 'I'll call the officer', and with that, the usher handed the judge a copy of the newly amended Form 609, and I entered the witness box and took the oath.

'There are three main objections to bail in this case, Your Honour,' I said, 'and they are as follows: I feel that if the defendant is granted bail he will commit further offences, fail to answer his bail and interfere with witnesses. To support the first of these objections, if Your Honour would consult the Form 609, on 16 July 1982, when the defendant appeared at this court, he was convicted of four charges, namely burglary, two cases of unauthorized taking of motor vehicles and theft. However, each of those offences was committed separately; he was arrested for each offence, he appeared at court, was released on bail and on every occasion he committed successive offences, being released on bail in respect of each of them, before eventually being remanded in custody. Exactly the same occurred with the five offences for which he was convicted, again at this court, on 2 May 1980, and more latterly in respect of the four charges at Highbury Corner Magistrates' Court on 11 March 1983, in respect of which he is currently the subject of a suspended sentence.

'Regarding the second of these objections, I believe there is a realistic possibility that the defendant would, if granted bail, fail to answer his bail. First, there is a conviction for failing to answer his bail; and in that case, the matter was not dealt with until he was arrested for a subsequent offence. And given that he is the subject of a suspended sentence, plus the inevitability of a substantial sentence of imprisonment if he pleads or is found guilty of this current offence, I believe there are substantial grounds for believing he will abscond to escape justice.

'Lastly, there is the matter of witness interference, and there is no clearer indication of that than when, at the time of his arrest, he lunged at Miss Jasmine Templeton-Adams, calling her a "fucking grass", and when the defendant had to be forcibly restrained. She is presently on bail as a co-defendant but one whom the Crown may almost certainly call as a prosecution witness when this case goes to trial. Those are my objections to bail in this case, Your Honour.'

The judge nodded. 'Mr McFarlan?'

Getting to his feet, McFarlan stated, 'It is true, is it not, Sergeant Kirby, that my client has no convictions whatsoever for violence?'

Before I could answer, the judge interrupted. 'Just a moment, Mr McFarlan, but if you refer to the copy of the form listing your client's convictions you will see that he has indeed been convicted of assault occasioning actual bodily harm.'

McFarlan's mouth fell open as he snatched up the Form 609 which I had handed him prior to the arrival of the judge; the one that he had not even looked at.

'Your Honour, this is outrageous!' he brayed. 'On the Form 609 which I was given at the magistrates' court there was no mention of this conviction – now, on this form, which Sergeant Kirby handed to me, just prior to this court sitting, up pops a conviction like a rabbit out of a hat!'

I explained to the judge the tardiness which had resulted in the conviction not being originally recorded and that I would bring this to the attention of my senior officers, and then I turned to McFarlan. 'Regrettable though this omission might be, Mr McFarlan, are you going to suggest that your client was not convicted of this offence?'

McFarlan opened his mouth to reply and then stopped as he saw the smile on my face; in an instant he suddenly realized that I knew what he had known all along. Thanks to the helpful clerk at the court, I was fully aware that when Wilson had appeared in court and had been convicted on the assault charge, he had been defended by McFarlan. Because there had been no mention of the conviction on the original Form 609, McFarlan had taken this as a perfect opportunity to lie blatantly that his client had no convictions for violence.

In a split second McFarlan made up his mind. 'Your Honour, I withdraw the application,' he muttered.

'I should have dismissed the application in any event,' murmured the judge, 'and next time you make a similar application, Mr McFarlan, you might, if I may say so, exercise a little more diligence in obtaining your client's instructions.'

And with that frosty rebuke, the usher called, 'All rise!' and, giving me the most poisonous look possible, McFarlan flounced out of court.

That evening, over a large scotch, the detective superintendent laughed as I recounted the tale, plus my suggestion regarding the possibility of feeling McFarlan's collar. He shook his head.

'Can't be done, Dick,' he chuckled. 'That slimy little fucker would just say that he defended so many low-lifes that he just happened to forget that particular conviction.'

'Let me pull him in, Guv,' I persisted. 'See what he's made of.'

But the superintendent smiled and again shook his head. I was disappointed, but he was probably right. However, I may have won the first round – in fact, Wilson later copped five years, which was a good result – but I hadn't won the fight. Not by any manner of means.

★ ★ ★

I came out of my corner for round two several months later. A 67-year-old spinster's apartment had been broken into, and during the course of the burglary she had been revoltingly murdered. A local specimen of pond-life had been arrested and had confessed to being the perpetrator; however, in the course of his admissions he mentioned that he had had an accomplice – a 14-year-old little scumbag named Shaun Pearson, the product of an alcoholic mother and an unknown father and the possessor of a string of convictions. These credentials, coupled with an almost complete lack of education, made him the darling of Islington social services.

'This is the little bastard's address, Dick,' said the detective chief inspector in charge of the investigation. 'Get round there quick and scrag the little fucker in.'

I grabbed a couple of aids and we shot round to the address; a tall, cheerless, crumbling tenement which was pretty well the norm for the area – graffiti everywhere, discarded fast-food cartons containing the unwanted portions of the various delicacies, the smell of vomit, the invasive and overpowering stench of urine.

From behind Shaun Pearson's front door came the thump-thump-thump of music turned up to full volume. Although I hammered on the door I knew no one could have heard my knocking, so I instructed the aids to kick the door in. As I walked into the hallway of that gruesome, unoccupied flat, I came across something I had never encountered before. The music blasted out from behind each door in the flat, and each door was locked. I kicked in each and every one of those doors, turning the music off as I went; each room was empty. Shaun Pearson had put the music on full-blast before locking each door and leaving the premises. That behaviour obviously said something compelling about his psychological profile, although what, exactly, was beyond me at the time; as a matter of fact, it still is.

And just then, who should enter the flat but Shaun Pearson? He stopped stock-still inside the front door, looking all around at the ruined internal doors.

'Who done this?' he shouted.

I took a couple of steps forward and grabbed him by the arm.

'Police,' I said crisply. 'Come on, you're under arrest for murder.'

Pearson struggled wildly.

'Have you got a warrant?' he shouted.

'Did you hear what I said?' I shouted back. 'You're under arrest for murder!'

'NEVER MIND ABOUT NO FUCKING MURDER!' screamed Pearson. 'DID YOU HAVE A FUCKING WARRANT?'

I wondered then, as I do now, what must have been going on in the mind of a 14-year-old boy whose only concern, upon being told that he was being arrested for the most serious crime in the criminal calendar, was whether or not I was in possession of a warrant to search his family's flat.

Since Pearson was a juvenile he had to be questioned in the presence of a responsible adult. His mother, who was in the process of getting staggeringly pissed in the company of the latest of Pearson's 'uncles', was nowhere to be found; not, of course, that she could even remotely be described as 'responsible'. However, his mother's brother – I describe him thus so that you will be aware that he was a genuine relative, rather than an uncle of convenience – was summoned. Uncle Bill, the possessor of a great deal of form – he had only been released from doing a stretch the previous month – duly turned up. And so did Pearson's solicitor, none other than Fergus McFarlan.

★ ★ ★

Following a consultation between McFarlan and his client, I interviewed Pearson in his presence of McFarlan and Uncle Bill.

To each question Pearson answered, 'Nah commen' – this being Islingtonian for 'No comment'.

I thought I'd try something which had worked in the past and, I hoped, might work now.

'A forensic examination of the murdered lady's flat is being carried out,' I said. 'It could be they're going to find fingerprints there; could be they've found some already. Do you want to deny ever going into her flat?'

At this Uncle Bill perked up. He knew exactly what I was getting at. It would be one thing to be tied in for a burglary; it would be something quite different if there were no other explanation for his fingerprints being at the scene of a murder.

'Shaun,' said Uncle Bill, urgently. 'If you've been in that flat, say so, right now.'

Pearson looked enquiringly at McFarlan, who grinned at him. This Pearson took to be his cue. He turned back to me and gave a smile, full of imbecilic pleasure.

'Nah commen!'

'Shaun!' repeated Uncle Bill, this time desperately. 'For Christ's sake! If you've been in that bloody flat, tell the man; don't you understand, you silly little sod? You think you're being so fucking clever, just saying, "No comment", don't you? You're bloody not! You're talking yourself right into a murder charge! Tell him!'

All of which didn't faze Pearson in the slightest. He and McFarlan were now all but openly laughing.

'Nah commen!'

And that was the end of the interview. Pearson was locked up again but only until he could be bailed.

'Thanks for trying to do the right thing in there,' I said to Uncle Bill.

'If you find his dabs in that flat, Guv'nor,' he replied, shaking his head slowly, 'that's his fucking lot, ain't it?'

I nodded but I wasn't going to hold my breath. And what's more, I was right; no independent evidence was ever forthcoming to tie Shaun Pearson in with the murder, and he was released. That was something which caused me grave concern, then and now. The thought of a completely out-of-control psychotic kid loose on the streets, knowing that he'd got away with murder once so he could do it again if he wished. In fact, if he could do that, he could do anything he pleased – all that was required was a venal solicitor on hand to coach him into saying, 'Nah commen' to every question that was asked of him.

Pearson's mother staggered into the nick later that evening, stupefyingly pissed, on the arm of a scrawny, tattooed Glaswegian who was similarly inebriated, and they made their own contribution to the proceedings.

'Yer see,' she told me with the sort of earnestness that only alcoholics can supply, 'it ain't 'is fort. Social workers tol' me, din' they? 'E's got behavioural difficulties.'

'Nah, nah,' interjected her companion. 'He's nae got behavioural difficulties; he's fuckin' sumple!'

That summed up the philosophy of the Islingtonian dross quite neatly. A woman is appallingly murdered, but of course, nobody's to blame. It's just that someone who happened to be 'fuckin' sumple' and when 'it ain't 'is fort' had got a piece of shit for a lawyer.

*   *   *

Time for a bit of closure. A couple of years went by and I was back on the Flying Squad doing what I enjoyed most – nicking big-time robbers. And in the course of feeling their collars I would inevitably end up at the Bailey.

I had just heard the sonorous words, 'and now, if you will retire to consider your verdict.' I sat there in Court 11, silently gathering my papers together, as the barristers and court officials streamed out of court. Would this pair of scumbags go down? God, I hoped so; I'd worked hard enough to keep them locked up until their trial, since every moment they were at large represented a danger to the public. Certainly, the evidence to convict them was all there and, given the circumstances of the case, it was sufficient to merit each of them having about fourteen years stuffed up their arseholes: the defence seemed to me, at least, to be a contrived piece of nonsense but even so . . . well, you never do know, do you? I sighed, stood up and walked towards the doors of the court which led out onto the third floor of the Bailey. As I left the court I was deep in thought when, all of a sudden, I was pulled up short by an authoritative voice.

'Oh!' someone exclaimed angrily. 'What are *you* doing here?'

I looked up and who should I see but Fergus McFarlan. Because he had caught me completely off guard, I replied automatically, 'I've got a case. . . ' before I suddenly pulled myself together. What in God's name was I doing explaining my attendance at the Central Criminal Court to this piece of slime?

I looked round the immediate area; nobody was about. I smiled.

'What am I doing here?' I repeated. 'Why, I'm admiring the architecture. That window over there, for example – see it?'

I pointed to the large third-floor window overlooking the street below.

McFarlan turned and looked. 'Well, what about it?'

'I should think you're just about the right size to go through it head-first,' I replied, 'and unless you fuck off out of my sight, you poisonous little wank, that's what's going to happen to you!'

'How dare you!' gasped McFarlan. 'I shall be making an official com– '

'If you do,' I interrupted him, 'you'll be making it from a nice comfy bed in St Bart's'.

St Bartholomew's Hospital – always known as 'St Bart's' – was just across the road from the Old Bailey. There must have been something in my eyes which caused the crooked little brief to scuttle away, nervously looking over his shoulder as he went – I've been told by Flying Squad colleagues that when I get really cranked-up, the ferocious look on my face is sufficient to put most people off their breakfast.

Well, I never saw McFarlan again, nor did he make a complaint, so I suspect that he believed that I was pulling his leg. But once again, I thought about him lying his head off in an attempt to get Tyrone Wilson bail, as well as being instrumental in setting that psychotic little bastard Shaun Pearson free to roam the streets and get up to God-knows-what. Up till now, we'd been honours even. So after this little encounter, had I won the best of three falls?

Well, I suppose it depends on your point of view. As a matter of fact, I'd used that 'chucking-through-the-window' ploy once before, on a pompous barrister at the Bailey. Of course, on that previous occasion I was only joking.

CHAPTER 6

A Slight Misunderstanding

Just the other day, I came in from my gym, puffed-out. That sounds very grand doesn't it – 'my gym'? Actually, I've semi-converted my garage so that it contains a second-hand multi-gym, a bullworker, a chest expander, some assorted weights (these last two items I purchased over sixty years ago) and a heavy punchbag. So that's my gym; however, in fairness, I have to admit to sharing it with my car, assorted tins of paint and, during the winter, several pots of geraniums.

It was the heavy punchbag I'd been pounding, and actually I felt quite proud of myself; usually I stumble around, half-heartedly and flabbily poking at the bag, but on this occasion I'd done quite well – my footwork was nimble and I darted sizzling straight lefts and right crosses into the uncomplaining piece of leather.

Now I was paying the price for my short-lived athleticism and, puffing like a grampus, I flopped down in an armchair and dropped my bag mitts on the floor, too tired to unwind the wraps from my hands.

'You want to take it easy, you know,' said Ann, mildly concerned by the sight of the sweat pouring down my face and my heaving chest. 'You're not as young as you were. Just as well you don't have punch-ups with villains anymore.'

It's remarks like that which tend to dent my male ego.

'Huh!' I responded indignantly. 'I could still give a good account of myself!'

But as Ann walked off towards the kitchen she laughed and called out over her shoulder, 'No you couldn't – you're an old fraud!'

I sipped a glass of water, and as I unwound the wraps I smiled. She had a point. Just as well I don't get involved in rough-houses anymore; I couldn't have a fight to save my life. And a fraud, too. I remembered a story in which a fraud investigation and a punch-up – through no fault of mine – were inextricably linked, and both situations were thrust upon me.

I never liked fraud investigations. I couldn't understand them; they were far too complex for my solitary brain cell. Other officers loved them; their eyes would gleam as they traversed columns of dodgy figures, and I came to rely on these officers. If they had a nice juicy grievous bodily harm to investigate, full of snot and gore, with which they were making no progress whatsoever, and I'd been landed with a fraud, I'd propose a swap. It was an offer which was inevitably eagerly accepted, and the other officer would shuffle away muttering about fraudulent conversion, falsification of accounts and warrants under the Bankers' Books Evidence Act, while I'd be happily up to my armpits in exit wounds caused by gunshots, incised and defence wounds and coming to terms with when a substance becomes 'noxious'.

However, the funny thing was, I did have some successes with frauds, but these achievements had little to do with my investigative skills; I relied rather on guile and low cunning. When a puce-faced company director called me into his office and thunderously accused a pale, trembling clerk of cooking the books, I'd take the clerk and the disputed accounts back to the nick, sit him down, give him a cup of tea and say, 'Y'know, you're a clever fellow. How you managed to cheat that old skinflint Johnson out of fifteen hundred quid is beyond me. How the devil did you do it?'

And perhaps because I wasn't denouncing him in doom-laden tones as his employer had done, or maybe because I was pandering to his vanity, on practically every occasion the clerk would give a half-chuckle and reply, 'Well, it wasn't too difficult, actually. Y'see, what I did was . . .' and then he would explain the scam, at my prompting, in minute detail so that a 5-year-old child could appreciate it. Since my understanding of fraud was on a par with the comprehension of a kid that age, I'd finally be able to grasp how the con had been worked and could charge the devious accountant. Only on one occasion did I come unstuck, and that was with a chap who worked in a bakery; after he'd admitted the fraud, it suddenly became clear to him how I'd duped the confession out of him and, enraged, he completely lost control and flew at me in a most un-accountant-ish sort of way. Fortunately, in common with many bakers, he was as puffed-up as the dough he kneaded, so this didn't present a problem.

Funnily enough, one of my last commendations was for a case of fraud, as was one of the first; however, since that initial one came from the lips of Sir Harold Cassel QC, who was as mad as a bag of bollocks, I suppose its authenticity could be challenged or at least be the subject of scornful comment.

But I'm drifting away from the main thrust of this story, where there were no confessions or commendations, just a whacking great punch-up.

*   *   *

It all started when I was told to investigate an allegation of fraud. I looked desperately around for someone in the office upon whom I could offload it, but with a palpable lack of success. Exactly what the finer points of this swindle were are of no consequence; suffice it to say, I had a mooch around and as a result came up with the name of Angus McPhee. This, I must make clear, was not as the result of a tip-off from a snout – it was due to my own investigative and detective ability, both of which, as you will shortly discover, were badly flawed – and it resulted in me, early one morning, knocking on the door of Angus McPhee's smelly abode in Holloway's Tufnell Park Road.

McPhee was a typical Glaswegian hard-nut – five feet tall and fag-paper-thin, red-haired and tattooed. Fighting, according to his file at Criminal Records Office, was something he knew quite a bit about, but there was no reference to offences relating to fraud. Still, he was relaxed enough when I told him precisely why he was being arrested. He denied unequivocally being in any way, shape or form connected with the fraud and told me he knew nothing about it. In fact, he provided me with a detailed alibi for the time the swindle was perpetuated, and then he came along peacefully. At Highbury Vale police station the station officer requested both his details and that he turn out his pockets, and McPhee dutifully complied. This was when matters started to go wrong.

'Right, Angus,' I said. 'I'm going to check out your alibi, so you'd better have a sit-down in the cells.'

McPhee regarded me calmly.

'I'm not going in the cells.'

'Well, we can't leave you wandering round the police station, can we?' I said, reasonably. 'Come on, mate, I'll be as quick as I can.'

'If you want me to go in the cells,' replied McPhee equably, 'you'll have to put me in there.'

As I took a step towards him, up came his fists. We then launched into a terrific tussle, rolling around on the charge room floor, feet kicking, both of us punching, with McPhee grabbing hold of anything which might delay his journey to the cells; tables, radiator pipes and doorways. I got him into the cell passageway, and the only vacant cell was the one right at the very end – isn't it always the way?

By now, our exertions had attracted the attention of the rest of the cells' inhabitants, who were awaiting transportation to the Magistrates' Court.

'Who's that?'

'It da littl' Bill!' (This was one of my more repeatable nicknames, courtesy of my parishioners from the Islingtonian black community.)

'Go on, Jock, give 'im a slap!'

Eventually, I shoved McPhee inside the cell and slammed the door. I was out of breath and furious, because I really hadn't expected such a set-to, given McPhee's previous equanimity. As I returned down the passageway, still the abuse from the inmates kept coming, ranging from the slanderous – ''Ow you like it for a change?' – to the offensive (and also mildly witty) – 'Hope he kicked you in the arse, so's you get brain damage!'

I banged a bruised fist on one of the doors. 'Shut up, you mugs, or you'll all get a lay-down at court!' and that had the desired, calming effect, until I walked out of the cell block and heard a muffled cry from an unknown prisoner: 'Wanker!'

'Thanks for your help!' I said furiously to the custody sergeant, who had remained at his desk the entire time.

'What, against a skinny little fucker like that?' replied the sergeant off-handedly. 'I'd have thought that he was the one who needed the help!'

I went upstairs to my office and sat down, simmering with fury. Right, I thought. I'm going to break that little bastard's alibi and screw him down for this fraud. But I didn't. When I started digging into McPhee's alibi, it stood up; and whoever had committed the fraud, it certainly hadn't been him. Luckily, Sammy the Snout owed me a few favours, particularly since he'd received an over-indulgent bursary from the Informants' Fund a week previously. I contacted him and, without any of his usual prevarication ('I'll keep me ear to the ground, Mr K'), he immediately provided the name of the real fraudster. To my extreme discomfort, he appeared somewhat surprised that I wasn't already aware of it since, as he stated, 'It's the worst-kept secret on the manor.'

I quickly pulled in the real swindler, and very unusually for me when dealing with fraudsters, roared at him, which left him trembling; he promptly confessed to the fraud which I was investigating and, to show good faith, two more. Since one of these was being investigated by a much-hated detective inspector from a neighbouring division who, it was generally felt, had given up investigating at the time when Christ was a carpenter, much of my equanimity was restored. Much – but not all. I still had McPhee to contend with. There he sat, comfortably in his cell, drinking tea from a polystyrene cup. I opened the cell door and cleared my throat uncomfortably.

'Look, I'm sorry, old son,' I said, 'but I made a right bloomer. You're free to go.'

McPhee drained his tea, said, 'Aye, that's OK', and shook hands with me. 'No hard feelings, eh?'

I never saw or heard from him again.

Why had McPhee reacted with such violence? Perhaps he felt that it was necessary to make a token protest about being banged up. Some token!

The account of our confrontation had rocketed round the nick, getting more inflated with each rendition. The story had been blown out of all proportion, with me, by now the hulking aggressor, picking on a tiny, quivering little stick insect named McPhee. It had, of course, filtered through to the detective superintendent and detective chief inspector, whom I met for a glass that evening. The superintendent was an officer I'd known for fifteen years. We had met one evening in a pub, when he was a first-class detective sergeant and I was an aid to CID; the following day, I was due to stand on an identification parade to decide my culpability (or not) in a case of grievous bodily harm, and he had given me wise and generous counsel. The fact that I had survived the identification parade gave him good cause to believe that he had a clear insight into my character. He thought the whole episode highly amusing and chuckled as I winced when the scotch I was drinking burned my still-sore lip.

There were, of course, no fulsome noises of approval for my catching the real fraudster, even though, apart from clearing up my own case, I'd squared up two more, including the one allocated to the chubby pimp of a detective inspector. I really didn't expect any congratulations. It was just as well.

The chief inspector, who rather unfairly had decided to accept the inflated version of events which had now become the main topic of conversation around the nick, sighed and shook his head.

'I dunno, Dick,' he muttered. 'You're a good DS, but sometimes I think it's the way you talk to people!'

There are some comments which are best ignored. Nowadays, when I think about less than helpful remarks like that, I go into the gym and look at the logo on my uncomplaining Everlast punchbag: 'Greatness is within'!

CHAPTER 7

Gordon

'Gordon,' said my wife in portentous tones, 'is one of just three people I know who I can describe as being a complete and thorough gentleman.'

Well, you don't argue with Ann Kirby when she makes such a magisterial statement – I don't, anyway – so I kept quiet and hoped that I would be included as one of the other two. In fact, I was doomed to disappointment, but never mind that; she was right, because Gordon is a blinkin' toff.

Gordon is tall, elegant and has the look of a courtier, someone perhaps who, if he were entrusted with state secrets, would never part with the details, either through indiscretion or force of arms. He always looks at home, whether he's wearing an immaculately cut tweed suit in the restaurant of a country hotel or black tie at the annual dinner of the Ex-CID Officers' Association. The son of a knight of the realm, and as smooth as a cucumber's codpiece, he's about ten years older than me, and I've decided that when I grow up I want to be just like him.

I first met Gordon when we were both attending an SAS reunion luncheon; I'm not entirely sure if he was a member of that esteemed regiment, because every time I've brought up that question he has effortlessly and with great charm brushed it aside.

As well as being a fellow member of the Special Forces Club, much of his police service has been shrouded in mystery, and he's disinclined to talk about it; but from time to time, when a bottle of Chilean Red has been broached and we're seated in his study, as the flames leap and crackle in the grate from the wood of a long-dead pear tree, I manage to induce him to recite a tale or two from his shadowy past.

Well over sixty years ago, Gordon found it necessary to discover precisely what a gang of criminals were up to. Unsuccessful attempts had been made to penetrate their ranks with informants, and the gang were notoriously guarded regarding anything they said on the telephone. But of course they had to discuss their criminal plans somewhere, and the best place of all was their flat, where they would be sheltered from eavesdropping by an unkind, law-abiding world. Or so they thought.

Gordon climbed into the roof space above their living room, surreptitiously drilled tiny holes in the ceiling and with the aid of some equipment which he delicately thrust into those holes – my queries as to the nature and the provenance of these items were smilingly discouraged – he settled down to a very uncomfortable ten hours, watching the crims and listening to their conversation.

The wind cut through both the tiles and the felt of that damp and rather claustrophobic enclosure, but it paid off; the gang were later rounded up, and it was thought neither necessary nor desirable to explain to them how the deeply incriminating evidence against them had been gathered. Following an appearance at the Old Bailey, they went off to a total of eighteen years' imprisonment, furiously scratching their heads and wondering who on earth had grassed them up.

'Of course,' murmured Gordon as he poured me a generous helping of Chilean nectar, 'the most ghastly aspect of the observation was that one had to keep absolutely still. The slightest movement up there would have alerted them to my presence.'

'What did you do with regard to your bodily functions?' I asked. Gordon, as you may have guessed, is not the sort of chap you'd ask, 'What happened when you wanted a slash?'

'Ah, well, you see, I'd taken the precaution of taking a hot water bottle with me,' explained Gordon. 'The trouble was, as the day wore on, it grew progressively fuller and heavier.'

I laughed. 'I hope that hot water bottle at least kept you warm in that draughty loft, Gordon.'

Gordon smiled. 'It did,' he replied smoothly, 'but not at a temperature exceeding 98.4° Fahrenheit!'

CHAPTER 8

A Silver Lining

Speaking of Gordon, I was having a drink with him one evening – and I can't for the life of me remember how this topic of conversation came up – when he reminded me that after the Second World War we were flat broke and had to beg the Americans for food; although that, I already knew.

But then he told me that from 1920 onwards all British 'silver' coins were produced in 50 per cent silver, alloyed with 50 per cent copper – so that from 1921 to 1946 inclusive, all silver coins were .500 fine. Amongst his other interests, Gordon is an expert on coins and antique silver so he's worth listening to, but he surprised me when he told me that in 1947 we had to melt down our silver coinage to repay the US for the 82 million ounces of silver we had borrowed from them during the war.

'Not a lot of people know that,' said Gordon, 'but it ought to be common knowledge.'

It explained why, from 1947 onwards, silver coins weren't silver at all; they were made of cupro-nickel, an alloy of copper and nickel. There were, however, still plenty of pre-1947 silver coins in circulation.

The Coinage Act came into force in 1971, and Section 10 stipulated that after 16 May 1969, the day parliament approved the Decimal Currency Act, it was illegal to melt down or break up any metal coin current in the UK or which had at any time after that date ceased to be so; the offence was punishable with a £400 fine or two years' imprisonment. That was only enforceable in the UK; it was legal if the coins were taken abroad.

However, on 23 July 1973 the Department of Trade and Industry permitted the export of various commodities, including silver coins minted prior to 1947. Because of the high world price of silver, it became extremely profitable to export these coins for melting down abroad and conversion into bullion. Therefore, a dealer who bought £500 face value of pre-1947 coins for £1,000 could take them to Amsterdam and sell them for £1,500. All the dealings were strictly cash, and the turnover was so rapid that the journey could be made three times in a week. The profit margin was enormous; in one month a dealer could theoretically increase his original £1,000 to £120,000.

See? Simple. Actually, it wasn't to me, because, as I've already confessed, I was an absolute dunce when it came to any kind of monetary transaction, fraudulent or otherwise.

Maurice Marshall, who joined the Met in 1953, had worked on the Flying Squad and Murder Squad and retired as a detective chief superintendent. He later became the president of the ReCIDivists' luncheon club so he has a fund of good stories. He's the most equable sort of chap, but when he had to explain to me, for the third time, in writing and in painstaking detail, the tale that follows, he did get a bit snappy.

'I must say I am disappointed that my "chatty" style of writing was not as clear as I intended,' he told me frostily, 'so may I try again?'

And this is the case which Maurice, as a detective chief inspector, investigated in 1974. He had a detective sergeant to assist him; it wasn't me, which was probably just as well, because if it had been, the case might not have had the successful conclusion that it did.

*   *   *

Ernie was one of three partners in a coin dealers' business. They were aware of the huge profits to be made by exporting these coins, but they were not aware that to take the coins abroad was quite lawful; in fact, they believed it to be totally illegal. On the morning of 23 April 1974 Ernie, who had collected 131 bags of these pre-1947 coins with a face value of £13,000, needed some help to export them, since they weighed in the region of 1½ tons. Malcolm was one of five couriers, his brother was another, and Martin, who was one of Ernie's partners, was a third. The coins were loaded into the boots of four cars, they took the ferry from Harwich to the Hook of Holland and the coins were duly sold to a bullion dealer in Amsterdam. The sale realized 220,000 Dutch guilders, and although Martin, being a partner, should really have held on to the money, it was Malcolm who took it.

The men returned on the night ferry, arriving on the morning of 25 April, when three of the men went straight to Ernie's house to await the arrival of Malcolm and his brother.

But Malcolm didn't arrive. Instead, his brother dropped Malcolm off at his own house, which was no more than 400 yards away from Ernie's, and it was there that three men who said they were police officers arrested Malcolm, put him into a blue Triumph saloon and, to the consternation of Malcolm's wife Hilary, drove off with him. Telling him they knew what he had been up to, the cops demanded his money, and Malcolm, under the impression that he had been involved in an illegal activity, handed the Dutch guilders over to them. Taking him to London's East End, they beat him up, threw him unconscious out of the car and left him there suffering from loss of memory.

Meanwhile, Hilary rushed round to Ernie's address and informed him and the waiting men of what had happened. There was great consternation. What to do? They had no doubt they had been involved in an illegal activity – how could they inform the police without incriminating themselves? For her part, Hilary made it quite clear that she *definitely* did not want the police involved.

Whilst this frantic discussion was going on, Malcolm was found in what appeared to be a dazed condition and was taken to the London Hospital. His injuries were only superficial, and although the doctors were sceptical regarding his amnesia, he nevertheless remained under observation for the next five days.

By now you'll probably have gathered that not only was the robbery by the alleged police officers a put-up job, but Malcolm was the originator and prime mover in it. However, it was important for Malcolm to keep up the pretence of amnesia, because it enabled him to keep quiet about the robbery until he knew whether or not Ernie had reported the matter to the police. Malcolm sent a message to Hilary, she went to see Ernie, and when he told her that he was going to contact the police, she in turn went straight to the London Hospital to inform her husband of this turn of events. From that moment Malcolm's memory miraculously started to return and he was able to give the police his version of the robbery – but what soon became quite clear to the investigators was that if Ernie had not informed the police, Malcolm certainly would never have done so.

This is where Maurice came into the picture, and it was clear to him that due to the number of discrepancies, the whole scenario stank to high heaven. But what was the answer?

As Maurice said to me, 'Was Malcolm telling the truth? Were any of the other couriers accomplices? Was Hilary complicit or even aware of the deceit?'

With practically everyone involved having previous convictions, this was a Gordian knot of epic proportions. Fortunately, this was 1974, ten years before the iniquities of the Police and Criminal Evidence Act and the Crown Prosecution Service were forced upon the police. Maurice Marshall dealt with the conundrum in true Alexander the Great style by slashing straight through the knot-full of clues, nicking everybody concerned and banging them up in police stations all over 'J' Division.

As Maurice went from one police station to another, speaking to one suspect, then another, cracks began to appear in their stories, each trying, bit by bit, to blame the others for their misfortunes.

'We played one off against the other and to do that we needed to keep the momentum going,' Maurice told me. 'These interviews had to be searching, sometimes pointedly so. The suspects' reply of "no comment" to a question was never heard; indeed, it would not have been tolerated!'

Some were released, only to be pulled back in again. Others were not, since it became clear that, despite the original suspicion, they were innocent.

'I recall the uniform superintendent at one station getting a bit anxious when one of the suspects had been in custody, uncharged, for nearly a week,' Maurice reminisced.

A big break came when the name of one of three brothers, Fred, was mentioned, and in he came. The house of cards was now well and truly collapsing, and Hilary admitted that there had been an arrangement made by her husband Malcolm to steal the money and that Fred was one of the three bogus police officers who had come to their house. She claimed that she had been under duress, being terrified of her husband, although she had played her part well, having provided photofits of two of the alleged robbers.

Husband Malcolm was the next to cave in; he admitted that he, Fred and a man named Vic were the main conspirators, and it had been arranged that they would 'make a hit' on the return from Holland. The Blue Triumph (hired by Vic) was waiting outside his address, and he, Vic and two other men – they turned out to be Vic's brothers, Terry and Joe – drove off to the house belonging to Fred's mother. The money was willingly handed over to Vic – with Malcolm expecting a cut at a later date – some injuries were self-inflicted, and then Malcolm was dumped in the East End and commenced his self-imposed five days-worth of amnesia.

Apart from originally naming Victor as one of the three bogus police officers, when Hilary was interviewed again she suddenly recalled that two of the other men were in fact Terry and Joe, Vic's brothers.

Terry and Joe were brought in and admitted their parts, but the search was still on for Vic – and the money. Maurice's investigation was pretty top-level; he discovered that an assistant bank manager had received a telephone call from Vic, the day before the alleged robbery, requesting the exchange rate of Dutch guilders into sterling. And on the day of the robbery Vic had gone to the Midland Bank at High Street North, East Ham, where he exchanged ten 1,000-guilder notes for £1,552.70p sterling.

The pressure was now on to such an extent that Vic surrendered to police on 15 May and handed over 209 1,000-guilder notes and £1,555 in sterling – in fact, slightly more than he had received in the transaction.

Had this ruse been successful, the conspirators would have had £34,210 to split between them – important money in 1974.

All of the conspirators with the exception of Hilary – Malcolm, Fred, Joe, Terry and Victor – were charged and convicted.

Coincidentally, in 1920, at the same time when .500 fine silver coins started to be minted in England, Jerome Kern's musical comedy *Sally*, starring Marilynn Miller, was staged in the USA. It was a sentimental rags-to-riches story which featured B.G. De Sylva's lyrics in the song, 'Look for the Silver Lining'.

If that's what a number of foolish and greedy conspirators were looking for some fifty-four years later, they were doomed to disappointment. All they found was the inside of a prison cell.

CHAPTER 9

Lofty Aspirations

'You'll never guess who I saw the other day!' exclaimed Keith, excitedly. 'Dougie Rankin!'

Before we deal with the matter of Dougie and his lofty aspirations, I want to introduce you to Keith Taylor, one of the more intrepid of my lunchtime companions. We've been chums for over fifty years, and our comradeship stems from the time when Keith was a police constable on plain clothes duty, tasked to find out who had been behind a spate of smash-and-grabs. He found out, all right, on his first night's patrol, catching them right in the act; and the duo responsible for the burglaries set about him. Now, Keith was (and still is) a pretty tough character, having been a member of 10 Para, but even so, this wicked pair inflicted the most grievous injuries on him. I was an aid to CID on a 'Q'-Car patrol that evening, and after I had a chance to inspect his injuries I had occasion to speak to one of Keith's tormentors. It's little kindnesses like that which have kept our friendship alive for so long.

When Keith imparted this astonishing news to me regarding Dougie Rankin, we were in the bar of the Special Forces Club. We were seated in the corner of the bar which the late Lieutenant Colonel Rupert Mayne (a former member of the wartime Force 136 who had narrowly missed assassination by an enemy agent) caustically referred to as 'Coppers' Corner' because so many of us swapped our secrets there.

'Dougie Rankin,' I echoed. 'Bloody hell, I haven't seen Dougie for over twenty years. In fact, it's more like twenty-five years. What's he up to?'

Keith explained that he had bumped into Dougie, just by chance, when he was walking through the City of London.

'He's got some big-wig job in a financial corporation,' said Keith. 'Doing very nicely for himself by all accounts. I invited him to lunch next Thursday – fancy coming along?'

I turned to Mustapha, the club's superlative barman, who was blessed with second sight. Without a word being uttered, he had accurately read my mind and poured me a generous glass of Rioja.

'I wouldn't miss it,' I told Keith.

There were some questions which I wanted to put to Dougie; questions which I'd been pondering for some time.

★ ★ ★

In fact, I'd known Dougie longer than I'd known Keith. We were uniform police constables and we gelled after we discovered that we shared the same kind of quirky humour, together with a fairly ambivalent outlook on the strict interpretation of suspects' civil liberties. Inevitably, this led to the odd misunderstanding, but Dougie and I managed to rise above the vagaries of outraged lawyers and their charmless clients and found no end of humour in those otherwise hostile situations.

But then I became an aid to CID and moved elsewhere, and Dougie and I lost touch. In fact, I don't believe I ever saw him again whilst we were serving police officers, but I do know that he also became an aid to CID; as the years passed, it became a fairly commonplace occurrence for me to open *Police Orders* and there, under 'commendations', would be Dougie's name (he was by now a detective constable), sometimes for a bit of derring-do but often for unravelling some kind of a complex fraud.

Although I hadn't seen Dougie I'd heard him, on the police radio in the late seventies. I was a member of the Serious Crime Squad and as such I had had a police radio fitted into my Ford Corsair 2000GT. As I drove through the night in East London I suddenly heard Dougie's voice on the channel specifically devoted to units on specialist operations. I was aware that he was part of a team which was hunting a very dangerous criminal and I knew I was close to where Dougie was transmitting his message; I was therefore tempted to call him on the air and ask if I could be of assistance. It was the type of situation upon which both Dougie and I thrived. However, I decided not to, and it was a wise choice, because (a) Dougie already had sufficient back-up, and (b) the senior officer in charge of the operation was so paranoid about security, he would probably have seen my intervention as a breach of the Official Secrets Act. So I left well alone, the target was arrested for murder without my assistance and in the fullness of time convicted, and Dougie notched up another commendation to add to his already impressive total.

And then – nothing. He'd vanished. I heard that Dougie had left the Metropolitan Police, but why? He hadn't been sacked – if he had, it would have been shown in *Police Orders* under 'dismissals' – so perhaps he'd received a better offer from the private sector. This, of course, was always possible but it appeared to me that he had

had a glittering career in front of him, quite possibly in the Fraud Squad, thanks to his expertise in unravelling complicated scams. I made a few desultory enquiries, but nobody seemed to know why Dougie had quit his post; and there, for about the next fifteen years or so, the mystery remained.

★ ★ ★

The restaurant in the City of London which Keith had selected for lunch was superb, but knowing Keith to be a first-class gourmet, I would have expected nothing less, especially when the first of his luncheon companions was a gourmand like me. It was a place where serious men went to eat serious food and perhaps, on this occasion, to extract a little information from the third member of our luncheon party.

People – especially CID officers with their eating and drinking habits – tend to change and, usually, expand over the years, but not Dougie. Keith and I were already sitting at the table when Dougie bustled in, and he hadn't changed a bit; tall, slim, good-looking and very expensively booted and suited. We greeted each other effusively, and over a couple of large scotches Dougie brought us up to date, telling us with a great deal of charm that he had been working in the banking and investment sector for some fifteen years. Matters of high finance are a bit above my head, but it turned out that Dougie was some sort of a very well paid stockbroker. His job took him all over the world, especially to the United States where, it appeared, he had acquired a property at Martha's Vineyard, as well as a prestigious one in this country, just outside Buckhurst Hill, complete with swimming pool. Blimey.

The waiter served the roast beef for which the restaurant was justly famous, and the sommelier poured some of the Bordeaux, a Château Larose-Trintaudon from France's Haut-Médoc region, into my glass. I tasted it – wonderful stuff. I nodded to the sommelier and told him, 'Better bring two more.' We old Flying Squad officers are sensitive souls, and I know instinctively when it's going to be one of *those* lunches.

So we relaxed and slowly munched our way through luncheon, as tales of old battles and confrontations were resurrected, often, I'm afraid, with embellishments and the characters of old despotic CID Guv'nors being assassinated, and it was a very jolly conversation. But still I wanted to know – what were the circumstances in which Dougie had left the police? It was . . . well, a delicate subject, but by the time the second bottle of Bordeaux had been lowered, I discovered that I possessed a newly-found courage.

I commenced proceedings by bringing up the subject of pensions. Keith and I had left within a year of each other, both with injury pensions, and I mentioned to Dougie that this had been financially beneficial because our pensions had been immediately index-linked, something which, had we served our full terms in the police, would not have occurred until we were fifty-five. Of course, I added, this would not have happened to Dougie, since as he had already told us, he had left the police prematurely.

'Which reminds me,' I said, carefully. 'When you left the Job early, was it because you had a better offer? Something like that . . .?'

I deliberately tailed the words off, leaving Dougie an opening should he wish to answer the question. Keith, I suddenly noticed, had become extremely alert, his eyes, like a hawk's, flickering between Dougie's face and mine; he was as interested as I in the reason behind Dougie's early departure.

'No,' replied Dougie, without any prevarication whatsoever. 'Nothing like that. I was given the option – get out or get nicked. As simple as that.'

I raised my eyebrows. 'Really?'

I put my answer in a tone which suggested polite interest, nothing more, when of course the reverse was the case.

Dougie drained his glass, which I immediately refilled.

'Yes,' he continued. 'It was after I had a visit from the Funny Firm.'

A number of departments in the Metropolitan Police have, over the years, acquired this nickname, but to the uninformed, in this context it meant that Dougie had had confrontational dealings with the Complaints Investigation Branch. It was this unit which dealt, to the exclusion of everything else, with allegations of impropriety made against police officers, and at the time of their meeting with Dougie, the department was probably known as 'A10' or possibly 'CIB2'.

I raised my glass and waited with great interest to hear what revelations would follow.

'Yeah, the Funny Firm came round my drum and gave me a spin,' said Dougie, adding almost casually, 'They found a car engine which had been nicked.'

'I s'pose you blanked 'em,' I commented, but Dougie shook his head.

'Nope. Stuck m'hands up to it.'

To say I was shocked was an understatement – this was certainly not the Dougie I had known, to cave in at the first sign of pressure. Then suddenly enlightenment dawned – or at least, I thought it did.

'Oh, I get it,' I said, knowingly. 'Those bastards told you that if you didn't stick your hands up they'd nick your missis, is that it?'

This was a ploy often used with great advantage by less than ethical A10 officers.

But again Dougie shook his head. 'Nope. Nothing like that. They just found it and I just stuck my hands up.'

Now I was thoroughly confused.

'Dougie, I really don't get this. A10 come round your gaff, find a nicked car engine and, without them bringing any pressure to bear, such as them telling you they'll nick mum if you don't come across, you say you stuck your hands up. I don't understand. You've nicked a few in your time and you must have made a few enemies. Couldn't you have said that someone who'd obviously got the arse with you had dumped the car engine in your back yard in an attempt to tuck you up, and the first thing you knew about it was when A10 turned up?'

'Well . . .' replied Dougie slowly. 'No. I couldn't.'

'But why not?' I expostulated.

Dougie sighed and with a touch of resignation shrugged his shoulders and replied, 'Because they found it in my loft.'

Keith later remarked that at that moment my jaw dropped so far he was surprised it hadn't hit the table top. But at the time, all I could think of to say, rather faintly, was, 'More horseradish?'

Four faces of the author

Above left: A wee nipper – innocence.

Above right: First day in the Met – apprehension.

Above left: Holloway – determination.

Above right: Retirement – reflection.

The greatest aids to crime-fighting

A Triumph 2500 'Q'-Car.

Left: A Jaguar 2.4 'Q'-Car.

Below: The 'J' Division Crime Squad.

Robbers at work

Robbers acquiring
£8,885.48 – for
about five
seconds . . .

. . . and their
getaway driver
being led away.

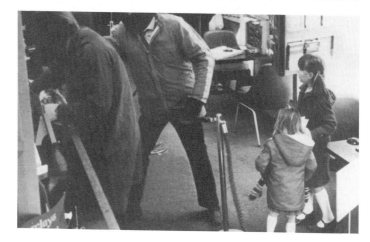

Robbers doing
what they do best:
terrifying people.

Five tough cops

Derek Webster.

Tony Yeoman.

Above left: Gerry Gallagher.

Above right: Mike Bucknole.

Left: Keith Taylor.

Business transacted on the telephone

Right: King's Cross, 1984. The author takes a call which would result in the arrest of double killer, Donald Mackay.

Below: Wiesbaden, West Germany, 1976. The author explains to an international swindler why it would be to his advantage to give himself up; Detective Inspector Charley Cheal, expressing incredulity, listens in.

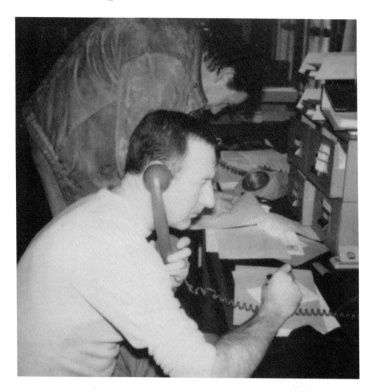

Physical exertions

Above left: The author in strict training, in the event that 'Angus McPhee' required a return bout ...

Above right: ... and an alternative strategy, should McPhee prove too much.

Below: The author defends himself with a housebrick against a much more dangerous adversary.

Four of the good guys

Ian 'Chiv' Chiverton.

Maurice Marshall.

Above: Ray Wood OBE.

Left: Julia Pearce.

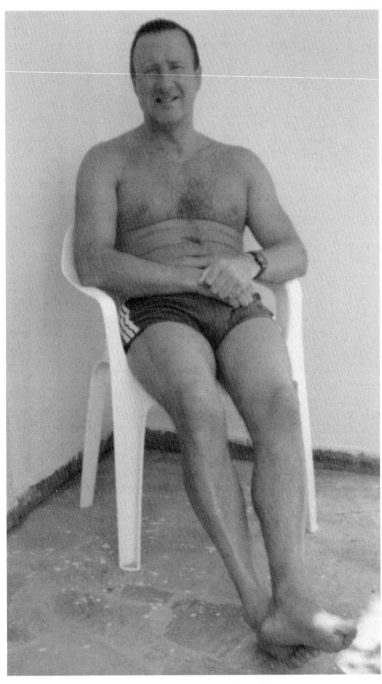

The author, 'looking [as a contemporary unkindly commented] like an armed blagger resting between bank raids'.

CHAPTER 10

Cloak and Dagger

There was a distinctive 'crack!' that I immediately identified as a shotgun being fired, and Charlie's head jerked up.

'That's probably the farmer potting a rabbit for his supper,' I explained, adding nonchalantly, 'but being a member of the landed gentry I'm used to that sort of thing, unlike a dazzling urbanite like you!'

We had just finished lunch on my terrace and we looked down the garden towards the farmer's fields and then the spinney which shielded us from the view of the River Lark and probably a supine rabbit *in extremis*. Ann had taken Charlie's wife for a tour to show off the fuchsias she'd grown from cuttings in her late father's garden.

Charlie knew how to get back at me all right.

'Got any more of that cheap French plonk?' he asked casually, and I tried to think of a suitably cutting answer but couldn't, so with pretended ill-grace I poured some more steel-dry Pouilly-Fuissé into his glass.

We sat there, relaxed. It was a warm, sunny day; a time for reminiscences.

'Were you with me when I nicked the bloke for having that Rembrandt away from the Dulwich Art Gallery?' I asked Charlie.

'Nah, that was before I met you,' he replied. 'I was young and pure in those days!'

'Huh! Pure as the driven slush!' I riposted, using a line from Dorothy Parker, and we both laughed.

Charlie took a sip from his glass. 'No, I remember that Rembrandt job, though. Wasn't there some sort of a row about it?'

'That was where the Metropolitan Police solicitor reckoned I'd tricked the bloke into confessing and wrote to his solicitor begging him to demand an ID parade,' I replied. 'Cheek! Luckily, the bloke's brief was Blackburn-Gittings; one of the straightest defence solicitors I knew; he wrote straight back saying he'd got his client's instructions, which was that he was guilty, so he didn't need an ID parade.'

'Not too many defence briefs like that to the pound,' commented Charlie.

'No, although I had Blackburn-Gittings against me on a blagging job. He firmly believed his client was innocent – course, he wasn't! – but he fought tooth and nail to get him off, and he did.'

Charlie smiled. 'You talking about that Rembrandt job made me remember a UC job. That got fucked up, although there wasn't a brief involved.'

Charlie was one of the Yard's top undercover (or 'UC') officers. On this occasion he was acting as a minder for the art 'expert'; they were attempting to recover a stolen oil painting which had been valued at £10 million.

'We were dragged around all over the place,' recalled Charlie. 'For an hour or more, just before dusk, we were in one rural area after another, round King's Lynn, before we were led into some woods. To be fair, they were a pretty professional team. In fact, they had the painting; they showed it to us. However, what they also had were two minders of their own – both wearing "old men" masks, both of them with sawn-offs. I gave the signal for the attack team to come in.'

Charlie shook his head.

'Christ, what a fuck-up. They'd only lost us in the semi-darkness, hadn't they? The attack team came in from the wrong direction, all hell broke loose and the villains had it on their toes.'

Charlie stopped while he swallowed a little more of the white Burgundy.

'I think that was one of the few occasions that I came close to getting topped,' he said, quietly.

There was a pause; Charlie was lost in his thoughts.

'Did you recover the painting?' I asked.

Charlie gave a short, bitter laugh. 'Dick, I had it in my hands . . . had it in my bloody hands . . . then it went all pear-shaped. The villains took it with them when they legged it. No, as far as I know, it's still missing. For all I know, it could be lying in some Norfolk field.'

He laughed again.

'The funny thing was, something good came out of that. It was the woods and the semi-darkness. It worked in my favour, just a few days later, for a job that was already on the go. Ever hear of the Jacobs brothers – Alfie and Jimmy?'

I nodded. 'Heard of them, but I never had any dealings with them. Horrible bastards, weren't they?'

'That's right. They were a pair of slags and very cunning, but when it came to professionalism like the team who nicked the painting, there was no comparison. We'd had the word that they were offering shooters for sale, and one of the UCs, Nicky – you remember him, don't you?'

'Yes, I do.'

'Well, Nicky was put into them as a middle man,' said Charlie, resuming the narrative. 'He met Alfie in a pub and he tore into Nicky from the word go. Told him he reckoned Nicky was there to stick him up to Old Bill, then suggested that Nicky himself was Old Bill.'

'How did Nicky handle it?' I asked.

'Oh, Nicky turned it around, said if Alfie had got Old Bill up his arse, what the fuck was he doing sticking his face up to them as well? All good, usual stuff. However, Alfie told him that if he was Old Bill, he'd got enough people round him to ID him. With that, he took Nicky out of the public bar and round to the saloon bar. There was Alfie's brother Jimmy, plus fifteen of the ugliest faces Nicky had ever seen. Alfie turned to them and indicating Nicky, he said, "Right, anyone know this geezer? Anyone think he's the filth or what?"'

'Hair-raising stuff!' I commented.

Charlie smiled. 'Apparently, everybody scrutinized him and a couple came right over and looked him up and down before he was off the hook. Nicky reckoned it lasted no more than two minutes but he said it felt like two hours.'

'I bet it did!' I said, with feeling. 'Poor bugger!'

'Still, as I told Nicky, I knew of the self-same thing happening with another UC guy; the difference was, after the first ID parade, they bundled him into a car and took him to another pub for a second one. They also made him strip off to see if he was wearing a wire.'

I shook my head. The very thought of being in that type of situation was sufficient to bring me out in a muck sweat.

'Mind you,' I commented, 'I can remember one Old Bill who went seriously off the rails' and I mentioned his name to Charlie, who nodded. 'It turned out he was working for a right evil firm; when they were going out on a buy, this bastard would be plotted up to see if whoever it was that they were doing business with was UC.'

'Yeah,' muttered Charlie. 'You can't get much lower than that.'

Both of us fell silent for a moment, thinking about a piece of garbage who carried a police warrant card and, for a price, was willing to sell out a fellow police officer to a murderous bunch of scum and place him in a deadly situation.

'Anyway,' resumed Charlie, 'Nicky set up a meet between the Jacobs brothers and me and Norm, another UC guy. We did it on a phone call and the first time we were going to meet was in the car park of a pub by Hainault Forest.'

'What was on offer?' I asked.

'It appeared they had a 9mm Sig semi-automatic to sell for six hundred and fifty quid.'

★ ★ ★

Around this time, the Ministry of Defence had purchased a number of these weapons. The Sig-Sauer P226 carried a clip of either fifteen or twenty rounds and it had been used by the FBI, the US Navy SEALS and various other Special Forces units and law-enforcement agencies world-wide. The Royal Canadian Mounted Police had fired 150,000 rounds of ammunition from this weapon; tests revealed that the rate of malfunction was 0.007 of 1 per cent, so it had a deservedly high reputation. Although it was expensive to manufacture it was light in weight and very accurate. Therefore it was highly desirable for Scotland Yard to get as many of these weapons off the streets as possible.

'The meet had been set for four o'clock,' said Charlie. 'It was late November and dusk was falling fast; that suited me for what I had in mind. In addition, I reckoned we owed those bastards a bit of payback for what they'd put Nicky through.'

He smiled.

'Alfie and Jimmy were up-and-coming gangsters,' explained Charlie. 'I knew that, because when they drove into the car park they were in a Mercedes 190E – very popular with "baby bandits" who hadn't yet made it to the 300 series.'

I smiled at Charlie's description of the brothers Jacobs, but he was right; a car in criminal circles says a lot about who or what you are. To emphasize this assertion, between 1979 and 1995, just 4,294 Porsche 928s, the big, low-back coupé, were sold in the United Kingdom. One of them had been acquired by SO10 Department, and it was in this hideously expensive vehicle that Charlie and Norm had been sitting.

'It was a quarter past four when they turned up,' said Charlie, 'and that suited me fine. Because with me and Norm standing by our car, they got out of the Merc and came towards us.'

Charlie took me right into the story.

Alfie nodded to him. 'All right?'

'No, not really,' responded Charlie caustically. 'Been left here, waiting like a cunt. Four o'clock, we was told.'

Alfie started to back-pedal and looked to Jimmy for support: 'Got held up getting the thing, weren't we?'

'Got it, have you? Good. 'Cos I've just knocked a one-er off the price for my troubles. Well, best you go and get it, old darling.' This to Jimmy.

Alfie and Jimmy stared gormlessly at each other, unused to this type of behaviour in carrying out illegal transactions, when they were usually in control. Jimmy went to the Mercedes, rummaged around in the boot and brought over a dark-coloured cloth bag, which he held out to the two UC men.

'Take a look, Norm,' said Charlie dismissively.

Norm was already wearing leather driving gloves; now he took hold of the bag, and out fell a Sig-Sauer P226. He squinted at it.

'It's so fucking dark here, I can't see fuck all,' he muttered.

And before either of the brothers could suggest the obvious solution of examining the weapon in the lighted interior of the car, Charlie suddenly said, 'Let one off – make sure the fucking thing works!'

'What – in the car park!?' screamed Jimmy.

'You can't do that – Old Bill'll be all over us!' shrieked Alfie, his voice several octaves higher than his brother's.

And now Charlie really took command of the situation.

'Where's the Old Bill, mate?' he asked, spreading his arms to emphasize the emptiness of their surroundings. His voice went up a notch. 'We're standing in a car park which is empty. It's almost fucking midnight, 'cos you two turned up late!' [This, of course, was a slight exaggeration.] 'Are you two paranoid or something? All you seem to do is go on about the filth being around – yeah! All the time you were dealing with Nicky, it was "Old Bill this, Old Bill that"! He told me, don't fucking deny it!'

By now Charlie had wound himself up to fever pitch.

'I'll tell you what, I'm getting the shits off you two. If Old Bill get hold of you, what're you going to do, go out like a light? I'll tell you what, mate, thanks but no thanks. I don't fancy doing work with worriers like you. If you ain't happy, walk away – that's what I'm doing.'

With that, Charlie nodded to Norm and both of them got into the Porsche. The UC men paused to sneer at the two astonished brothers, before Charlie turned on the ignition; the roar from the 5,396cc V8 engine seemed to echo their contempt. He slipped the car into gear and drove off out of the car park. In spite of the darkness, he didn't even bother to put the lights on.

*　*　*

'So the brothers still had the gun with them?' I asked.

Charlie chuckled. 'This is where it all comes together. The operational team had arranged for a traffic patrol car to be stationed close to the meet, out of sight. There were a couple of C11 surveillance guys hidden in the undergrowth on the edge of the forest. The fact that I hadn't put the lights on was the signal that they'd got the gun in the car – if we'd driven off with the lights on it would have meant that they hadn't got the gun and that they should let it go. About half a mile away, the Merc was stopped by the traffic patrol car and the gun was found under the carpet in the boot. Course, they screamed that they'd no knowledge of it and that they'd been fitted.'

'What happened next?' I laughed.

'We heard from several sources of information that they were looking for Nicky in order to blow his fucking legs off and that if they ever met me or Norm again, we'd be shot on sight.'

'But why didn't you do the buy in the car park, so that they could be nicked there and then with the weapon in their hands?' I asked.

Charlie shook his head. 'Too risky. I never intended to purchase the gun. Once they'd fixed the meet in the car park, it was considered that it wasn't a suitable location to mount an attack. It was a large, open car park, there could have been anybody, a dog walker for instance, coming out of the forest, crossing the car park . . . no. The risk was too great. But if the brothers had turned up without the gun, but were willing to do the deal elsewhere, we'd have given the "no lights" signal and then moved off after them, and the surveillance would have moved with us and we'd have taken it from there.'

'There's a hell of a lot to think of,' I said, admiringly.

Charlie shrugged. 'You've got to think on your feet. Like, on one occasion, me and the other UC had a fight outside a pub – I was saying the guns were OK, he was saying they were shit – and the target took fright when we started scrapping and cleared off rather than get involved. He got pulled by a traffic car, south of the river, with four handguns in the boot. It took the dairy off us [removed suspicion, in other words]; in the worst case scenario, it'd just have made us look like grasses.'

'Was that what happened with the Jacobs brothers?'

Charlie laughed. 'As I say, they weren't top-league but they had some smart briefs. Their barrister applied at Snaresbrook Crown Court for three men – me, Norm and Nicky – to be produced by the Crown, as it was believed that one or more of us was an informant. However . . . recent case law had been laid down and prior to the defence application, the prosecution made an application of their own – without the knowledge of the defence – that the three of us were undercover officers and that our sole aim was to bring a firearm out into the open, so that it could be seized and the prisoners arrested by conventional police. Afterwards, the judge heard the defence application, then ruled in favour of the Crown.'

'But if he hadn't . . . ?' I asked, already half-knowing the answer.

'Oh, the CPS would've offered no evidence and the whole case would've collapsed. A lot of work to recover one gun, I know,' smiled Charlie, wryly, 'and at the trial Jimmy pleaded to possession, because he had the least convictions. He got nine months, and Alfie walked. Still, that's how close cases come to being winners or losers.

'Not enough really, was it?' I said.

Charlie smiled and shook his head – then he laughed. 'D'you know what the unkindest cut of all was? It came from one of the operational team. He said that when Norm and I were in that car park we looked like two silverback gorillas who'd escaped from London Zoo and nicked a Porsche! Bloody cheek!'

CHAPTER 11

Check Everything – Trust Nobody!

Gerry Gallagher was what used to be described as 'a character' in the Metropolitan Police; as far as I'm concerned, he still is. With both of us in retirement, I telephoned his office, and his secretary told him diffidently, 'There's a Dick Someone on the phone for you.'

'He's the finest Dick you're ever likely to meet!' roared Gerry in response.

We first met on the Flying Squad; a huge, genial giant from Ireland, Gerry impressed everyone with his capability. Known as 'The Big Irish Guy', he was courageous and knowledgeable, and utterly unflappable in the witness box. On one occasion, during the trial of the receivers of a stolen lorry-load of goods, Gerry was on the end of a blistering attack concerning his probity during the interview of one of the prisoners. His voice becoming ever shriller, the defence barrister denounced Gerry for denying his client legal representation, assaulting and planting evidence on him and falsifying a confession. At the end of this peroration there was a short silence in court.

'I wonder why your client should say that?' Gerry enquired mildly. 'I thought we got on so well together!'

Every time I see Gerry in attendance at a CID-inspired dinner or luncheon, he always roars with laughter as soon as he sees me. This, I suppose, could have a rather disconcerting effect on someone who suffers from low self-esteem, but I know exactly what Gerry's laughing about. By the time I've crossed the floor to the bar, he is laughing so hard, tears are running down his cheeks; he grabs hold of me, beats me on the back and bellows, 'Jesus, what a lark that was!'

Well, yes, seen in retrospect, I suppose it was, and Gerry's laughter is so infectious, I can't help but join in; but at the time I remember thinking, 'Dick, my boy, this is well and truly your bloody lot!'

This is what happened.

* * *

Right from the start, let me admit that the fault was mine. Not because 'they' were involved (which I really couldn't help), but because I didn't check every aspect of 'their' work. By 'they' I mean a certain constabulary whose identity I am going to cloak, because I have some fairly unpleasant things to say about them. I had long believed that their uniform branch was so crushingly stupid that their movements could be charted by following the marks made by their knuckles being dragged along the pavements. As for their CID, replacing their ability with the expertise displayed by the cast of the one-time Brooke Bond PG Tips television commercial could only have been regarded as beneficial.

And if you think my sentiments are unduly harsh – good. Because if I now have grey hair, if in times of stress the muscles in my face twitch, and if when I imbibe I take a glass too much, it is directly attributable to one of this loathsome constabulary's Scenes of Crime Officers (SOCOs). All of the foregoing seems rather obscure, I know; I merely want to set the scene for what's to follow.

My Flying Squad team and I had been keeping tabs on a gang of armed robbers, although not as tightly as one would have wished, due to other work, the constrictions of the overtime budget and the vagaries of the informant who, let it be said, was not the sharpest knife in the drawer. Because just when we least expected it (and of course, on the morning when we weren't keeping the gang under observation) – bosh! – a security van was knocked off, and the raiders, with the aid of a sawn-off shotgun, lifted a large amount of cash and escaped in a stolen car. Since the team that we were looking at appeared to be the prime suspects, this was bad enough; what made matters irredeemably worse was that the offence had occurred right on the borders of this ghastly constabulary.

We raced across London, but by the time we arrived, the local officers had already started taking statements from witnesses – the content was, of course, utter gibberish – and their SOCO had found a rucksack which had obviously been discarded by the fleeing robbers.

'I've checked it – there's nothing in there,' he said, airily and handed me the rucksack, which he had already bagged up and sealed.

The constabulary detective inspector made whining overtures that they should oversee the investigation, but with true Flying Squad aplomb he was contemptuously told to 'Shut it!' and, taking possession of the statements and the exhibit, we returned to the Yard, deposited these items and held a council of war. In addition, the indolent informant was collared, spoken to rather sharply and told to get his skates on.

As a result, during the next couple of days, there was a great deal of Flying Squad activity in South London which resulted in quite a number of local gangsters having their feathers severely ruffled. The snout had certainly pointed us in the right direction, but this was where I started floundering; anywhere south of the Thames was a foreign country to me where, for all I knew, women ate their young and the local inhabitants painted themselves with woad. But Gerry made a significant contribution to the proceedings; he knew the local toerags of Walworth and Deptford far more intimately than I, and in consequence, his feather-ruffling was far more efficacious. As a result, two out of the three robbers were arrested, a large amount of incriminating evidence was recovered and there was more than enough with which to charge and remand them in custody. In addition, the getaway car had been found, together with some discarded balaclavas and other robbery paraphernalia. So far, then, so good.

It takes robbers no time at all to carry out a blagging or dispose of the loot, and in a couple of days the £11,000 that this bunch had stolen had been put to good use on a wild spending spree. Behind one door that was bashed in we found the property they'd acquired, including a pair of crocodile shoes which cost one of the robbers £300; in fact, he hadn't had time to wear them (in any case, I believe they were the wrong size), but most important of all, the items which they had purchased were now strewn all over the floor of the flat, accompanied by the receipts. It made our job a lot easier; all the items and the receipts were collected and the stores were promptly visited to obtain statements from the assistants who had served the blaggers, before they forgot what they looked like.

There's something I need to mention here. Apart from being a very tough customer, Gerry had an abundance of Irish charm and this he put to good use when he interviewed the elderly manageress of the expensive West End shoe shop and obtained a very useful statement from her. Told that her presence would likely be required at the Old Bailey, the lady assured Gerry, her eyes shining, that she would be only too happy to be there. Please bear this in mind for later on.

With the prisoners locked up, now came the task of cobbling together all of the evidence to produce a watertight case at court. Apart from checking the statements, I did as I always did; my team and I went through the exhibits with a fine-tooth comb to see if anything, no matter how small, had been overlooked. In the initial stages of gathering evidence it was all too easy to fail to notice something which originally appeared to have little significance to the case but was later found to be of vital importance. However, in this particular case, it appeared that nothing had. Then we came to the sealed rucksack.

'Better have a look, just to make sure,' I said, adding with a laugh, 'You know what that lot are like!'

I pulled open the sealed wrapping and searched through the rucksack; the laughter froze on my lips. In the rucksack's pockets were a number of shotgun cartridges, plus damning documentary evidence which linked the bag directly to the robbers.

Consider the position. I had received a sealed package containing the rucksack from the SOCO who claimed he had searched it – which he quite conspicuously had *not* done – without finding anything. And now, several days later, I had opened the package to discover that it contained the most incriminating evidence. It was a tailor-made situation for the defence to allege that these items had been planted, with yours truly being the number one suspect. The implications of this scenario were not lost on my associates, because four horrified pairs of eyes stared at the contents.

'Jesus!' said someone. 'Who's going to believe us?'

'Nobody,' muttered another member of the team, which I thought was rather defeatist but accurate.

After a bit I said, 'Well, what can we do? We can't say we *didn't* find it! We're simply going to have to say exactly what happened and tough it out!'

Eight months went by before the case was called at the Crown Court. A barrister whom I had previously encountered at two separate trials defended one of the robbers; he was renowned for his vituperative attacks on police officers' characters, especially mine. However, on this occasion, he had a little extra help.

With the lazy, inept SOCO in the witness box, the following cross-examination took place.

'Would you describe yourself as a competent Scenes of Crime Officer?'

Yes, sir.'

'A diligent one?'

'Yes, sir.'

'And when you found and took possession of this rucksack at the scene of the crime, did you thoroughly and diligently search it?'

'Oh, yes, sir.'

'Did you find anything inside it?'

'No, sir.'

'No. Because I assume, if you had, you would have separately bagged each item and made a note of your findings?'

'Yes, sir.'

'So having thoroughly searched the rucksack, without finding anything inside it, you put it into a bag, sealed it and handed it to Detective Sergeant Kirby – is that right?'

'Yes, sir.'

'I see . . . would it surprise you to learn that Detective Sergeant Kirby will say that when he opened that sealed bag he discovered in the pockets eleven shotgun cartridges and correspondence allegedly linking my client to the rucksack?'

'Yes – it would surprise me, sir!'

'IT WAS ALL PLANTED, WASN'T IT?!'

'It – it wasn't me, sir! I knew absolutely nothing about it!'

'SO KIRBY PLANTED IT! IS THAT WHAT YOU'RE SAYING?'

'It must have been! I assure you, sir, it was nothing to do with me!'

There was much more of the same before this dozy, useless little twerp tearfully squirmed his way out of the witness box. It sounds like perjury had been committed by the SOCO, doesn't it? In fact, I don't think so – I believe that he had got into such a state, he now firmly believed that he *had* searched the rucksack and had found nothing. But he wasn't finished yet – oh, no. He had one further significant contribution to make for the defence.

The following day, I was in the witness box. I won't weary you with details of my cross-examination regarding the finding of the items in the rucksack; it was entirely predictable. In addition, a few more robbers' stock allegations were tossed in for good measure: that I had threatened them, concocted the notes of interview, grabbed handfuls of head hair from them and popped the hair inside the balaclavas which had been found inside the getaway car – you know, the usual stuff. And then suddenly, the defence barrister looked up with delight.

'Look, members of the jury!' he bellowed, pointing to the public gallery. 'There sits the Scenes of Crime Officer who gave evidence yesterday! Although His Lordship had released him from the court yesterday, he's returned today! I expect he's as eager as the rest of us to discover how Detective Sergeant Kirby of the Flying Squad planted the evidence in the rucksack!'

This, without doubt, was one of the lowest moments in my career. What the bloody blue blazes was he doing there? With hindsight, I wouldn't be surprised if the defence team had told the SOCO to turn up in case he had to be recalled and that he should sit in the public gallery, and this drearily stupid little prat, completely ignoring the judge's instruction that he was released from court, had whimpered, 'Oh, all right, then.'

But whatever the case, apart from his incredibly inaccurate testimony, his second appearance at court had caused immeasurable harm. Thus the jury had to decide: had I, Duplicitous Detective Sergeant Dick Kirby of the Stop-at-Nothing Flying Squad, planted the incriminating evidence, or had the SOCO – with a mixture of laziness, incompetence and sheer stupidity – failed to properly search the rucksack? Using precisely the same words to the jury as the defence barrister had during our two previous encounters – 'Every police force has its share of rotten apples, members of the jury, and my goodness, it would be difficult to find an apple more rotten than Detective Sergeant Kirby!' – the jury returned from their deliberations to unanimously find the two robbers guilty.

The judge had some abrasive comments to make to the robbers, to whom he gave ten years each; and rather more fulsome comments to me.

It didn't stop one of the robbers pursuing his claims of my alleged impropriety from his prison cell; it was one long rant, and apart from the stock allegations already mentioned, I was also accused of introducing a bogus witness into the proceedings (who that was supposed to be, I've no idea) and of conspiring with the prosecuting barrister to bring about the robber's downfall. From beginning to end, the official complaint investigation continued for a year, before my team and I (plus the prosecuting barrister – he was interviewed as well) were completely exonerated of any wrongdoing. The SOCO, of course, was never accused of any kind of misconduct.

In the years which followed I remembered that case for several reasons. It was a clever bit of investigation and, what was more, it branched out, because several other teams of robbers had been interested in the same prize. They, too, were swept up, convicted of conspiracy and sentenced to long terms of imprisonment. There was a lesson learnt, as mentioned in the title of this chapter: check everything; trust nobody! But my enduring memory of the case came after I tottered out of court following my mauling.

Outside stood Gerry, whose evidence corroborated mine and who was completely oblivious as to what had occurred in court. Usually a picture of calm, Gerry was completely out of breath, his chest heaving, his face red.

'It's that lecherous old biddy from the shoe shop!' he gasped. 'She's been chasing me all round the Bailey!'

'Ah,' I said and nodded. 'Right.'

'Anyway', said Gerry, breathing a little easier and nodding in the direction of the courtroom. 'What's happening in there?'

'Nothing much,' I replied. 'By the way, you're next!'

CHAPTER 12

Ray's a Laugh!

I'd known Ray almost as long as I can remember. He was a hugely popular member of the luncheon attendees, so you'll excuse me if I devote quite a bit of space to him; and those who knew Ray will know that no such excuse is needed – Ray was the best of all of us. And for those of you who didn't know Ray, you're in for a treat.

He was a musician, a humanitarian, a Freemason who worked tirelessly for charities and in so doing raised thousands of pounds, and the president of the local St George's Society; and he was a police officer, as everybody knows. He was a very talented Flying Squad and Regional Crime Squad officer, but to those who knew him, he was principally an outstanding undercover officer. He could be a dodgy art dealer, a gun-runner or a contract killer. Sometimes UC officers worked in pairs, and one celebrated UC officer told me that when he and Ray worked as an uncle and nephew team of lorry thieves, 'I was never happier than being in the back of a lorry, surrounded by swag with me Uncle Ray.' After displaying the type of bone-shaking courage symptomatic of so many undercover officers, he retired right at the top of his profession, if not in rank, then in the number of commendations he received, as well as a decoration.

Raymond George Patrick Wood joined the Metropolitan Police a few months after me and he looked like nobody's idea of a police officer. Short and slim, he possessed the most melancholy eyes peering out from his black-framed glasses. His whole demeanour suggested naïve innocence, and he was tailor-made for the local yobs to ridicule. Those who did never tried it a second time; his deceptively slim frame hid an ability to punch hard, with either hand. For Ray to have remained in uniform for very long would have been an absolute waste, and his talents were soon put to the test in plain clothes, identifying and arresting the drug dealers in the area. Before long, Ray became an aid to CID, and after notching up an impressive number of arrests he was transferred to 'K' Division, where we briefly worked together again. Alas, we became victims of our own success; our arrest rate was so phenomenal that the detective inspector split us up, so that both of us might break in new recruits to the CID.

Ray became one of the Yard's top undercover officers. He had a close affiliation to the National Society for the Prevention of Cruelty to Children and he infiltrated paedophile groups, posing as someone as depraved as themselves. It is almost impossible to assess the trauma which this happily married man, with children and grandchildren, experienced; it was due only to having such a stable home environment that he was able to cope. I don't know how many children Ray saved from the clutches of these abominable perverts; dozens, certainly, and possibly hundreds. On one occasion, a 3-year-old girl was about to be gang-raped (and possibly worse), and Ray not only saved the girl from harm but incredibly and almost impossibly, at the same time, *managed to preserve his cover as a paedophile.*

All this took its toll on him, and in later years he suffered the most atrocious ill health. I remember having a drink one evening with him, and he told me that during the past few years he had been given the demanding task of training up other paedophile undercover officers.

'How many are there now?' I asked.

Ray smiled, sadly. 'Still only me,' he replied. 'The rest couldn't hack it.'

* * *

With some 250 people filling the Peelers Restaurant at the Yard, the noise was deafening. It was hardly surprising; a lot of folk wanted to honour Ray at this, his retirement function. Tributes to Ray's ability as a detective followed one after the other until, eventually, it was Ray's turn to respond.

'Everybody has a tale to tell here,' said Ray, 'and it seems invidious to single one person out, but there's a story that I want to tell about someone who's here tonight. To save him any possible embarrassment, I shall refer to him by his pseudonym – Dick Kirby!'

A great roar of laughter erupted, from me as well, because I knew that any story that Ray was going to tell was bound to be a corker.

'Dick and I were young PCs,' said Ray, 'and to bring our figures up, we decided to do a bit of ATS.'[1]

---

1 ATS stands for automated traffic signals, or common or garden traffic lights, and in those days, one officer would stand in a position to see the traffic lights and the other would secrete himself some little distance

On this particular occasion, I had been the spotter and Ray was the stopper, eagerly awaiting my signal to flag down the first errant driver.

'Suddenly,' continued Ray, 'I saw Dick wave as a long black limousine crossed the junction. I stopped the car and went round to the driver, who was an oriental gentleman.'

'What seems to be the trouble, officer?' intoned the driver smoothly, his accent reminiscent of one of Oxford's better colleges.

'Would you mind waiting a moment, sir?' asked Ray. 'A colleague of mine would like a word with you.'

The driver took a large cigar from his mouth and deposited about half a crown's-worth of ash on the roadway.

'I do hope this won't take too long,' he sighed. 'You see, I'm the cultural attaché for the Peoples' Republic of China and I'm in the most ghastly hurry.'

'With that,' said Ray, 'Dick Kirby sauntered up. Looking down at the driver, Dick slowly waved a cautionary finger in his face and slowly and deliberately said, "When red light show-ee, you no go-ee!"'

The audience roared their appreciation at a course of action which many, I feel sure, thought symptomatic of me, and then, as the laughter finally subsided, Ray added, 'The Cultural attaché was so impressed by the man-management skills of the Metropolitan Police, he not only took Dick's number, he took mine as well!' – and a fresh shout of laughter went up.

Now it just goes to show how long ago this all was; the passage of time had dimmed my memory so much, I couldn't readily recall this blip in my career, but Ray swore it was the whole unvarnished truth. It didn't matter. It was a lovely story and now I'm beginning to believe it really did happen.

Ray retired from the Metropolitan Police aged sixty, having served for over thirty-two years at what can truly be described as the sharp end of policing. He had been awarded sixteen commissioner's commendations, he was given the Freedom of the City of London and he was also appointed OBE. This decoration has often been bestowed upon officers in the Metropolitan Police holding the rank of deputy assistant commissioner or above, but never before to a detective constable; in this, as in many other aspects of police work, Ray was the first.

---

beyond; as an injudicious motorist drove through a red light, so the first officer would signal the second, who would gamely leap into the road and stop the vehicle, leaving the first officer to join them and report the motorist for contravening the Road Traffic Act.

But he was not ready to put his feet up and relax. Despite his failing health, he continued to work for the next ten years, this time for the security services in different parts of the world, carrying out the most hazardous and secretive undercover work.

He died on 22 June 2011, aged seventy-one; I read William Ernest Henley's poem *Invictus* at the requiem mass which, as can be imagined, was attended by hundreds of mourners.

★   ★   ★

Wherever old 'tecs meet up, it is inevitable that stories about Ray will be recounted. The subject matter is pretty well irrelevant; the nub of the tale will be to demonstrate Ray's humour and quick-wittedness.

Ray's undercover work started, as I've mentioned, when he was a uniform PC; he had arrested a young man in possession of a large block of cannabis resin and at the North-East London Quarter Sessions he had been found guilty of possession with intent to supply.

The Judge – who possibly gave Ray rather more credence as an expert on drugs than he actually deserved – asked, 'Tell me, officer, in your opinion how many 'reefers' [as they were then called] would this block of cannabis make?'

Ray told me, 'I hadn't a bloody clue!' – but never one to admit defeat, he replied, 'In my opinion, one thousand.'

The defence barrister went into a hasty, whispered conversation with his client, before rising to his feet and saying to Ray, 'My instruction, officer, is that no more seven hundred reefers could be obtained from that piece of cannabis', to which Ray, greatly relieved that the matter had been clarified, replied, 'In that case, sir, I bow to your client's greater judgement!'

One of my favourite tales comes from Ray's days as a member of the Flying Squad. He was in an observation post and he had seen a team of armed robbers leave a premises, their leader carrying a holdall which bore a distinctive logo. The gang drove off, obviously to carry out a robbery, but the surveillance team then lost them. Nevertheless, a robbery did occur, and when the team later returned, the gang's leader was still carrying the distinctive holdall. Ray sent an R/T transmission to the Squad, who steamed into the address and arrested the gang; the stolen cash was recovered and the holdall was seized, which contained a variety of weaponry used in the hold-up.

At the subsequent trial at the Old Bailey, Ray was subjected to an extremely hostile cross-examination by the gang leader's barrister, whose intention was to prove to the jury that if his client was carrying a holdall at all, it most certainly was not the one with the distinctive markings containing the incriminating firearms. The questioning went something like this.

'Officer, how far away were you from my client when you – allegedly – saw him carrying the holdall which is exhibit eight in this case?'

'About twenty-five yards, sir.'

'And can you be sure that it was this exhibit that he was carrying?'

'Yes, sir, absolutely. I remembered it from the very distinctive markings on the side. That was the holdall he took out of the premises and also the one he brought back, there's no doubt in my mind about that.'

'I see . . . officer, do you always wear glasses?'

'Yes, sir.'

'How far away from you am I?'

'Oh, I'd say about five feet, sir.'

'Yes. About five feet. I'd agree that that's a fair assessment of the distance between us.'

There was a pause.

'Can you see me clearly?'

'Well, fairly clearly. I mean, I know you're there.'

'Officer, would you remove your spectacles and pass them to me?'

Ray did so, and blinked myopically around the courtroom. The barrister looked at Ray's glasses, gave a theatrical sigh, shook his head and asked that they be passed to the jury. Slowly, each member of the jury inspected Ray's glasses, the lenses of which closely resembled the bottoms of beer bottles, and then they looked at Ray, appearing quite naked without his glasses and gazing around the courtroom, blinking helplessly, and they, too, sighed and shook their heads.

Eventually – the judge and the prosecuting counsel also inspected the spectacles – they were handed back to the defence barrister, who fired one parting shot before he returned them.

'Officer, previously when you were wearing your spectacles you said that when you were looking at me at a distance of five feet – as indeed, that is the distance I am from you now – you remarked, and I quote, "I knew you were there". Tell me this. Now – without your spectacles, can you still see me?'

Ray shrugged his shoulders helplessly. 'Right now, sir, you're just a blur.'

'Thank you, officer,' said the barrister and he handed the glasses back to Ray, who gratefully put them on again. 'So it comes to this, doesn't it? At a distance of five feet, without your glasses, I'm just a blur. At the same distance, wearing your glasses, in your own words, "You know I'm there". And yet, at a distance of twenty-five yards – in other words, *fifteen times the distance between us* – you are actually asking the jury to believe that you could see my client carrying a holdall which you now unequivocally identify as exhibit eight – the one in this court?'

Ray shuffled about uncomfortably in the witness box before he hesitantly replied, 'Well . . . yes, sir.'

'I see,' replied the barrister and smirked at the jury. 'No further questions.'

Ray remained in the witness box and coughed apologetically.

'Actually, I meant to say that at the time I was using a set of powerful binoculars'!

★   ★   ★

I want to finish with a story that Ray recounted to me fifty years ago. It is quite an extraordinary tale, and Ray got the bones of it from Albert Ford, whilst he was waiting for his escort.

But in the strange way in which coincidences appear in the investigative world of the police, years after Ray recounted the story to me, I met up with the man whom I shall refer to as Trevor Hopper. Trevor, as you will discover, was an old-time villain and a snout, although at the time of our meeting he was an informant no longer. By then he had passed his sell-by date and was now an elderly gent and no longer involved in criminality, therefore of no use as an informant. But I knew who he was, in the same way he that knew me, and from time to time, as a Flying Squad officer, whenever I was in the Romford area, I would pop into The Bull for a lunchtime sandwich and a glass. If Trevor was present, I'd stand him a drink as well and we'd have a chat. It was during one of these meetings that he recounted the story of Albert Ford, and his input filled the gaps and gelled exactly with the story which Ray had told me, so many years before.

★   ★   ★

Albert Douglas Ford was the type of man that the security services dream of having on their books; to all intents and purposes he was invisible. Nobody noticed him as he walked along the street; he did not stride, head up, shoulders back, with a military bearing commanding attention and respect. By the same token, he did not slouch or shuffle in a way which might cause passers-by to wonder if he was ill, or so down on his luck as to make them speculate whether they should offer him half-a-crown. No. At the time when this story unfolds, Ford was aged fifty-two; he was of medium height and build, his hair and eyes were grey, as were the flannel trousers he usually wore. His sports jacket had seen better days, but not to such an extent that passing tramps might eagerly demand to know if he had no further use for it, and his feet were encased in 'Hush-Puppies', a popular if relatively inexpensive brand of footwear at that time. Ford did not smoke, did not drink, was unmarried, possessed no friends and had few acquaintances. He was employed as a storeman at May & Baker's Factory in Dagenham, and his trademark brown overall and clipboard made him even more anonymous. No one in the company was ever heard to say, 'Have a word with Bert Ford about that.' Instead, they said, 'Go and see the storeman – y'know, what's-'is-name.'

All of which suited Albert Ford down to the ground. He did not want to be on matey terms with anybody. The less social intercourse between him and the rest of the workforce at May & Baker's the better. If he was not engaged in conversation he could not be induced to tell an outsider anything about himself – anything which might cause him to betray the guilty secret which he had carried around for the past twenty-seven years.

* * *

Ford hung up his overall and clipboard punctually at five o'clock as he always did, walked out of the factory, crossed the busy Rainham Road North and headed towards Dagenham East tube station. As he walked past the main entrance to Dagenham police station he failed to notice the man who had left the front counter and was emerging into the street. But this man, whose name was Trevor Hopper, had noticed Ford and gave a start, because he thought he recognized him; he decided to make sure and strolled after him. Hopper paused as Ford stopped outside the station to purchase a copy of the *Evening Standard*, before showing his season ticket to the guard at the barrier and walking through. As Ford walked down the stairs to the platforms, Hopper stopped; he had no ticket, neither had he any idea in which direction or how far Ford was travelling. Fortunately for him, at that moment the guard was called away to the ticket office, and Hopper slipped through the barrier, snatched up a discarded newspaper from a refuse bin and followed Ford, who was now waiting on the left-hand side of the platform for a London-bound District Line train.

By the time the train pulled into the station, Hopper was fully satisfied that the man that he was observing over the top of the newspaper was indeed Bert Ford. Well, well. Ford boarded the train, and Hopper got into the same carriage, keeping well away from his prey and pretending to busy himself with his newspaper. The train trundled on, through Dagenham Heathway, Becontree and Upney stations. At Barking, Hopper once more carefully scrutinized Ford in case he was going to change to the Tilbury to Fenchurch Street mainline train, but Ford remained in his seat, still immersed in his newspaper.

The train set off again, stopping at East Ham station, but still Ford remained seated; however, just before the train pulled into Upton Park station, Ford got up and walked to the doors. The train came to a halt, there was a pneumatic sigh as the doors opened, and Ford stepped on to the platform. Hopper rose to his feet and nipped out of the carriage just before the doors shut, then followed Ford as he walked towards the exit. Ford again showed his season ticket and walked out of the station, but Hopper was held at the barrier while he paid the irate ticket collector his fare from Dagenham East. This took longer than expected, but he had seen Ford turn to the left as he exited the station. As Hopper quickly walked into Green Street he urgently inspected the thoroughfare for any sign of Ford, but without success; the task was made more difficult by the number of other commuters going home. Hopper walked in the general direction that Ford had taken, anxiously scanning the pedestrians, and then all but collided with Ford, who walked out of a confectioner's where he had just purchased a packet of sweets. With a muttered apology, which Ford ignored, Hopper entered the shop, waiting for a few moments before returning to Green Street and hoping against hope that Ford had not realized that he was being followed.

He hadn't. Nothing was further from Ford's mind as he reached the busy junction with Plashet Road and crossed the street. Hopper followed the back of the man wearing the faded brown jacket and grey flannels and saw him turn right into Cromwell Road. Crossing back to the other side of Green Street, Hopper looked down Cromwell Road and saw Ford walk up to the front door of one of the terraced houses, insert a key in the lock and go in, shutting the door behind him. Strolling down the road a few minutes later, Hopper made a mental note of the number of the house and smiled to himself. His work was over, and he might do himself a bit of good.

The reason why Hopper had been leaving Dagenham police station at that particular time was because he had been charged with receiving a quantity of gents' suiting, and it was part of his bail conditions to sign on at the police station once a day. Hopper's arresting officer had told him that if he wanted a result at court he'd have to come up with some pretty nifty information. This, thought Hopper on that Wednesday afternoon, could be it.

*   *   *

However, it was not a view shared by the arresting officer when Hopper imparted his information after meeting up with him in an Elm Park pub the following evening.

'Leave it out, Trev,' he laughed. 'You'll have to do a bit better than that, old son!'

But he took Ford's details and address, and the following day, he made a couple of telephone calls from the CID office. The result surprised him, and when he put the receiver down he laughed and shook his head. It was not something that he wished to tackle himself; he had far too much on his plate in any event, but still . . .

'Oi, Jimmy!' he called, as a detective constable walked through the office. 'Who's on Kilo one-one?'

When Jimmy replied, 'Ray,' he smiled again. 'Call him up and get him to come and see me, will you?'

That was Friday.

*   *   *

The following morning, Saturday, saw Cromwell Road pretty well deserted at ten o'clock. Except, that is for the slight figure who emerged from the junction with Jephson Road. Short, with a thick mop of dark, curly hair, the casually dressed young man strolled along Cromwell Road and peered through a large pair of black, horn-rimmed spectacles at each of the premises in the row of rather shabby-looking Edwardian terraced houses.

Finally, he stopped in front of one of them and walked up the short pathway to the front door, where he noticed a number of doorbells. Each had a name written next to it, either bold or faded according to the length of time the tenant had been there. He pressed the top bell and could hear it ringing from inside. There was no response. The young man pressed the bell again and again, but there was still no answer. On the third occasion he stuck his thumb on the bell and kept it there.

Suddenly there came the sound of one of the first-floor sash windows being wrenched open. There, framed in the open window, stood Albert Ford. He was wearing a singlet and (although the young man could not see them) striped pyjama trousers. Ford's usual equanimity had deserted him. His regularly recurring dream of falling through space had substantially robbed him of sleep the previous night. Because it was a Saturday, he had been having a lie-in and was understandably peeved at his doorbell being persistently rung.

'What d'you want?' he shouted.

The young man looked up at him and silently mouthed some words.

'What?' shouted Ford, his hand cupping his ear.

The caller gesticulated and mouthed some more noiseless words.

'What did you say?' bawled Ford, staring at the figure below him looking quite nondescript in a sports jacket which was only marginally more respectable than Ford's own.

But the visitor simply stood there, waving his arms about and opening and shutting his mouth, giving the impression of speaking but in fact uttering not one word. Ford had now come to the conclusion that he was either dealing with a mute or an escapee from a lunatic asylum, and after a few more moments of this rather one-sided conversation he decided that enough was enough.

'Wait there!' he roared and, taking a step backwards, slammed the window shut.

The young man heard the sound of footsteps clattering down the stairs, and the front door was jerked open.

'What the fuck do you want!' bellowed Ford.

The visitor, whose name was Ray, surveyed him calmly.

'Are you Albert Douglas Ford?'

Ford nodded.

'Born on 5 May, 1920?'

Again, Ford nodded. 'So?'

'So I've got some news for you, Mr Ford,' said Ray, equably. 'You see, when you reported for duty with the 1st Parachute Brigade on 11 September 1944, they did expect you to stay a bit longer than two days – and you're nicked!'

The station officer at Forest Gate police station looked apprehensively at an ashen-faced Albert Ford, who sat slumped on the bench in the charge room.

'Well, I dunno, Ray,' he muttered *sotto voce* as he furiously scratched his head. 'I mean, it's over twenty-five years ago, now. Is anyone going to be interested?'

The two Redcaps who turned up from Aldershot Barracks, three hours later, were certainly interested. Of course, both were far too young to have been involved in the ill-fated Operation Market Garden but they were aware that, four days after Ford's sudden absence, 10,000 men had been parachuted into Arnhem. Initially, the men had been asked to hold out for two days – in fact, they held out for nine, against incredible odds – and fewer than 3,000 of them got out. Of the rest, 5,000 (including 3,000 wounded) were taken from Holland into captivity in Germany; the remainder were killed.

Corporal Green, the taller and meaner of the two Redcaps, had a special empathy with Operation Market Garden because his father, like Ford, had been a member of the 1st Parachute Brigade. Green's father had been rather a more conscientious combatant than Ford, because he had participated in the operation and had lost an arm during the savage street fighting in Oosterbeek.

So now, some twenty-seven years later, Corporal Green's eyes narrowed as he surveyed Ford.

'Left yer mates in the lurch, did yer?' he growled, and as Ford started to say something in his defence he was silenced by a mighty roar from the military policeman.

'STAND UP, YOU FUCKING TUBE!' – and Ford was marched out at double-time for an unforgettable trip to the glasshouse.

* * *

This rather extraordinary arrest by one of the crew of the 'Q'-Car Kilo one-one was talked about for some considerable time and it became part of the legend of Ray Wood.

But as Trevor Hopper's arresting officer had suggested, Hopper really would have to do much better than catch a deserter to get a half-way decent result at court. In fact, he did. Within days of his spirited tailing across East London, a local tearaway requested Hopper's assistance in unloading a lorry-load of bronze ingots, due to be hi-jacked the following night. This, as the arresting officer remarked, was 'much more like it', and as the stolen lorry came to a halt in Bulphan, Essex, the hi-jackers, the lorry driver (who was well and truly implicated in the theft) and all six unloaders (with the notable exception of Trevor Hopper) were all captured on the plot.

Some time later, Hopper, at his trial for receiving the natty gents' suiting, pleaded guilty. Given his amount of form, he should have copped a couple of years' porridge. Instead, he found himself the recipient of a suspended sentence and later, a modest payment from the Informants' Fund and a rather more sizeable one from the haulage company's insurers. He accepted, with fairly good grace, the necessity of splitting the rewards with his arresting officer.

Thereafter, Trevor faded from the scene. His arresting officer who, with a combination of luck, guile and Masonic influence, neatly avoided entanglement with any of the Metropolitan Police corruption trials of the 1970s, rose steadily through the ranks and eventually retired, having achieved very senior rank. He took his not insubstantial commutation and pension overseas, and this, together with certain investments (the provenance of which was highly dubious and which would not have withstood detailed investigations), provided him with a rather sumptuous lifestyle. His whitewashed villa where, I believe, he lives to this day is aptly named 'Rich Pickings', and his neighbours believe that he is a retired businessman. They are right.

But now we return to my meeting with Trevor Hopper, who settled back in a chair in The Bull in Romford Market Place and sipped his pint of bitter. He smiled as he told me about the time, all those years ago, when as a young paratrooper he had been briefed for sixteen different operations between 6 June and 10 September 1944, and how, as each one was cancelled he had, in company with his fellow jumpers, felt pretty pissed off. He also remembered the slag who had cheated him at cards in the camp in Lincolnshire, and it was lucky for the health and beauty of Paratrooper Albert Douglas Ford that he had made himself scarce when he did.

'Funny, wasn't it, Trev, spotting him like that, as you walked out of Dagenham nick?' I said. 'By that, I mean it was funny you hadn't seen him before, what with you signing on every day.'

Trevor Hopper grinned and swallowed the rest of his bitter.

'Wasn't funny at all, Dick,' he replied. 'Y'see, I was supposed to sign on at four o'clock every afternoon. On that day I got held up and I got a right bollocking from the sergeant, who threatened me with a nicking because I was an hour late. If I'd been on time I'd have missed him altogether. Fancy another?'

CHAPTER 13

A Closed Book

In 1971, Detective Sergeant (First-class) Henry Stevens GC was serving with the Flying Squad when he was part of a Scotland Yard team sent to Northern Ireland. Following his return, he was awarded a commissioner's commendation, which read, 'For valuable assistance leading to the arrest and conviction of two men in a dangerous and complicated case'.

Some forty years later, I was chatting to Henry and asked him, 'That Northern Ireland business, Henry – what happened when you were over there?'

'I don't talk about it,' was his bland response, and he added, 'and therefore you won't write about it either!'

Don Brown was a detective inspector on the Flying Squad and he was another officer who travelled to Ulster on that occasion. He received an identically-worded commendation from the commissioner. I spoke to his widow, Linda, about it.

'I wasn't married to Don at that time,' she told me. 'Later, I knew he got that commendation, but because he was on the Flying Squad at the time, I assumed it was to do with the arrest of armed robbers. I didn't know it was to do with Northern Ireland. Don never spoke about it.'

Approximately twenty years after Henry and Don went to Ulster, I went there too.[1] Like them, I was a member of the Flying Squad, and like them – amongst other matters – we were looking at a number of murders. Following my return to the mainland, like those other Squad officers, I was commended by the commissioner and the citation read, 'For courage, dedication and detective ability in connection with a sensitive major enquiry'.

Really, it was just as ambiguously worded as the commendation twenty years earlier had been.

---

1 For further details of these brave men see (for Stevens) *The Brave Blue Line: 100 Years of Metropolitan Police Gallantry*, Pen & Sword Books, 2011, and (for Brown) *The Wrong Man: The Shooting of Steven Waldorf and the Hunt for David Martin*, The History Press, 2016

When I wrote my first book[2] I included a couple of short, humorous anecdotes about Ulster – nothing to do with what I'd been doing, just amusing stories, one involving the judiciary and the other, the Parachute Regiment.

After the book was published, I was approached by a senior – and I mean a *very* senior – police officer.

'In any further books that you might write, Dick, you won't be mentioning what happened over in Ulster, will you?'

Although it was very pleasantly said, it was very firmly meant.

In recounting the tale that follows, I don't believe for one moment that I've broken any confidences; it's a case where hard knocks were received, and it makes you wonder how many of us could have recovered from such a scenario.

*   *   *

In Northern Ireland there were areas which were designated 'Bandit Country': Republican areas which were extremely hostile, where the smell of hatred from the residents for the Royal Ulster Constabulary (RUC) and the security forces practically wafted up off the pavement at you. RUC stations throughout the province were regarded as legitimate targets by the IRA and like Tara, the County Meath residence of the Kings of Ireland in times gone by, they had massive fortifications – they needed them. And when police officers wished to visit an RUC station within an IRA stronghold, they had to drive to the nearest 'safe' RUC station and telephone the station in question, who would send out an armoured police vehicle to transport the officers in and out of the area.

That was the position in which I found myself whilst I was serving in that troubled Province. I had to make an enquiry at the collator's office in one of these stations; for a number of reasons, it was not an enquiry which could be made over the telephone.

So my RUC minder and I were picked up to be transported to this RUC station right in the heart of Bandit Country. The first thing I noticed was the car; I believe it weighed the best part of five tons. The body was armour-plated and would have been able to withstand an attack by anything short of a rocket; the windows were an inch thick and so heavy they couldn't be opened. No matter how hot the weather, those windows stayed

---

2 *Rough Justice: Memoirs of a Flying Squad Detective*, Merlin Unwin Books, 2001

resolutely shut. Air conditioning was used – although I often had apprehensive thoughts about what might happen in the eventuality of a gas attack. The next thing brought to my attention was the driver and his colleague. I've been on record as saying that the men and women of the RUC were the bravest, most committed and professional police officers with whom I ever had dealings, and I adhere to that. But these two – both tall and cadaverously thin – were seriously weird; during the journey they cracked the most conspicuously unfunny jokes to each other and screamed with hollow, tinny laughter which was utterly devoid of mirth. The other thing which rather unnerved me was their eyes. They were utterly blank, as though they had been cast in metal. They resembled the eyes of dead men. I had seen these eyes before; they had belonged to the terrorists against whom the RUC were so bitterly opposed. Perhaps it was something which the two opposing forces unwittingly shared: having witnessed sights which were so frightful that it had necessitated the shutters coming down on their eyes to mask their true feelings.

So I was glad when those two huge iron gates clanged shut behind us as we entered the yard of the RUC station, with vigilant, heavily armed RUC men on guard scanning the outside area. My minder and I entered the station and headed toward the collator's office. Just then, a passing RUC officer called out, 'What about ye?' to which my companion replied, 'The best!' Obviously they wanted to chat, so I continued towards the collator's office. Just then, I heard my minder call out, 'Dick – hang on . . .' but I ignored him. I'd already had enough of this dreadful place and I wanted to get in, complete the enquiry and get out as soon as possible.

And then things happened very quickly. When I opened the door to the office I saw a small man, obviously the collator, sitting at a desk, and as I entered, his head jerked up and he jumped to his feet, simultaneously wrenching open one of the drawers in his desk. There was a 'click!' and at that moment my minder joined me in the doorway and shouted out, 'Ronnie, it's me, son! It's OK – he's with me!'

The collator – Ronnie – stared at me with those awful blank eyes which, it seemed to me, were symptomatic of this dreadful area, and then he switched his gaze to my minder and nodded, I suppose in recognition. There was a second 'click' as he uncocked the SP101 Ruger revolver, which he then replaced in the desk drawer. With a 2¼-inch barrel and weighing just over 1½lbs, the all-steel sidearm is not especially large but it is chambered to take the powerful .357 Magnum cartridge.

The enquiry completed, I waited until we'd returned to the satellite station and were back in our own car before I spoke about Ronnie. As the sun was setting and we sped back to the comparative safety of Belfast, I had no doubt there was a story waiting to be told.

'Sure, Ronnie was a good peeler,' commented the minder. 'A tough wee fella. He was out on patrol with another couple of cops, when they got called to a burglary. It was a set-up.'

He shrugged. 'Happens all the time. Got ambushed in a one-way street and those IRA bastards opened up on them; bad luck the peelers were in a thin-skinned vehicle.'

It was probably the casual way in which the story was recounted which made it all the more horrible. The IRA team had attacked the police vehicle with high-velocity weapons; and of course the protection offered by the thin-skinned body of the car was no protection at all. Ronnie's companions were literally blown to pieces – and after the jackal assassins had scuttled away into the side streets and police assistance arrived, Ronnie was pulled from the car. Incredibly, he had not a scratch on him – the gunmen's bullets had completely missed him. But he was plastered from top to toe in his companions' blood, brains, bones and shredded clothing, and as poor old Ronnie looked down at himself and started screaming, he was accompanied by the shrieks of laughter from the groups of Republican housewives who poured out of their homes and who always seemed to find infinite amusement in scenes of carnage in which the security services, or Protestants, were the victims.

Ronnie spent months off sick, receiving a great deal of counselling, and if he had retired on an ill-health pension, no one would have blamed him; indeed, many would have praised him for taking such a sensible course of action. But he refused to give up and although he was unable to perform front-line duties again, eventually he was found the post of collator. Mind you, Ronnie wanted to ensure that he was never caught unprepared again, so the authorities let him keep his Ruger.

Suddenly confronted by a complete stranger, Ronnie had acted instinctively; so even though I was within a gnat's whisker of getting my head blown off, I could see his point of view.

At that time, Interpol regarded Northern Ireland as the most dangerous place in the world to be a police officer. The risk factor was twice as high as in El Salvador, which was said to be the second most dangerous.

To an outsider, going into Northern Ireland in those days was bound to leave a mark on you. Henry and Don didn't talk about what happened over there; and neither did I.

When I came back, my eldest son, Mark – he was then about twenty-five years of age – said, 'What was it like over there, Dad? What happened?'

I thought for a bit and then I replied, 'Perhaps I'll tell you one day . . . not now.'

But I never did and now I never will. After all, it happened a long time ago, didn't it?

CHAPTER 14

Trigger Happy

When there was a situation that required an armed presence by police, it was always a good idea to call in the professionals – and over the years, although its designation changed, we knew the unit as 'PT17'. Selected from the ranks of uniformed officers, many of them came from military backgrounds. During my time they were used for static plots, so if an armed suspect was in a premises, either as an occupant or in a hostage situation, it was PT17 who were used; and very professional they were, too.

However, in those days, when mobile surveillance was carried out on a team of robbers and it was not known where they were going to strike, PT17 were not used; that was the remit of other armed officers, such as the Flying Squad.

Many Squad officers were trained in the use of firearms. I was sent on the very demanding course and failed dismally; wrong temperament, I suppose! The same applied to another officer who, when he routinely fired off six shots and missed the target completely, dealt with this lack of success with his characteristic good humour.

Not so the furious instructor, who confronted him and snarled sarcastically, 'Do you think you could ever kill a man?'

The errant officer placed one hand on his hip, flashed his eyes and murmured seductively, 'Eventually!'

So, as I said, leave it to the professionals; although I must admit that during that course a question mark was raised. There was a firearms instructor I disliked because of his disposition; he seemed to me to be highly strung, and there was something else as well. He drew from its holster his own personal sidearm and showed it to a number of students so that they might admire it, then handed it to one of them.

But then, when he took it back, he spoke to it – I'm not joking, he actually *spoke* to his fucking revolver!

'There,' he crooned softly. 'Somebody else held you – did you like it? Now, you've come back to me!'

Jesus, I thought, I wouldn't want you on any armed operation that involves me!

In fact, a couple of months later, that's *exactly* what happened. I arrived at a situation where a dangerous armed suspect was supposed to be in a flat and PT17 were already in position. There I saw that same instructor, weapon drawn, behind a wall. A loudhailer was used to advise anybody inside the flat to come out with their hands raised, and the two occupants of the flat (neither of whom was the wanted man) came out and gave themselves up. The operation was stood down, and everybody relaxed – all save one. I couldn't take my eyes of that instructor; having holstered his weapon he was visibly shaking all over, as though possessed with Sydenham's Chorea, more commonly known as St Vitus' Dance. Perhaps he was. Despite many more operations with PT17, I never saw him again. I hope he asked for professional help, and for everybody else's sake, as well as his own, I hope he got it.

*   *   *

After the abductions of Muriel McKay and the heiress, Lesley Whittle, a whole new approach was brought into play for kidnap investigations. Right from the start, there was a news blackout; the first thing the public knew about it was when the hostage was rescued and the perpetrators were arrested. That was because C11 Department took charge of the operation and used all their expertise – telephone intercepts, electronic probes, hostage negotiators, surveillance – to bring the matter to a successful conclusion. Also, they would have an armed arrest team ready to go in, extricate the hostage and arrest the bad guys. Usually, the arrest team would be drawn from the Flying Squad or, as in this particular case, the Anti-Terrorist Squad.

Actually, I knew the 'criminal mastermind' in the case; Arthur was an old-time safe-blower from the 1940s, so he was well past his sell-by date. Heaven knows what possessed him to get involved in kidnapping the 12-year-old son of a wealthy industrialist and a subsequent ransom demand, when at his age he should have been ensconced in a bath chair and fed cocoa past his toothless gums, whilst cackling softly to himself.

But there you are; he did get involved and, as the participants in the 2015 Hatton Garden heist proved, there's no fool like an old fool.

Arthur was probably dreaming of the riches sure to come his way to supplement his state pension, when the front door of the Wandsworth flat he was occupying was suddenly blown off its hinges, he was roughly seized, flung to the floor and the business end of a Model 36 Smith & Wesson revolver was jammed in his ear. That model was never held in particularly high esteem for its accuracy by those who used it, but Arthur must have quickly come to the irrevocable conclusion that at that range, if things went wrong – like, for example, him struggling – the hallway of that wretched council flat would quickly be redecorated with a slight hint of brains.

He therefore submitted quietly to being handcuffed, the other kidnappers were also subdued with the minimum of fuss and the terrified boy was released, so everyone was pleased – with the exception of the authorized shot who, when he removed his revolver from Arthur's ear and was about to holster it, discovered a huge glistening lump of disgusting earwax hanging from the barrel!

It served a purpose, however; Arthur was able to hear quite clearly the judge at the Old Bailey sentence him to seven years.

★   ★   ★

Staying south of the river, one story that did make me laugh was about 'Mad Mitch', who was a large, horrible and violent character who lived up to his nickname; he was certainly certifiably insane. Amongst his many convictions for violence, he had already served a sentence for attempted murder; when his girlfriend upset him (and apparently it hadn't taken much) he ran her down in his car, stopped, then reversed over her, carrying out this steamroller operation – backwards and forwards – several times. It was amazing that the poor woman survived. Five police officers had sustained injuries during that arrest; one still suffered from blinding headaches, and another had been medically discharged from the force. In addition, three shattered truncheons had to be returned to the stores for replacement.

Rather incongruously, perhaps – given his previous convictions – Mitch was currently wanted in connection with a large-scale fraud, but he was rightly considered so dangerous that his arrest demanded determined action. Detective Constable Fred Wells and Mitch were known to each other; in fact, Fred had been the arresting officer in the steamroller incident, so there was no love lost between them. Fred had been issued with a service revolver for this latest arrest – in fact, it would have been considered lunacy if he had not been – and he discovered that at a certain time on a certain day Mitch would be walking past a certain South London police station.

At the specified time Fred was waiting around a corner that Mitch was sure to pass; and when he did, Fred – no lightweight himself – leapt out, grabbed Mitch by his collar and stuffed the end of the revolver's barrel up Mitch's right nostril.

'Right, you're nicked', snapped Fred, and Mitch slowly swivelled his eyes, sparkling with insanity, in Fred's direction.

He recognised his adversary instantly.

'Hello, Mr Wells,' he said in his barmy undertone. 'Guess what? I'm going to kill you!' to which Fred replied, 'Shut it, you slag!' as he dragged and pushed Mitch towards the nick.

'No, I mean it!' whispered Mitch. 'I'm going to tear your fucking head off!' – and there was little doubt that, given the opportunity, he would have done exactly that.

There was an ominous 'click' as Fred thumbed back the revolver's hammer. It was now in 'single-action' mode, meaning that if a light touch was applied to the trigger, the gun would fire. This would hopefully not happen, providing Fred kept his index finger straight along the trigger guard, but he didn't; he now had it curled around the trigger. A highly charged situation had become even more volatile.

Still with the revolver jammed up his nostril, Mitch was propelled into the police station, and as he passed the surprised station sergeant in the charge room who was dealing with two altogether more placid prisoners, they heard him say, 'You as well, Mister Sergeant – you and those two cunts – I'm going to kill you all!'

Down the cell passageway they went, with Mitch giggling insanely, until they reached a vacant cell. Fred pushed Mitch inside and, relieved of the pressure of the revolver against his proboscis, Mitch uttered his final threat.

His voice barely audible, he whispered, 'When I get out of here Mr Wells, I'm going to kill you – I'm going to find you and kill you! I don't care how long it takes! You won't be able to hide from me! And I'll tell you something else – I'm going to kill your family! I'm going to make you watch – and then I'll kill you, last of all!'

In the cell passageway, Fred raised his revolver.

'No,' he said, simply. 'You won't', and with that, he pulled the trigger. 'Click!' went the gun. 'Click, click!'

'Oh, blimey – I forgot to load it – sorry, Mitch!' apologized Fred, and the slamming of the cell door coincided with Mitch's primeval scream which caused the superintendent in his office on the second floor to wonder what on earth was going on in his normally peaceful station.

By the way, no evidence was offered in the large-scale fraud (in which Mitch had played an admittedly miniscule part) at the Inner London Crown Court; during the interim period, the staff at Brixton prison, including the prison doctors and psychiatrists (as well as one or two fellow inmates and their families), were subjected to the same threats and intended end result that Mitch had levelled at Fred Wells and his family. It appeared to everybody concerned that incarceration in a secure psychiatric unit for an unspecified amount of time was the best plan for him.

CHAPTER 15

Aliens Have Landed!

This may be a highly disturbing chapter heading for you to read – but don't worry. I'm not trying to emulate Orson Welles, who as a chubby-faced, 24-year-old, up-and-coming prodigy in American theatre and radio wrote and narrated an adaptation of H. G. Wells' 1898 novel *The War of the Worlds*. In Wells' story, set in the Victorian era, seemingly invincible invaders from Mars overrun the Earth. Forty years later, on 30 October 1938, Wells' near-namesake broadcast his up-to-date version of the classic novel on the CBS radio network in New York.

During the broadcast, the phrase 'we interrupt this programme' was used with devastating effect to describe a rocket landing in New Jersey and how the goggle-eyed crowd who observed this phenomenon had been incinerated by Martian heat-rays. As the programme continued, other 'newsflashes' were interpolated into the script, informing the listeners that huge extra-terrestrial machines had been seen wading across the Hudson River.

In fairness, many of the duped listeners had tuned in after the hour-long programme had started, and because few people possessed telephones, they spilled out into the streets to demand from their neighbours what on earth – or perhaps, out of it – was going on. Garbled versions of what had apparently occurred were blurted out, many people claimed to have actually seen the Martians and there was widespread panic.

The following day, the *New York Times* headlines declared, 'Radio Listeners in Panic, Taking War Drama as Fact'; 3,965 miles to the east, in Berlin, a certain Adolf Hitler (who had invasion plans of his own) contemptuously stated that the broadcast was 'evidence of the decadence and corrupt condition of democracy'; and over a million and a half Americans were permanently cured of constipation. In addition, Hollywood made Welles an offer he couldn't refuse, and his future and his marriage to sexpot Rita Hayworth were assured.

So no, this is not a reincarnation of the broadcast from the twentieth floor of 485 Madison Avenue, New York City, over eighty years ago – but there are many of the same ingredients in the story which follows: disbelief, contempt and panic.

*   *   *

The four area offices of the Flying Squad investigated armed robberies within their boundaries, and the report of one such offence landed on my desk in the North-East London office at Rigg Approach. Three black youngsters had dashed into a building society in Plaistow armed with what purported to be a gun, terrified the staff, demanded cash, which was duly handed over, and dashed out again. I headed off to the premises, as did a Scenes of Crime Officer and a photographer, and I spoke to the shaken witnesses and obtained statements from them. But that apart, there was little else – I could find nobody outside the building society who had seen where the gang had run to, or could give a description of any vehicle they had climbed into, or knew which direction they had headed off into – and the Scenes of Crime Officer had detected nothing which was going to be of help in a future prosecution. The building society's CCTV camera might have yielded clues as to the identities of the perpetrators, but unfortunately the person responsible for loading the cassette into it had neglected to do so. I had to admit that, given such a paucity of information, this case was rapidly heading for the 'No-hoper' category.

The story merited little space in the *Stratford Express*, and although the paper mentioned a hint of a reward and that 'anyone with useful information should contact Detective Sergeant Dick Kirby of the Flying Squad', nobody did.

So I contacted C11 Department at the Yard and asked them to send one of their identikit experts to see the victims; and having done that, I carried on with more promising investigations and promptly forgot about the case.

Identikits had been the brainchild of Hugh McDonald, a Los Angeles deputy sheriff; he had produced a book containing interchangeable transparent flaps, each of which had a facial feature – eyes, nose, hairline, mouth, etc. – which could be used to build up a composite picture of a criminal suspect. McDonald came over to England and gave a three-day course on the use of identikits to thirty-one officers. On the day that the course ended – Friday, 3 March 1961 – the body of Elsie May Batten, the owner of an antique shop off the Charing Cross Road, was found. Two antique daggers had been used to stab her to death. Witnesses were found and described the prime suspect as being a mixed-race Asian man. Detective Sergeant Ray Dagg, who had attended the identikit course, built up a picture of the suspect which was not only circulated in two police publications, *Confidential Informations* and *Police Gazette* (the latter was published throughout the country, the former being restricted to the London area), but was also shown on television and published in the media. Four days later, Police Constable Hilton Cole was on patrol in Soho when he stopped and arrested a man who resembled the identikit picture. This was not surprising; Sergeant Dagg had assembled the image so skilfully that the result actually looked like a photograph, and although the suspect, Edwin Bush, initially denied knowing anything about the murder, he later confessed to having robbed and murdered Mrs Batten and was duly sentenced to death and hanged.

So the initial test of the identikit was a resounding success; it improved over the years – by now it was known as photofit – and it had resulted in a string of successful convictions. But it would not do so, I had thought, in this particular case, when a couple of weeks later I received an envelope through the internal dispatch. When I opened it, there were the photofits of the Plaistow building society robbers – and what an odd lot they looked! They looked nothing like a gang of black robbers. In fact, what they really looked like were aliens – all of them had heads like inverted dewdrops, and I was reminded of the deeply unpleasant Mekon of Mekonta who was Dan Dare's ('The Pilot of the Future') adversary in my boyhood copies of the *Eagle* comic. I reached for the telephone and dialled C11's number.

The author of the aliens' pictures was Detective Sergeant John Woodhouse, who joined the Job one week after me. I heard about John long before I met him; he had been posted to the 'Q'-Car of Bert Wickstead's creation, 'Juliet One-Three', which had a roving commission to patrol 'J' and 'K' Divisions, plus Essex and Hertfordshire and, it appears, anywhere else that caught their fancy. The reason why I – and quite a few other aids to CID – had heard of him was because of his phenomenal run of success on the 'Q'-Car. These news items were passed on to us in caustic tones by our detective sergeants: 'I see Woody from 'J' Division has had another good knock-off; you lot had better ask him how he does it!'

How *did* he do it? We were beginning to hate Woody – thereafter, it seemed to us, he got made up to detective constable, then posted on to the Flying Squad in record time; and it was not until some time later that Woody imparted the secret of his success to me.

By then I knew the name of Jack Murray as a very successful (if rather dubious) businessman, but he was an unknown quantity when Woody first met him, years earlier.

'At the time, I was leaning on a grass for a bit of work, and he propped up Jack Murray's name,' Woody told me over a glass. 'He was only about eighteen or nineteen then, he didn't have any form but he was associating with some tasty, experienced villains, although I never did find out what the connection was. The grass told me that Murray didn't carry out jobs himself – he was too cute for that – but he was a receiver. He lived with Mum and Dad on a council estate at Rainham, so I turned the address over, but there was nothing in the flat. Then I had a look in the bike shed and there I found some stolen jewellery and, rather than involve his parents, Jack stuck his hands up to it. He went to court, and I let him out on bail and put the pressure on him to start snouting for me, but he wouldn't have it at any price. A week later, I pulled him again; I'd found out that the engine in his prized Ford Corsair was nicked, so he was charged and appeared in court. Once more he was given bail, and once more I suggested that he went to work for me. Once more he refused. The following week, I paid another visit to his parents' address; lo and behold, there was more dodgy gear in the bike shed. This time when I nicked him, I said to him, "You know Jack, when you go to court this time, I expect the Beak will wonder why you keep getting bail. In fact, I don't know if I can think up excuses as to why you *should* get bail. What's more, Jack, the Beak might think that no matter what I say, you should be banged up in Brixton until your trial, and since you've never had a lay-down before you might find it an uncomfortable experience. But if you do want bail, I dare say I could tell the Beak of a good reason why you should get it and you could do yourself a bit of good at the same time by going to work for me – and there might be a few bob in it for you as well." Well, the penny finally dropped, and Jack started to give me some good info regarding his mates, hence all those arrests I made on the 'Q'-Car. But by the time that tour on the 'Juliet One-Three' was over, we'd come to the end of a rather uneasy relationship; he was never really happy with the idea of my hands gripping his nuts!'

John's career as an active Flying Squad officer (and as the originator and choreographer of the Flying Squad Morris Dancers' Troupe)[1] had been suddenly curtailed after a malignant

---

1 For further details, see *A Copper at the Yard: Inside the Real Sweeney*, Pen & Sword Books, 2012

growth had been discovered, and after some skilful surgery, one of his lungs had been removed. This was followed by months of chemotherapy and recuperation, after which he had returned to work – but not as a Flying Squad officer. He was shifted across the corridor on the fourth floor at the Yard to C11, the Criminal Intelligence Department, for duties of a less strenuous nature. His first job was to chart the progress, the haunts and the associates of a Triad gang (coincidentally, one of my cases), so with this Oriental connection, his recent surgery and the dark humour which all detectives possessed, he was nicknamed 'One-Lung Woody'.

However, I also knew him to be very skilled at his work as an Identikit officer so I was somewhat perturbed at these . . . well, Martians.

'John,' I said, 'these photofits you sent me . . .'

'What about 'em?' interrupted John brusquely.

Obviously, I had caught him at a bad time.

'Well, do you think you've captured a good likeness?' I asked, rather tentatively.

The reason for my reticence was that John had enjoyed considerable success as a schoolboy boxer, and I didn't want to aggravate what was obviously his present, scratchy disposition.

'What d'you mean, "a good likeness"?' snapped John.

'It's just that . . . well . . . they look like . . . well, sorry, mate, but they look like aliens!'

'I don't care what they look like!' roared John. 'That was the way the witnesses described them, they were satisfied with the results, and if you don't like them, that's your fucking bad luck!' and with that, he slammed the phone down.

John, I should add, is a good friend of mine and for him to have acted like such a Big Girl's Blouse was completely out of character.

There was nothing else to assist with the case, so I decided to make up a 'Wanted Docket' with what I'd got. This docket was a large foolscap envelope and into it went all the statements and documentation pertaining to the case, so that if this team were identified in the future and I wasn't present, the officer who was interested in the investigation could go to the crime book entry, where he would see 'Wanted Docket No. 36 refers' and then be able to pick out the docket for all the evidence. In this particular case, I had to admit, it was a highly unlikely scenario. But having done that, there was one last matter to complete.

Whenever somebody was circulated as being 'wanted' – as these three obviously were – their names would be shown in either *Confidential Informations* or *Police Gazette*. But whilst I was unaware of the names of the robbers, I did have their photofits, so I labelled them 'Suspects 1, 2 & 3'. Then I typed out three forms – in those days the form was known as a CRO 73 – with their descriptions, attached the relevant photofit to each of the forms and put them into the tray of a senior officer. The forms required his signature, and then they could be sent off to the Yard for insertion in *Confidential Informations*; just as Edwin Bush's identikit picture had been, back in 1961. And with that, I had virtuously empty 'In' and 'Out' trays and went off on holiday with a clear conscience.

A couple of weeks later, relaxed and tanned by the Cretan sun, I returned to work. I sat down at my desk with a cup of coffee and caught up with the various publications and news. But as I casually flipped through the pages of *Confidential Informations*, I suddenly realized that there was no reference to my three building society robbers.

I went into the senior officer's office – there, in his 'In' tray, were the three CRO 73 forms, complete with the photofits, just where I'd left them over two weeks previously. I was surprised; I knew him to be absolutely, stunningly bone-idle, but not even to scrawl his signature on the bottom of three forms really took the biscuit.

'Why didn't you sign these and send them off?' I asked crossly. 'I did them weeks ago, before I went on leave.'

'I'm not signing them,' he replied simply.

I was nonplussed. 'Why ever not?'

'Look at them,' he said, waving at the forms. 'They look like Martians. I'm not putting my signature to something like that. If word got round that I'd authorized this to go to the Yard, people would never stop taking the piss out of me.'

In fact, he was already the subject of ridicule for his absolute inertia in taking any kind of decision whatsoever, but that was by the by, because that was that – sign them he would not. I was furious, snatched up the forms and stamped out of his office. When something like that happened, it was not unknown for a wheel to come off over something else connected with the case, and in the ensuing internal investigation every scrap of documentation would be scrupulously examined – and for Forms CRO 73 not to have been submitted was a disciplinary offence. On this occasion, I thought to myself, 'This is one time I'm not going to cover up for that windy bastard – if there is an investigation and I'm asked why the forms weren't forwarded to the Yard, my reply will be, "Because I've got a senior officer who's not only as lazy as arseholes but he's as weak as piss as well."'

But it didn't come to that. A few days later, I received a telephone call.

'Is that DS Kirby?' said an excited voice. 'This is DC Perkins from Plaistow, Skip – just to let you know we've nicked three black kids for a blagging at a building society and they've put their hands up to your one as well!'

'That's great!' I exclaimed. 'Bloody well done to you – how'd you do it?'

'Oh, we were out and about, saw these three hanging around by a building society, and before we could stop them they went inside, and then we nicked 'em as they came out – stuck their hands up straight away!'

'Bloody good that you were close enough to nab 'em,' I said admiringly.

'That's right,' laughed Perkins. 'Mind you, if they had got away, we'd have picked 'em up later. There was no missing them – it's funny, Sarge, I'd never seen black kids like these three before. I know it sounds funny but . . . well, quite frankly, they looked like fucking aliens!'

CHAPTER 16

Aids to CID and Other
Suspicious Persons

In order to comply with Sir Robert Peel's strictures regarding the prevention of crime, laws had always been passed to deal with this, the first of which was the Vagrancy Act, 1824, which had been implemented five years' prior to the formation of the Metropolitan Police. This law was passed principally to deal with returning troops from the Napoleonic Wars who were wounded, disabled or in any other way unemployable and likely to make nuisances of themselves. Those falling foul of the Act were deemed to be 'idle and disorderly persons, rogues and vagabonds and incorrigible rogues'. Yes, Britain knew how to look after her ex-service personnel, even then.

Section 3 of the Act dealt with homeless persons – they were deemed to be 'wandering abroad' – and also beggars, for whom the punishment was one month's imprisonment. It was known as 'a woodman's', because the first month of any prison sentence meant that the prisoner slept on a wooden cot without the benefit of a mattress.

By far the commonest offence under Section 4 of the Act was that of 'being a suspected person, loitering with intent to commit a felony' – other offences included indecent exposure and being found in an enclosed premises for an unlawful purpose – and the punishment was three months' imprisonment, or 'a carpet', because that was the amount of time it took the inmate to weave a carpet on the prison loom. Anybody found guilty of a subsequent offence under that section of the Act (since he was now deemed to be 'a rogue and a vagabond'), stood the risk of being committed to the court of quarter-sessions for sentence under Section 5 of the act, having been adjudged to be 'an incorrigible rogue', in which case the sentence was twelve months' imprisonment – 'a stretch'.

This section of the Vagrancy Act also dealt with being in possession of housebreaking instruments by day, in which cases the prosecution had to prove that the accused person had them in his possession for a larcenous purpose. Section 28 of the Larceny

Act 1916 dealt with the possession of those items by night, when the onus was on the accused person to prove they were for an innocent purpose. I shall deal with the anomaly regarding this particular offence a little later in this chapter.

And there was Section 66 of the Metropolitan Police Act, 1839, which gave the police power to stop persons or vehicles in or upon which they had reason to believe stolen property could be found. If a person was in possession of items about which there was a suspicion that they were stolen or unlawfully obtained and for which he could not provide a satisfactory explanation, he faced a fine of £5 or two months' imprisonment.

None of these pieces of legislation now exist; all of them have been repealed. But they were all on the statute books when I joined the Metropolitan Police and they were a terrific weapon against street crime, as were the now defunct Aids to CID.

Aids were drawn from the uniform branch; although they were still essentially uniform officers they wore plain clothes, and the way in which they conducted themselves would depend on whether or not they were inducted into the CID proper, with the rank of detective constable. Usually, the whole transitional process took anything between two and four years. It was then the only way to get into the CID; it had been for many years – and, I firmly believe, the *best* way.

Aids to CID worked in pairs – their partners were known as 'bucks' – and their role was the prevention of crime. Of course, as they patrolled the streets, if they walked slap-bang into a robbery or a burglary which was in progress and they arrested the perpetrators, all well and good. But the aids were principally there to stop, search and arrest suspicious-looking members of the community who, they suspected, were in possession of offensive weapons or stolen property or who were preparing to commit crime. This meant keeping observation on a thief or groups of thieves until they had, for example, stolen lead flashing from a roof or committed a series of acts which would put them into the category of 'suspected persons'. Therefore, the majority of arrests under this section of the Vagrancy Act were for 'Sus dips' or 'Sus handbags' – these two offences, of course, relating to larceny from the person – and for 'Sus houses' and 'Sus cars'.

'Me and my buck were posted permanent night-duty,' recalled Bill (one of the older ex-tecs) reminiscently. 'There'd been a spate of screwings on an estate and we were told to go out – and stay out – 'til they'd been nicked. That was during the fifties – cor, bleedin' cold, it was. If we'd had a brass monkey with us, the RSPCA would've had us nicked for cruelty! Nearly two weeks we spent inside a deserted bungalow; then we saw 'em. A couple of geezers trying back doors. We nicked 'em for Sus houses and they got a carpet apiece. Course, there wasn't any commendations or nothing like that; the CID said we were just doing our job. But the fact was, while that pair were inside, the number of screwings in the area dropped to almost nothing.'

Aids did not deal with reported crime; that was the province of the CID, and it wasn't the only thing that differentiated them, either. Both the CID proper and the aids put in tremendously long hours; the distinction was, the CID were paid a niggardly allowance, whereas the aids, being uniform officers, were paid overtime. The number of hours they worked was added up and they were free to take time off – if their duties permitted it – but if they did not, after three months the accumulated number of hours which were recorded on a 'Time Off' card went in for payment. This could provoke hostility between them and the CID, especially with the detective sergeant (first class) who traditionally was in charge of the aids.

'Our first-class was a bastard,' commented Bill. 'Me and my buck, we'd done so much work, each of us had a hundred hours on our cards, and it was just coming up to three months for it to go in for payment. And we needed that dough; my mate was in lodgings, me and the missus were in married quarters, and both of us were saving up for a deposit on a house. Know what that fucking first-class did? Me and my buck came on duty at two o'clock and he says to us, "A load of cars have been broken into in the station car park; if any are broken into up to ten o'clock tonight, you and your mate are back to uniform. However, both of you have got too much time on your cards, so I'm telling you to take eight hours time off, starting now." See, we were bollocksed, weren't we? If we went home and cars were broken into, we'd be back to uniform; the only alternative was to sit up at the car park in our own bleedin' time and try to nick whoever was doing 'em.'

'Did any cars get broken into that night?' I asked.

Bill nodded. 'Two.'

'Were you sent back to uniform?'

Bill shook his head and grinned. 'Nah. Me and my buck went up to the car park, and after a bit a couple of tearaways came along and started making themselves a bit busy. We nicked 'em for Sus cars.'

'What about the cars which were broken into?' I asked.

'That was our get-out, see? We could prove that when that happened we were down the nick, dealing with our prisoners. Couldn't be in two places at once, could we?'

Bill laughed. 'Plus, of course, to all intents and purposes, we'd made arrests off duty; we got commended by the Beak for vigilance – plus, of course, once we'd nicked 'em, we were back on duty, again. Nothing that bleedin' first-class could do about it.'

Of course, it also raises the question that Bill and his buck could not have been held accountable for the cars being broken into, since they had been given an order to book off duty, but in those days that rationale really didn't come into the equation.

The demise of the aids came in 1963. The late Detective Sergeant Harry Challenor MM (who during a seven-month period as an aid notched up 105 arrests, the majority for Sus) was in charge of the aids at West End Central police station.[1] During a period of civil insurrection in the West End of London, three of his aids were found guilty of planting bricks on innocent people at a demonstration and were imprisoned; Challenor (similarly a brick-planter) was found unfit to plead and was sent to a psychiatric hospital. Following an internal investigation and a public enquiry, the aids system was abolished and the aids were replaced with temporary detective constables. It made little difference; they were still referred to as 'aids'.

Right from its inception in 1919, the Flying Squad had used the 'sus' laws, especially to effect the arrest of 'dips'; in 1928, when the Squad was responsible for 429 arrests, 215 of these were for 'Sus dips'.[2]

Later, the Squad had its own 'Dips Squad', which was how 8 Squad was referred to. They had considerable success arresting pickpockets at racetracks and other public events, plus there were additional benefits – 'dips' are known to be notorious grasses, and the Dips Squad received some excellent information over the years which was disseminated to and acted upon by other members of the Squad. All that came to an end after sixty lucrative years following the decision by a stupendously stupid deputy assistant commissioner, who had spent practically all of his service in uniform and who ordered that the Dips Squad be

---

1 For further information regarding this charismatic character, see *The Scourge of Soho: The Controversial Career of SAS Hero Detective Sergeant Harry Challenor MM*, Pen & Sword Books, 2013

2 For further information regarding this elite unit, see *The Sweeney: The First Sixty Years of Scotland Yard's Crimebusting Flying Squad, 1919–1978*, Pen & Sword Books, 2011, *Whitechapel's Sherlock Holmes: The Casebook of Fred Wensley, OBE, KPM, Victorian Crime Buster*, Pen & Sword Books, 2014 and *Scotland Yard's Flying Squad: 100 Years of Crime Fighting*, Pen & Sword Books, 2019

disbanded. He had no comprehension of the results obtained by the Squad, and his despotic decision was rather like asking Errol Flynn to apply for the post of caretaker at a pubescent girls' school; not really within his job description or capabilities.

★ ★ ★

Sometimes it was difficult to establish absolutely the offence which was being committed. One pair of aids saw a well-known villain in a crowded market place pushing up behind women with shopping bags, one after another, and it was clear he was up to no good. Eventually, the aids walked over and felt his collar.

'Wot?' expostulated the aggrieved felon. 'Wot exactly am I supposed to have done?'

'Take your choice,' replied the older and wiser aid. 'Sus handbags or three indecent assaults.'

'Blimey, I'll take the sus, Guv,' replied the thief hurriedly. 'I don't want it put about that I'm a nonce!'

He pleaded guilty at court, was weighed off and the younger and less experienced of the two aids learnt a substantial lesson in the management of the criminal classes. The older was what was known as a 'Tutor Aid'. In years gone by, if an aid was to be selected for the Criminal Investigation Department, he had to have passed the Civil Service Examination. Many of those who failed the exam were excellent thief-takers but nevertheless were returned to uniform. Some – a very small number – were so outstanding, not only in their ability to arrest thieves but also in their encyclopaedic knowledge of the people of the area, that they were retained as tutor aids, to instruct new aids to CID on how to conduct their duties. These tutor aids were greatly admired by the CID proper and were worth their weight in gold.

One of the most famous of the tutor aids was Ted Collier, who worked on 'G' Division. He had twenty years service behind him when, in 1941, he instructed Ian Forbes, later to retire as a supremely capable deputy assistant commissioner, in the art of aiding. In 1945, when Bert 'Iron Man' Sparks was posted to Commercial Street as the new detective inspector – he would later head the Flying Squad – he and other officers, including Ted Collier, chased five thieves who had been seen on the roof of the Salvation Army Hostel. The suspect being chased by Sparks was gradually distancing himself from his pursuers when Collier put his fingers in his mouth and emitted his distinctive and particularly piercing whistle. The thief came to an abrupt halt, turned, walked back to the officers and surrendered, commenting sadly that if

Ted Collier had spotted him, there was no point in even trying to escape.

However, some of the tutor aids exercised rather more enthusiasm in their duties than the discipline code (or indeed the criminal justice system) would have permitted. Bill, lost in his memories, was in full flow.

'You won't remember old Harry Travers,' he said. 'He was an old pre-war copper. Although he was only an aid, he did a bit of work with the Ghost Squad.[3] Mustard, he was. Later, when I knew him, he was a tutor aid.'

Harry, it transpired, had his eye on a team of three local tearaways. They were very strongly suspected of breaking offences but they were cunning; they left not a clue behind to link them to their handiwork, and no one knew the identity of their receivers. On several occasions they had been arrested, and their haunts and those of their associates had been searched, but all without success. They were rightly regarded by the local police as a bunch of professional piss-takers. Crafty they might have been; however, in the field of slyness they were about to come up against Harry Travers, who held a black belt in the arts of duplicity.

Into a canvas holdall Harry put a fearsome collection of housebreaking implements (HBI), which he placed on the crossbar of his bike before he and his buck set off across the mean streets around City Road, just as dusk was falling. Bicycles were often used by aids in those far-off days of police-work; they could cover a much wider area and they used hand signals when they spotted each other at road junctions if they had discovered something untoward which merited their combined talents.

It was not too long before Harry spotted his larcenous trio; clearly, to his practised eye, they were up to no good. He could see the direction in which they were heading, so taking an alternate route he pedalled furiously away and arrived at the junction towards which the three screwsmen were heading, several minutes before their arrival. Having checked that the coast was clear, Harry dumped the incriminating bag right on the corner, rode off, met up with his buck and gave the signal to inform him that something was brewing; then the pair of them cycled back to the junction. As they rounded the corner, there were the three felons, not only busily sorting through the bag they'd found but

---

3 For further information about this unit, see *Scotland Yard's Ghost Squad: The Secret Weapon Against Post-War Crime*, Pen & Sword Books, 2011

also gleefully distributing the contents about their persons – and they were nicked for possession of housebreaking implements.

'That was a bit borderline, don't you think?' asked Dave, who was one of the regulars listening to the tale.

'Oh, I don't know,' replied Chris, another habitué. 'I mean, they didn't have to pick them up, did they?'

'Anyway, what happened to them, Bill?' I asked.

'What happened?' echoed Bill. 'They pleaded guilty, of course.'

'Bloody hell!' muttered Chris.

'Yes, two reasons mainly. First, they knew they were well overdue for a nicking, and with Harry feeling their collars, they realized their time was up.'

'What was the second deciding factor in them pleading guilty?' asked Dave, but Bill disregarded the heavy irony in Dave's voice.

'Oh, Harry was nothing if not fair,' he replied, cheerfully. 'The time was just coming up to nine o'clock. These herberts knew full well that if they were caught in possession of HBI in daytime under the Vagrancy Act, the maximum penalty was three months' imprisonment; to be caught with them under the Larceny Act, in the hours of darkness – and darkness officially started at nine o'clock – it was five years' penal servitude; or, in the event that they'd previously been convicted of felony, ten years. So Harry just said to them, "When d'you wanted to be nicked, boys – just before nine o'clock, or a few minutes afterwards?" No contest really, was it? They'd been taught a much-needed lesson and they all drew a carpet, quite happily!'

CHAPTER 17

Rough Justice

Throughout the pages of this book are tales of no-nonsense police work in which the justice meted out might be described by some as being rather rough. But I recall a couple of cases in which someone on the other side of the law felt himself aggrieved and decided to administer a little zero tolerance of his own. Generally speaking, I'm all for resolving minor disagreements without involving the police, but not when things degenerate into mob-handed vigilantism as they did in the first of these two cases.

Before I describe what happened, I want to mention Arthur Haley's best-selling novel, *Roots*, which was published in 1976. It told the story of Kunta Kinte, one of the Mandinka people from what is now known as The Gambia, who was sold as a slave in 1767 and taken to America. Unable (or unwilling) to attempt his given name, the owners of the plantation to whom he was sold decided to re-christen him 'Toby'. Kunta Kinte initially rebelled at this rebranding of his identity and was given a bashing as a punishment for his recalcitrance.

The book provided Haley with a Pulitzer Prize, and soon after, a very popular television series which won several awards, with LeVar Burton playing the lead, was shown in the States and later in this country. Just bear this in mind for what's to follow, because it gives an insight into the motivation of some of the people involved.

I'd taken over the running of the 'J' Division Crime Squad in 1980 (it had been dubbed 'The Magnificent Seven' in the press following the convictions of nine people for burglary and receiving), and whilst the aids were usually sent out patrolling the streets to detect and prevent crime by stopping and searching suspects, I also checked the crime book entries of the surrounding stations so that I was aware of types and patterns of crime which were emerging.

It was while I was in the CID office at Barkingside that I became aware of a rather shocking matter that immediately attracted my attention. It appeared that the younger brother of a local tearaway had been attacked and forced to drink a bottle of vodka by what was described as 'a bunch of Teddy Boys'; and now the older brother sought revenge. Discovering the name of the person – Jenkins – allegedly responsible for the attack on his younger sibling, he gathered together some friends from a local pub and went to Jenkins' address for a reckoning. Mr Jenkins Sr opened the door of his council house to four rather determined-looking young men who demanded to see his 16-year-old son, but he decided that he didn't like the look of them at all, so told them that his son was in bed and shut the door. When they knocked again, he opened the door and waved them away, but the ringleader punched him in the face, breaking his nose, while two of the others held him while he received a thorough beating. The ringleader then went outside and gave a wave; it was the signal for pandemonium to break loose. Approximately fifteen other youths who had been hiding around the corner rushed forward and into the house, wrecking it; a neighbour would later describe how a bicycle had been picked up and thrown through a window.

It was the sort of behaviour that just could not be tolerated; it had to be stamped on immediately, and I spoke to the detective chief inspector.

'Guv'nor, can you put this one down to me? There's a lot of people involved in this, potential prisoners as well as witnesses, and it's tailor-made for something like the Crime Squad to deal with.'

The DCI readily agreed, and I called the Crime Squad in for a briefing.

Not a great many people wanted to come forward as witnesses in a case like this, because of the possible repercussions, but we found sufficient numbers to build the framework of a case. The younger Jenkins denied forcing the ringleader's brother to drink the vodka; he said that a group of them had had a consensual swig out of the bottle. Maybe, maybe not. But even if it were true, in no way could it justify what the newspapers later referred to as 'House Rampage of Terror Gang'.

Several of the gang were named. And this was where the connection with Arthur Haley's novel came in. Just a few months earlier, a number of them had grabbed hold of a black kid, tied him to a tree and whipped him with a lump of rope, telling him that he should refer to himself as 'Toby'. What astonished me was that when this was reported to the police it was handled by the uniform branch, who told the perpetrators that they shouldn't do it again and wrote it off as a piece of youthful boisterousness. I thought it disgraceful; this wasn't a bit of playground rough and tumble between little kids – the perpetrators were in their late teens and early twenties. It also revealed the sort of nastiness which had inspired the attack upon the Jenkins' household.

With a list of names, we carried out synchronized raids to gather in the gang simultaneously; but, as is often the case, it didn't go to plan. Some were brought in, others weren't at home, but those who were brought in were questioned, and other names were forthcoming. We walked into a pub which I'd been told they frequented; there were two of them at the bar, I recognized them from the descriptions we'd been given, and in they came.

Some were released, there being insufficient evidence to charge them, and some, I feel sure, we never identified. But eventually, nine young men aged between seventeen and twenty-three were committed to stand their trial at Snaresbrook Crown Court on charges of conspiracy to assault.

It was a fairly uneventful trial as far as I was concerned; some of the prisoners had made admissions, some partial admissions, and others none at all; all of them pleaded not guilty. As is common with conspiracies, culpability varied greatly from the hard core at the centre to the runners and riders on the periphery.

One young man was among those who could accurately be described as being 'easily led' and who, I think, was really a decent young fellow. So when his barrister – also a reasonable sort of chap – took a bit of a chance and said, 'Can you tell the court, Sergeant Kirby, where, in your view my client featured in this conspiracy?' I replied, 'Whilst it was clear to me that he was indeed involved in this conspiracy, it's only fair to say that in my opinion he was right on the edge of it.'

'Thank you,' said the barrister and wisely sat down.

The young man in question was one of five of the defendants who were acquitted; the other four were given six months each, with the ringleader getting an extra six months for breaking Mr Jenkins' nose.

As I walked out of court I was rounded on by the father of the young man I'd spoken up for; I suppose it was the relief of a concerned father who believed that his son stood a chance of going to jail.

'You've put my family through purgatory!' he shouted. 'You had no right to arrest my son – I'm going to complain— ' and then a voice cut across his rants.

'No you're not,' said his son's barrister. 'You're not going to complain at all. You're going to thank Sergeant Kirby for having the common decency to provide me with the ammunition to get your son off. When I asked him that all-important question, he could have said that your son was deeply involved in the conspiracy;

he didn't. Now, just be grateful that your son's not joining his mates in the cells to start six months' imprisonment.'

Whether or not I did receive an apology, I don't recall. Not that I could have cared less; it was all water off a duck's back to me.

However, I mention it not only because of the aspects in this case of rough justice in reverse, but because of the oddity of receiving a commendation from a defence barrister. This, I assure you, was something that only happened to me once – mind you, my chum Derek gazumped me there; in the second of these cases, he actually got a commendation from a blackmailer at the Old Bailey!

* * *

Derek Webster imbibes with us at those luncheons, but sadly far too infrequently because he lives so far away. He's the best of companions, a big former rugby player (and later a member of the RFU Judiciary Discipline Panel), much admired by his contemporaries, often commended for excellent police-work and one of the finest detective constables I ever met. Nowadays he always sonorously greets me with the words of the report which I submitted to the Metropolitan Police Solicitors' Department in respect of the investigation that follows: 'The facts of this case read more like a garish novel than that of happenings in sleepy Chigwell on a sunny, Sunday morning . . .' There, you see? I was even then juggling with literary phraseology and hyperbole.

Derek had about a year's less service than me; we met at Barkingside police station after I'd been transferred there in 1979 from the Serious Crime Squad. The 'Sunday' to which I've just referred was a day in which only a skeleton CID staff was on duty; Derek was one of just two officers and he would have been justified in calling out senior management and a few more troops to deal with what occurred; typically, he did nothing of the sort but just cracked on and dealt with it himself.

Early on that Sunday morning, a car had pulled up outside a house in Meadow Way, Chigwell, a fairly salubrious area. Two very large Mancunian lorry drivers got out of the car and knocked on the front door; the reason for their visit was not a social one. The occupier of the house, Mr Green, had carried out a deal with a haulage contractor who lived in Kent and who claimed that Mr Green owed him a considerable amount of money. The contractor had demanded payment on several occasions, but

Mr Green had either refused to pay, was unable to do so, had attempted to defer payment or denied any such contractual agreement; whatever the circumstances, he had made it quite clear he was not going to part with a brass farthing. It appeared that the haulage contractor had made a phone call to a third party in Manchester, who had sub-contracted two thugs, provided them with Mr Green's address and requested that they 'lean' on Mr Green to hand over the money.

However, upon answering the knock at the door, Mr Green – no lightweight, himself – refused payment, whereupon one of the thugs, Black, 'leant' unnecessarily hard on him by punching him in the face. Black happened to be wearing a large ring, and the impact of this resulted in several sutures being inserted in Green's nose. The resulting furore raised by Mrs Green and the children caused the two heavies to flee, but not before the registration number of their car had been noted. The police were informed, hence Derek's involvement.

Derek took a detailed statement from Green and his family which included descriptions of the two thugs, and a registered owner check revealed that the driver of the vehicle lived in Manchester. Derek telephoned his counterparts at Greater Manchester Police, who acted very swiftly, identifying from Derek's description the driver – who had a fair amount of form – and his likely associate; at Derek's request, both men were arrested.

The two thugs were brought back to Barkingside, interviewed and made full and frank confessions in great detail, naming the haulage contractor and the middleman who had organized their ill-conceived jaunt down to London.

The following morning, I walked into the CID office at Barkingside, and the detective chief inspector had a quiet word with me.

'Derek's copped a right tasty blackmail; I know he's capable, but a job like this needs a DS in charge. Just keep an eye on things, will you?'

Of course, I didn't need to 'keep an eye on things' at all; supremely capable as he was, in the space of twenty-four hours Derek had made two impressive arrests, and now I got stuck into the investigation because the haulage contractor needed to be spoken to. Nowadays, Derek tells me that I told the man from Kent he was under arrest for attempted murder, which all but put him in a swoon. I don't recall that, but I do know that he obtained the services of a particularly unpleasant solicitor, and although the contractor agreed that Green owed him money, he had said and done nothing which caused the unwarranted demand to be made.

There was no supporting evidence – the two thugs had said that their instructions had come from him via a third party, but they had not spoken directly to the contractor so this was hearsay on their part, and regrettably he was released without charge.

This left the middleman, Brown, also from Manchester; he was brought in to be interviewed by Derek and me. Just as we were about to commence the interview, a breathless solicitor rushed in; who had called him, I don't know, but it must have been at short notice because he was out of puff, and there was something else as well . . .

In any event, Brown was questioned, with Derek taking notes of the interview; the solicitor was also taking notes. At the conclusion of the interview, the prisoner was asked to read and sign Derek's notes as being correct; he refused, as did the solicitor. There was sufficient evidence to charge Brown with blackmail, and the three men were committed from Redbridge Magistrates' Court to stand their trial at the Old Bailey.

Now, I've already mentioned that Derek was well liked by his colleagues; but the fact of the matter is, he was often popular with villains as well, because he dealt with them in a decent, friendly fashion, and these two thugs were no exception. Black, especially because he had a fair amount of form, thought he was going to be committed in custody to the Bailey and he was concerned because his wife was in poor health. Derek smoothed things over and ensured that he was released on bail; after that, as far as Black was concerned, Derek could do no wrong.

The evidence against the two heavies was overwhelming; against the middleman, Brown, it was not so compelling. This was pointed out to the two thugs – and if they pleaded guilty, the evidence which would convict them could not be used against Brown. But if they pleaded not guilty, all of the evidence would go in. They would tell the jury exactly what it was that Brown had told them to do and then they could be cross-examined on their evidence. That was the decision they had to make: let the slippery Brown, who had put them up to this caper, get away with it? Let their mate Derek down? The thugs were not overburdened with brains, but this really was a matter of Hobson's Choice.

So all three pleaded not guilty to blackmail. Brown was represented by a left-wing barrister famed for his bellowing, barracking attacks on witnesses. All of the evidence went in, and Black came in for some scathing, sneering cross-examination. In fact, because of his lack of comprehension, a lot of it went over Black's head until, hearing the tittering laughter coming from the jury, he suddenly realized that the barrister was making fun of him.

Giving the barrister much the same look as he had given the occupant of Meadow Way several months previously, Black very quietly and forcefully said, 'Don't you take the piss out of me!'

Like many bullies, the barrister was now on the back foot. Ever since entering chambers he had felt that donning a wig and gown would afford him sufficient protection in court to say pretty much anything he liked to a witness; but now his bluff had been called. Possibly thinking that, any second, Black was going to vault out of the witness box at him, he whimpered, 'I wasn't!'

'Yes, you were,' answered Black and, warming to his task, he added, 'just like you tried to take the piss out of that detective the other day!' (This, of course, was Derek.) And now, thoroughly warmed up, he roared, 'BUT YOU COULDN'T, COULD YOU? BECAUSE HE WAS BLOODY BRILLIANT!'

And really that was the end of the defence case. It had not been helped when previously I had been cross-examined on the matter of the note-taking during Brown's interview. In the witness box I had been handed the notes allegedly made by the solicitor; I looked at them and saw that they bore little resemblance to the accurate notes which Derek had taken down.

'Can you explain the discrepancy in these two sets of notes?' sneered the barrister.

'I believe I can,' I replied. 'The notes made by Detective Constable Webster are, of course, wholly accurate. I was there when he wrote them, and when your client and his solicitor refused to read or sign them, they were read and signed by DC Webster and myself. Therefore these notes, contemporaneously made, are a correct record of the interview.'

The barrister gave a theatrical, exasperated sigh. 'Then why is it that the solicitor's notes are so different to DC Webster's?'

'Because the solicitor was drunk,' I replied, and as I did so I heard a gasp from the jury. 'I noticed that when he sat down, apart from being out of breath, he also smelled strongly of spirits. His explanation of both was that he had been at a party when he had received the phone call about his client and he had rushed all the way to the police station.'

All three were convicted and all went off to prison, the two thugs cheerily waving to Derek as they left the dock, but Brown looking rather downcast. We sat down afterwards in The Feathers for a well-earned glass.

'It was a result, those two giving evidence like that,' I said to Derek. 'I wonder who put that idea in their heads about pleading not guilty?'

Derek smiled, shrugged his shoulders and sipped his pint. Affable he may be, but at times awfully enigmatic as well.

And after all that, we went our separate ways. Derek was understandably snapped up by the Regional Crime Squad, I went to the Flying Squad, and that was the end of our working relationship. How I wish we could have worked together on the Flying Squad; between us, like my Saturday morning pictures hero, Flash Gordon, in the third of his adventures, I believe we could have conquered the universe.

Right: Roelant Savery's purloined painting.

Below: A 'pavement job' – a spectacular Flying Squad arrest.

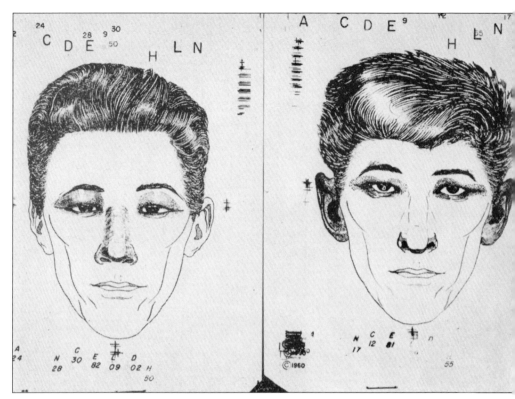

Above: The very first identikit impressions . . .

Left: . . . which led to the arrest of murderer, Edwin Bush.

Above: John Woodhouse, identikit assembler *par excellence* . . .

Below: . . . and photographed outside the Old Bailey by a C11 surveillance operative.

Commendation time

Above left: Mick Carter.

Above right: The author.

Below: Graham Seaby.

What was once regarded as the top crime-busting centre of the western world.

The Old Bailey – sometimes (not always) a dispenser of justice.

Caught in the act

A robber – supposedly in possession of dynamite – making a withdrawal.

Left: A thief, similarly making a withdrawal, from the Flying Squad commander's safe.

Below: Safety deposit key impressions made by London's top 'key-man'.

Standard police weaponry . . .

Above and below: . . . although the villains had access to rather more diverse munitions.

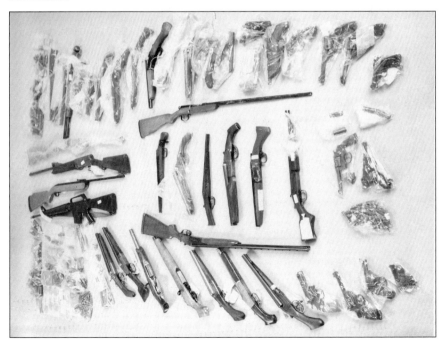

The author being terrifyingly 'goosed' by the President of the ReCIDivists'
Luncheon Club, Julie Hillman . . .

. . . but finding comfort with Ann, the love of his life for sixty years.

CHAPTER 18

The Loan Ranger

Something which once featured large, on an annual basis, under the control of the CID, and which has now gone the way of all things, was the loan club.

The loan club – and there were many on the manor – was usually run from a pub. The members would pay in whatever sum they could afford each week in order to purchase their Christmas presents; and during the year, loans would be arranged for those who required them, usually for a short term and at a very low rate of interest which, of course, had to be fully repaid prior to the pre-Christmas payout. The treasurer was a well-known, upright citizen of the area – usually a businessman – who relied upon the local CID to accompany him to the bank on payout day and return with him to the pub where, over the course of the day, he would pay the money out to the investors. Since it was common knowledge in the area that a large sum of money would be on the premises, it required the presence of a couple of aids to stay in the pub all day until the very last customer was paid out, and for this service they were liberally supplied with beer. Since they were also armed with service revolvers, any emergency could have escalated into a very tricky situation indeed, although to the best of my knowledge, thankfully nothing of the kind ever occurred.

And within a few days of these transactions being completed, the local CID Christmas party would occur. This would be attended by local publicans, market traders, scrap metal dealers, second-hand car salesmen, bookies and other respectable businessman of the area. They, like the three wise men of so long ago, came bearing gifts to such an extent that the party funded itself, and many CID officers tottered off home afterwards clutching a spare donated bottle or two under their jackets. And of course, the treasurer of the loan club would also make an appearance, ready to show his appreciation for the local CID officers' contribution to the safe distribution of the club's accumulated cash.

Additionally, it was not unknown during those festivities for the station's typists to succumb to the blandishments of libidinous detectives. Rather like the eponymous heroine of Adolphe Adam's ballet, *Giselle*, who found herself deceived by a prince in disguise, the betrayed stenographer would usually be discovered in the New Year curled up, weeping, inside the drawer of a filing cabinet.

These parties, you will be unsurprised to learn, do not happen today. Any self-respecting, currently serving police chief would faint on the spot at the very thought of anything of the kind taking place, but consider this. Such a meeting was invaluable to a working detective. If he didn't know all of the guests when they arrived, he did by the time they left. As the liquor flowed and tongues were loosened, a great deal of useful information passed between all the parties which helped the detectives know who was doing what, to whom and, what's more, why. If you like, it was an intelligence-gathering exercise, and what was gleaned from it could, in the long run, be very beneficial to the local community. So any serving senior officer who, upon reading these words, starts stammering and expostulating about breaches of the disciplinary code and possible corruption, might like to consider his position the next time he accepts a Sikh businessman's invitation to visit a *gurdwara*, dresses up in very strange-looking kit and stuffs himself with exotic grub. There's no difference, really. He thinks he's doing the local community a service, and perhaps he is. Unfortunately, any meaningful information that's being passed between the other guests is probably in a language he can't comprehend.

* * *

I arrived early for lunch with the chaps in the run-up to Christmas – the traffic had been kind to me and there were very few fellow ex-tecs in the bar. But Jim Sharpe was there, and we got into conversation. Jim was someone I only knew from attending these luncheons; we had never worked together. In fact, much of his service had been spent in North or North-West London, as well as the Regional Crime Squad and the Flying Squad, and he had joined the Metropolitan Police approximately ten years before me. Like me, Jim had never risen above the rank of detective sergeant but he was one of those officers who were the backbone of the Force. At every police station where he had worked he knew the manor and its inhabitants inside out.

Jim grinned at the glass of sparkling water which I was drinking.

'You wouldn't have been drinking that at the Christmas party a few years ago,' he laughed.

I nodded and said, 'I'm told they don't have CID Christmas parties any more, Jim.'

He snorted in disgust before taking a swallow of his bitter.

'No Christmas parties?' he scoffed. 'Whoever heard of such a thing?'

'I remember when I was on the Squad going to three parties a night on the run-up to Christmas,' I said. 'Apart from the parties, there were the loan clubs. They don't have them anymore, either – or if they do, the Department's not involved with them, that's for sure.'

At that, Jim Sharpe smiled slyly.

'I can tell you a story about a loan club, years ago, when I was on 'X' Division,' he murmured. 'Want to hear it?'

This is the story that Jim told me: how he came to the rescue of a beleaguered loan club treasurer – or perhaps, how Jim transformed himself into 'The Loan Ranger'.

★   ★   ★

During the early sixties Jim frequented The Jester public house; it was fairly close to his local nick and it was a well-run establishment. Many of the local scrap metal dealers and market workers were customers, and it was a place where Jim could have a quiet, relaxing drink and pick up often worthwhile snippets of information. It was also the base for one of the area's loan clubs, to which Jim subscribed a modest amount each week.

The treasurer was Alec Michaelson, the proprietor of a toyshop in the High Street, and ten days prior to Christmas, it was Michaelson whom Jim saw in the saloon bar of The Jester and realized immediately that something was wrong. Michaelson's normally ruddy, smiling face was pale and anxious.

'Jim, can I have a word?' muttered the treasurer, sitting down at Jim's table.

His eyes darted from right to left, as though fearful of being overheard.

'Sure, Alec,' replied Jim. 'What's up?'

Alec Michaelson was a worried man indeed. One of the loan club members had borrowed £150 – a substantial sum at that time – and with pay-out just days away, he had not only failed to repay the loan, he had actually *refused* to pay it!

'That's not all, Jim,' added Michaelson. 'The word is, he's just won two hundred nicker at the local bookies! And *still* the bastard won't stump up! Jim, can you do something – go round his address and make him cough up the cash?'

'Hmm!' replied Jim.

What Michaelson was suggesting might well be construed as demanding money with menaces; a felony punishable, when the Larceny Act of 1916 had first been placed on the statute books, with penal servitude for life (and in the event that the culprit was a male under the age of sixteen he could be privately whipped!). And even if a benign Director of Public Prosecutions decided that there was insufficient evidence upon which to prosecute, there was still the police discipline code – known to cater for everything between being born and dying – to contend with. No. What was required here was perspicacity – a commodity which Jim Sharpe possessed in spades. That, and a modicum of low cunning.

'Alec, what's this finger's name?' he asked.

* * *

Brian Coombe was what was known as 'a tapper'. He lived mostly on his wits, sponging money; he considered that any debts or liabilities which he incurred should not be repaid, as a matter of honour. And although Alec Michaelson was an astute businessman he preferred, because he liked to help out the community of which he was a member by running the loan club, to think the best of people and had failed to spot this flaw in Brian Coombe's personality.

But Jim Sharpe knew different; although he had not had any direct dealings with Coombe he was aware that he was a whiny little crook with a couple of minor convictions for false pretences whose disinclination to cough up this borrowed money (even though he was well able to) was a character defect which would need to be rectified, sooner rather than later.

'Sergeant Sharpe, CID,' was how Jim introduced himself at Coombe's council flat as he flashed his paste-board warrant card at him and walked straight in, almost as though he'd been invited. Pausing only to turn off the blaring television in the lounge – Jim considered this an unnecessary intrusion – he plumped himself down in one of the sagging armchairs and waved towards one of the others – 'Sit down, Brian.' Jim had, of course, taken control of the whole situation – not a bad policy, as I'm sure you'll agree.

'Brian, I've come to mark your cards. Now, I know about your debt to the loan club' – and as Coombe opened his mouth, either to expostulate or explain, Jim held up an admonishing hand. 'Just hear me out. That loan is nothing to do with the police – understand? It's what we call "a civil dispute" and whether you settle it or not, it's up to you – it's certainly nothing to do with me, understand?'

Jim noticed Coombe's audible expulsion of breath, a result of his relief that he wasn't going to be nicked.

'No . . . it's just that . . . well, I shouldn't be telling you this,' continued Jim, 'but strictly between you and me, that Alec Michaelson's a bit of a nasty, vindictive little bastard.'

Coombe frowned. Michaelson had certainly never struck him as possessing that sort of personality; in fact, he regarded him as being something of a dope.

'Y'see, the word is, Michaelson wants you hurt. Hurt bad, is what I heard, just to spoil your Christmas. I mean, why else would he hire the McGuigan brothers?'

At the sound of the name, Brian Coombe's jaw dropped. The brothers had a well-justified reputation for violence; they were from gypsy stock and apart from their ability in bare-knuckle fighting 'on the cobbles', they also owned a scrap metal yard. When they had decided to expand their business empire they had made an offer to a fellow dealer in non-ferrous metals to acquire his yard; he had refused their proposal. The reason for a crane mysteriously toppling onto the recalcitrant dealer's shed shortly afterwards (with him inside it) was reluctantly recorded as 'misadventure' by the coroner at the inquest which followed, there being no other evidence to the contrary. However, the entire neighbourhood knew different.

'Of course,' continued Jim as he got to his feet, noticing as he did so the blood draining from Brian Coombe's face, 'I expect it could be bollocks. But just to be on the safe side, it might be an idea to make yourself scarce. The reason I say that is – well . . . I suppose you'd think it's a bit selfish on my part. Y'see, I'm on duty all over Christmas and if possible I'd like to spend a bit of time with the family. And if I copped what could well turn out to be a murder enquiry, it'd fuck things up. Yeah, I know. I *am* being a bit selfish, ain't I? Still, if you vanished, just till after Christmas, say . . . or New Year . . .'

Jim frowned.

'Well, perhaps Easter, just to be on the safe side. I expect the McGuigans would've forgotten all about it by then, don't you think? It's not as if they're the sort to harbour a grudge, are they? Well, I'll be off. Ta-ta.'

It is doubtful if Brian Coombe, his mouth hanging open, heard the 'click' of his front door shutting. The McGuigans not harbour a grudge? He'd thought that Old Bill was well-informed – Christ, he didn't know shit!

★   ★   ★

Half an hour after his return to the station, Jim was called to the front counter. There stood Alec Michaelson.

'Jim, I don't know what you did, but that little bastard Coombe just turned up at the shop and paid me the hundred and fifty nicker in full! He was in a right state – he kept on babbling, "You'll call them off, won't you? You'll call them off?" I didn't know what the hell he was going on about and what's more, I didn't care! Here – where's that Widows and Orphans box?'

With that, Michaelson stuffed two £5 notes into it.

'See you at the Christmas party, Jim!'

And half an hour after that, Jim was called down to the front counter once again, and there stood Brian Coombe, who grabbed hold of Jim's hand and shook it enthusiastically.

'Thanks, Mr Sharpe, thanks for taking the time to warn me about what was going to happen! The money's all paid back – d'you think I ought to make myself scarce, just in case, like?'

Jim patted his shoulder reassuringly.

'Leave it to me, Brian,' he said, soothingly. 'I'll make sure that everything's squared up,' and was gratified to see another ten quid disappear into the Widows and Orphans charitable fund.

*   *   *

'Nice story, Jim,' I laughed.

In fact, I had been involved in a situation where comparable chicanery had been utilized and a grateful customer had similarly deposited a generous donation in a collection box in respect of the same charitable concern, but Jim's account was far funnier!

CHAPTER 19

Official Entries

'**D**id you see that Blenkinsopp died?' asked Barry, one of the regular luncheon attendees, as we sipped our drinks at the bar.

'Yeah, I saw it on the back page of the *Pensioner*.'

I was referring to the quarterly magazine for retired Metropolitan Police officers, the *London Police Pensioner*, where on the back page (and usually on several pages before it) are recorded the names and other details of police pensioners who've been posted to the great charge-room in the sky.

'Pity I hadn't heard about it sooner,' I added. 'Then I could have attended the funeral and pissed all over the bastard's grave.'

Barry nodded, knowingly. 'Yes. I suppose, given a bit of notice, you could have attended the funeral service having consumed asparagus the night before. That would have added a little – well, *je ne sais quoi* – to the piquancy of your urine.'

On emotive subjects such as Blenkinsopp, Barry could always be relied upon to bring a little sophisticated humour to proceedings, especially because he was aware of our encounter; but Blenkinsopp was forgotten as my chum Keith Taylor walked up and there was something that I wanted to ask him, so we spoke of more palatable matters. But as I drove home I thought of Blenkinsopp again . . .

Claude Blenkinsopp was a tall, corpulent officer who had the most pompous, overbearing manner and a sonorous voice that set your teeth on edge. He also had one of the shortest careers ever as an aid to CID. His partner went to the first-class detective sergeant and told him, 'I can't work with this idiot anymore, Sarge.' When the reason was explained – Blenkinsopp had been targeting juvenile shoplifters and had tried to induce them to grass up their little mates on the promise of being rewarded with tubes of Smarties – the first-class sergeant agreed; Blenkinsopp was on a one-way ticket back to uniform, and everybody in the CID breathed a collective sigh of relief.

But Blenkinsopp hadn't quite finished with the CID. Back in uniform, he took promotion to sergeant and, for some unaccountable reason which I've never been able to fathom, he was posted to a divisional 'Q'-Car. There were two types of

'Q'-Car which worked consecutive shifts – the CID one and the uniform car; the latter was crewed by a uniform sergeant in plain clothes, the driver and an aid to CID. In this way, the division received sixteen hours-worth of attention, although with arrests and observations this was often extended to 24-hour coverage, which was a pretty satisfactory state of affairs.

Of necessity, the uniform sergeant had to be an officer who had displayed a natural ability for crime-fighting, and the ones I knew who were posted on the 'Q'-Car possessed this facility – so goodness knows what went wrong on this occasion. But Blenkinsopp had Bert Wiggins – a real 'old-time' aid – on the car with him; and this was a recipe for disaster. Now I knew Bert and I liked him; he had a very jolly sort of personality and a nice line in chat and he was an admirable drinking companion. However, I had never worked with Bert; something for which I was very grateful, because he had a well-deserved reputation for sloppy practices and cutting corners with breathtaking abandon.

One of the first lessons trainee police officers are taught is the necessity, once an arrest is made, to make notes of the arrest as soon as is practicable. The reason is obvious: the circumstances of the arrest are still clear in the officer's mind, and it's therefore a matter of common sense to commit them to paper at the earliest opportunity. However, it is not always possible; if, for example, a prisoner were to be brought into the station for burglary and suddenly blurted out the particulars of his accomplice, then the search for and the arrest of the prisoner's associate would have to take precedence. Similarly, if a police officer were to be badly injured he would not be expected to start scribbling down what had happened until after he had received medical attention. But in the vast majority of cases it was possible to make notes of the arrest. When I brought a prisoner into the station, once he had been booked in (and providing there were no unexpected circumstances), I would sit down and, over a cuppa, in collaboration with the other officer present at the arrest, would record the evidence of his arrest in my pocket book. Both of us would then sign it, after which I would hand the book to the sergeant who had booked in the prisoner and ask him to initial my entry. It was a practice followed by the vast majority of police officers. But not all. And definitely not by Bert Wiggins.

Once he had brought in a prisoner, as far as Bert was concerned, it was time for a drink. So he would scribble the prisoner's name down in his pocket book and that would be that – when the case went to court the following day, and if the prisoner pleaded guilty, there was no need for any more expanded notes. If the prisoner pleaded not guilty, however, Bert would then insert fuller details of the evidence into his pocket book. In fact, he possessed several spare pocket books for this purpose.

Fate finally caught up with Bert after an arrest on the 'Q'-Car with Blenkinsopp, who had been cowed by Bert's stronger personality. Following the prisoner's initial appearance at court (where no plea was taken) and the next, when he pleaded not guilty and a date was set for the trial at the Magistrates' Court, Bert had inserted a more expansive account of the arrest, which Blenkinsopp duly countersigned. All went well until the defence barrister demanded to examine Bert's pocket book. When he did he discovered that several successive entries of arrests had been made prior to the one which Bert had referred, all of which post-dated Bert's entry – and the jig was well and truly up. The scandalized magistrate took decisive, immediate action – he threw out the case and demanded an immediate police internal investigation. The Police Complaints Unit (A10) had just been formed and they set to work with a will. Bert's desk revealed a rich haul of pickings. First, there were a number of pocket books, all with different entries, all out of sequence. Then there were items of prisoners' property which Bert had 'forgotten' to restore to them. There were also items of prisoners' property which in any event could not have been restored to them: the knuckleduster and the open razor in particular should have been sent to the Prisoners' Property Store for disposal. There was an old tobacco tin which was found to contain a number of pound notes. This, of course, could probably have satisfactorily been explained away, except that they were all forgeries. They had been handed to Bert by defrauded shopkeepers, and Bert should have made an entry in the crime book, then written 'forgery' across each note and sent it off, with a Form CRO150, to the Counterfeit Currency Squad at the Yard. Bert told his accusers that he had 'intended' to do so; he felt it prudent not to mention that the forged pound notes had formed an important addition to his beer money at the pub.

At the discipline board that followed, Blenkinsopp who, as the senior of the two, was charged with lack of supervision, caved in, cravenly lollied Bert up a treat and received a slap on the wrist. Bert, of course, was fired in double-quick time.

Even at his leaving drink, the irrepressible Bert managed to find humour in the situation, and we toasted him; a crook and a scoundrel he might have been but he was still an amusing companion. Blenkinsopp was, of course, nowhere to be seen, and I suppose he scuttled away, cockroach-like, to goodness-knew where. Well over fifteen years was to pass before our paths crossed again.

*   *   *

It would be really nice to be a detective of storybook fiction – where you're presented with one case and one case only and you work at it to the exclusion of everything else – but life, unfortunately, isn't like that. I was investigating an armed robbery as a member of the Flying Squad and I had already obtained a number of compelling pieces of evidence which, when I identified and arrested the robbers, would hopefully slot into the sequence of things as surely as night followed day. But I needed time to unravel a whole lot of information, and it was time I really didn't have; plus, I had other cases to investigate, other suspects to arrest, informants to meet, courts to attend and other ongoing surveillance operations run by my contemporaries in which to participate. And then I received exceptionally top-grade information, from a highly-placed informant, as to the identities of two of the robbers, and one clue after another started to fall into place. But I really didn't want to arrest them immediately. I had received other information that they were planning another robbery. I knew the location of the intended robbery and I decided to let them come to me; so the area where it was going to take place was well and truly staked out by the Flying Squad.

But it didn't happen. The information I'd received about the next robbery did not come from the same source that had provided me with the identity of the robbers, and, to be fair, the intelligence was rather shaky. I had coupled it with other information and enquiries which I'd made in the hope that two and two were going to make four – and they didn't.

So I decided to arrest them for the original robbery on the evidence that I'd got. I worked it all out in minute detail, much like a military operation – if they did this, or said that, then I'd take an alternative course of action. However, there was one part of the operation which was highly important. Because the Police and Criminal Evidence Act was now in force, prisoners were to be allowed access to legal representation from the word go. However, this could be circumvented in two ways: firstly by having them held incommunicado, secondly by initially denying them legal access. Therefore, if robbers were caught in the act – going across the pavement – and it was felt that further arrests or the recovery of evidence could be jeopardized by anybody knowing that they had been arrested, the robbers were held incommunicado until those enquiries could be carried out, and nobody was informed that they had been arrested.

However, if it was known the robbers had been arrested – and that was what had happened in this case – and money from the robbery was adrift, plus the identity of anybody else involved, then it was quite in order to deny the robbers legal representation until the suspects could be questioned about these matters. It prevented them telling their solicitors so that the money or suspects could make themselves scarce. And if this prompts you to cry, 'Oh, but solicitors would never do anything like *that!*' then you really shouldn't be reading this book.

So that was my plan – initially deny them legal access – and this had to be authorized with an officer of the rank of superintendent or above. I'd discussed the matter with a Flying Squad detective superintendent, and he agreed with my decision and stated that he would attend the police station once it was confirmed that they were in custody, to authenticate the prisoners' custody records.

Yes, because as soon as a prisoner entered the police station, a custody record was started by the custody officer, who held the rank of sergeant. Into this record every single incident – removal from the cells, visits, meals, requests – would be slavishly entered by the custody officer.

It was my sheer bloody bad luck that the custody officer in charge of my prisoners was Claude Blenkinsopp.

★   ★   ★

The years had not treated Blenkinsopp kindly. The rank and file loathed him, because as soon as a prisoner was deposited, Blenkinsopp would worry the arresting officer, terrier-like, to the point of hysteria, to ensure that every 'i' was dotted and every 't' crossed. In particular, he was insistent about pocket books – never having forgotten the incident with Bert Wiggins, Blenkinsopp was going to ensure that nothing of the kind ever happened again. He wanted entries made in the officer's pocket book in front of him, then and there, so that he could initial them.

By the time I brought my prisoner in, the other Flying Squad team had already lodged their prisoner, and as I laid eyes on the podgy form of Blenkinsopp I controlled, with an enormous effort, my lip which had started to curl.

'This prisoner,' I said, 'has been arrested for armed robbery. I want him denied legal access until I've had the opportunity to discover the whereabouts of the stolen money and the identities of his associates. This has been agreed with a detective superintendent, who will be arriving shortly to give his authorization on the custody record.'

And I don't think I could have put it any plainer than that. Blenkinsopp recorded the details of the prisoner before bustling him off to the cells.

When he returned he said, 'Right – I want to sign your pocket book.'

'That,' I replied, 'would be a bit of a wasted exercise, because there's nothing to sign – I haven't written anything in it yet.'

'Just put down the time of arrest and sign it, then I'll countersign it,' he gabbled, and I could see sweat beading on his forehead. Blenkinsopp's pomposity had vanished; gutlessness had taken its place.

'I shall do nothing of the kind,' I replied. 'But I'll tell you what I am going to do. I'm going upstairs to the canteen to order my breakfast and while I'm waiting for it to arrive I shall write down my notes of arrest – you know, "as soon after the arrest as practicable", remember? And when I've finished and signed them, then you can countersign them, and not before. Got it? Now, do something useful – go down the cell passageway and check that you've actually locked the cell door to ensure my prisoner hasn't escaped.'

In fact, I think he did just that, and I went off to the canteen. When I returned to the charge room having consumed my breakfast I handed my pocket book to Blenkinsopp.

'There you are; those are my notes of the arrest. I finished writing them at 8.20 and that's the time I've entered in my pocket book'.

I looked at my watch.

'The time's now 8.25 – put the time down when you countersign it.'

Blenkinsopp stole a furtive look at the charge room clock – it showed 8.27, so that was the time he wrote down when he signed my pocket book, bless him.

I was now set to interview the prisoners, but before I did I took a look at the custody record. To my horror, I saw that Blenkinsopp had recorded that my prisoner – and the other prisoner as well – were to be held incommunicado!

'You bloody idiot!' I gasped. 'I told you that he was to be denied legal representation – not held incommunicado!'

'No, you didn't! No, you didn't!' stammered Blenkinsopp.

Quite obviously, he'd got himself lathered up into a state of panic and in wanting to get everything right, had got everything wrong.

The 'yes-you-did', 'no-I-didn't' argument went on for several minutes before I said, 'I'm telling you, I *did* say that he was to be denied legal access; I'd discussed this with the superintendent, who'll be arriving shortly and who'll back me up. When this record is produced in court – as I expect it will be – I hope you realize that you'll have some explaining to do.'

'I'll just say I made a mistake,' muttered Blenkinsopp.

It transpired that there was overpowering evidence against the two robbers, and they were charged. Therefore, several months later at the Old Bailey, it was absolutely necessary for their legal team to try to pull every dirty trick out of the hat to get them off. However, some of the tricks were not dirty at all and were served up to them on a plate.

'Tell me,' said the defence barrister, 'when you arrested my client, at his home address, in the presence of his wife, did she ask to which police station her husband would be taken?'

I agreed that she had asked that question and I had provided the answer.

'Then since his wife knew of his arrest, plus the station at which her husband would be held, I'm at a loss to understand why you asked that my client be kept incommunicado?'

'I didn't,' I replied.

The brief raised his eyebrows. 'Really? That's not what's written on the custody record by – ah – Sergeant Blenkinsopp. Are you saying that he deliberately falsified this record?'

'No, I'm not saying that,' I replied. 'As you're aware, the Police and Criminal Evidence Act was a new act at the time when that record was made, and denial to legal access and being kept incommunicado were matters which, I imagine, could be easily confused. As you will see, if you examine the rest of the document, when the denial to legal access was authorized by the superintendent, the mistake was made clear.'

'Yes,' sneered the barrister, turning to the jury. 'By a superintendent of the *Flying Squad*!'

I noted uneasily that one or two members of the jury were nodding their heads in agreement at the emphasis on those words.

So Blenkinsopp was called to confirm that he had made a mistake. But that's not what he said in the witness box. He stated, quite categorically, that 'incommunicado' was the expression

I'd used. Blenkinsopp had been found wanting once before; he would ensure that never again would he voluntarily be put in that position. The superintendent was called to explain what had happened, but of course he was a member of the duplicitous Flying Squad and any explanation he could give would have to be regarded as beyond the pale.

Despite overwhelming evidence, it was enough to put doubt in at least some of the jurors' minds; they were unable to reach a unanimous verdict, and there was a re-trial. It may have been disappointing, but it was a million times better than an acquittal.

In the interim period, some of the wobbly evidence was strengthened, and although Blenkinsop returned to inform a new jury of his pack of lies, eventually (and at a great additional cost to the public purse) the robbers were convicted and were sentenced to substantial terms of imprisonment.

That was the last I saw of that podgy cockroach, Blenkinsopp. I suppose he continued panicking and fussing over every dot and comma until he reached retirement; maybe that was the reason why he didn't have a long and happy retirement, because he had nothing left to whine about.

I try not to speak ill of the dead, but I've made an exception in Blenkinsopp's case.

CHAPTER 20

A Slight Case of Abduction

If, during these pages, I bang on about 'Q'-Cars and especially aids to CID, I make no apologies for doing so. As you'll have gathered, these now redundant aspects of policing in the Met were two of the most valuable tools for crime-fighting in London.

One of the most effective Aids' Squads was the one based on 'G' Division in the 1960s. Thirty young uniform aspirants to the CID were under the command of Ian 'Jock' Forbes, a detective chief inspector, then a detective superintendent (and later Deputy Assistant Commissioner Forbes QPM), a very tough veteran of the Flying Squad.[1] Many of those aids became members of the CID, some reached high rank and others were decorated. Terry Brown was awarded the George Medal for his part in the arrest of the highly dangerous, gun-toting Walter 'Angel Face' Probyn. In spite of his youth, Brown was extremely well-informed and was commended on twenty-one occasions for displaying courage in arresting armed robbers and other violent criminals. Up until 1 October 1967 he had been Police Constable 271 'G'; the following day, he was a detective constable, posted to the Flying Squad. There – and with the Serious Crime Squad – he would remain for the next ten years.

Whilst the Aids' Squad was in operation they were a force to be reckoned with. Not only did they nick anything that moved on the streets around City Road, Dalston and Stoke Newington, they nicked anything that didn't. They were feral.

Nipper Read used their talents when it came to arresting the Krays, but as he diplomatically remarked to me, 'I think Ian permitted them rather more latitude than was strictly necessary or desirable!'

But the aids went the way of all things and were replaced with temporary detective constables – aids in all but name.

---

1 For further details of that intrepid gangbuster, see *The Guv'nors: Ten of Scotland Yard's Greatest Detectives*, Pen & Sword Books, 2010

In turn, young uniformed police constables who, like their predecessors, aspired to become detectives, became members of Crime Squads, and properly managed, they too became formidable crime fighters. A burglary squad was run out of Chelsea during the 1980s. At that time, the division had the highest burglary rates in the Metropolitan Police; instead of being simply content to investigate the burglaries, half the squad took the war straight into the enemy's camp. They used their informants to pinpoint the burglars working the division; having identified them, they staked out their addresses (irrespective of where they lived) and tailed them when they left home. As soon as they set foot within the precincts of 'B' Division they were stopped and searched. Many were arrested, especially for 'sus'. The message soon got around to the felons that 'B' Division was a good place to avoid. From being top of the leader board, 'B' Division fell to the bottom, leaving only the insalubrious area of Heathrow with a lower burglary rate.

And it was a Crime Squad who made a sizeable contribution to the resultant investigation, after a murder was committed on Fulham's manor.

* * *

The scam committed by the two men was becoming more and more commonplace. Posing as dealers, they arranged deals for large quantities of drugs, but when it came to the exchange, they produced guns instead of the promised drugs and took the cash instead. The buyers kept quiet and took the scam on the chin.

One such exchange took place in the lobby of a small hotel. Just as the two men were relieving their victims of £30,000, using a sawn-off shotgun, a hotel guest entered the lobby. Seeing what was going on, this plucky young man decided to intervene and tackled the gunman. He was promptly shot in the knee, then the gunman stepped over his supine body and put a second shot into his forehead. As the young man's life ebbed away, the two robbers fled with the cash.

This was too much for the dealers; they readily imparted the names of the two assailants to the police, and a murder enquiry was launched.

The detective superintendent who had recently arrived on 'F' Division, covering Hammersmith, Shepherd's Bush and Fulham, was Graham Seaby. Initially, he was greeted with, if not suspicion, then certainly some reservations, by the detectives. He had obtained a Bachelor of Law (Upper Second Honours) degree, and in those days anyone with an academic background was viewed with misgivings. But Seaby had been an active copper before his spell at university; now he was about to display that during his seventeen years' service he had not lost his considerable talents as a thief-taker.

It was the second of the two robbers who was arrested; he pleaded that he had nothing to do with the murder and that he was purely a common-or-garden robber. It was not too long before investigative and scientific forensic police-work provided a sufficiency of evidence to charge both men with murder; that is, when the gunman, 'Michael', would be caught.

So, with his associate charged and remanded in custody, the hunt for Michael began; the investigators knew *who* he was but not *where*.

'The gunman – Michael – was one of four brothers notorious in Fulham in a criminal family controlled by a domineering mother,' Seaby told me. 'The eldest brother, Patrick, was serving four years for drug dealing. Informants told us that Michael had been flown out to Spain by Fulham criminals – such was the power of the family. There was no extradition treaty with Spain at that time. The solution? To convince those who had flown Michael out to fly him back in again.'

Easier said than done? Don't you believe it.

Although the offence had taken place in Fulham, Seaby was running the investigation out of Hammersmith police station. There was more room and better facilities there; plus, that was where the 'F' Division Crime Squad was based.

Twenty young aspiring detectives were led by two hard-nosed detective sergeants and they were brought straight into the investigation. They were tasked with executing ten search warrants each day, every day, at the addresses of known Fulham criminal families and charging as many of them as possible. The procurement of those search warrants did not present a problem; the Justice of the Peace responsible was the mother of the murdered man.

What happened next is best described by Seaby:

The charge room soon started overflowing with Fulham residents who had had their doors kicked in at 6.00am – so much so that the crime rate fell by 95 per cent. In a short while I had an approach from the 'community' as to how normality could be restored. Their response to bringing Michael back was that they would do so, but not without the consent of Michael's family.

My response was to arrest the mother for perverting
the course of justice, and she was remanded in custody at
Holloway. Her legal team immediately applied for a writ of
Habeas Corpus, and I had to justify her arrest to a judge at
Knightsbridge Crown Court. When the judge rejected the
defence application, the eldest son – Patrick – went berserk
in prison, smashing up a TV and furniture and terrorizing the
other inmates. I had a message from the prison governor saying
the son was demanding to see me.

I saw Patrick at the prison. He wanted his mother out of
prison. I told him what he had to do. He told me that to do that
he needed access to a telephone which could not be overheard
or intercepted; mobile phones were unknown at that time.

I signed a piece of paper, and Patrick was released into my
custody. He was placed in a cell at a police station and made
comfortable with some decent food and some beer. We then
sealed off his family home. Patrick was taken home and left
alone to make his telephone calls. Then he was returned to his
police cell before being returned to prison the next day.

It was three days later that a car drew up outside the police station.
Two sturdily built men reached inside and dragged the occupant
out, across the pavement and up the steps of the police station, then
draped him over the front desk. The recumbent lodger was heavily
sunburned and would have answered to the name of Michael
except that he was even more heavily 'stoned'. The introduction
to the desk sergeant was made by his solicitor, who said, 'I believe
the detective superintendent wishes to speak to my client.'

The interview was duly carried out, but due to Michael's
incapacity, not until three days later. In the meantime, Graham
Seaby had self-imposed contractual obligations to discharge.
First, the mother was released from Holloway; next, Patrick was
transferred to another prison and it was ensured that no action
would be taken against him for the damage caused during his
temper tantrum.

It was not only Patrick who displayed ill-humour. Seaby's
crusty detective inspector blew his top when he discovered that
the desk sergeant had inserted on the charge sheet that he was
the arresting officer. Tearing up the charge sheet in front of this
wilting lily, the DI berated him, and after Seaby had signed the
replacement charge sheet, the DI told him, 'When we get another
sticky one, Guv, I hope you're leading it.'

It was a landmark in Seaby's career; any suspicions that the
department might have harboured regarding the degree-educated
youngster disappeared, and he gained real acceptance. As Seaby

told me, the detective inspector's remarks 'were about the best compliment I had ever been paid'.

Michael duly pleaded guilty to the murder at the Crown Court and received a life sentence; his accomplice successfully argued that he was only guilty of robbery, a defence that was accepted by the jury, and he was sentenced to six years' imprisonment. After the case, Michael's defence solicitor, who had introduced his comatose client to the less than ethical desk sergeant, joined the investigators for a celebratory drink, wryly telling Seaby, 'Game, set and match to you on this one, but I look forward to the next one.'

Seaby spent the remaining thirteen years of his service being what he described to me as 'a very happy superintendent', because it permitted him to carry out field work rather than 'ride a desk', a view he shared with my friend, the late Detective Superintendent Bob Higgins. It enabled him to travel the world, serving with the Yard's legendary Murder Squad, which included a secondment lasting almost two years to the Trinidad and Tobago Police where, given the rank of deputy commissioner, he investigated allegations of corruption and several questionable deaths.

During the last year of his service, still as a superintendent, Seaby was appointed Branch Commander of SO2 Department at the Yard, which meant he had control of a Special Operations budget. Despite his misgivings about doing a desk job, it suited him down to the ground since it enabled him to involve operational officers in deciding where to direct money. Front line policing benefitted and office refurbishment for senior officers lost out.

Before his retirement in 1994, Seaby had enhanced his academic credentials by becoming a Master of Philosophy; his thesis described the motivation and cultivation of criminal informants. He challenged the entrenched departmental view that informants were inspired purely by monetary gain – and what was more, with his investigation into the Fulham murder case, he had the credentials to prove it.

CHAPTER 21

Sheer Coincidence

TonyYeoman is a chum of over fifty years standing; because he lives so far away he doesn't attend the luncheons, and that's a pity – he possesses sufficient charm to light up a room and, quite apart from being a brave, resourceful Flying Squad officer, he also has a fund of witty stories plus a number of devastatingly cutting 'put-downs'. If anyone decided to apply a strong after-shave, Tony would quietly intone that 'it had the redolence of the interior of an old whore's handbag.' Only once did I get the better of him, and on that occasion his sighing, regretful riposte was, 'What a pity your parents never actually *married!*' So the other day, when I mentioned the name of a certain cordially disliked CID officer, Tony sniffed disapprovingly and murmured, 'If you should bump into him – and I sincerely hope you don't – pray give him my compliments,' then added, 'And tell him that I hope the fleas from a thousand camels infest his scrotum!'

Tony and I met up as aids to CID and we had a number of minor successes: arresting a youth for stealing money from a dwelling house and then, a week later, arresting two men for the theft of a motor vehicle, which we later recovered from a garage in Rainham.

No sooner had we finished the paperwork in respect of the two car thieves than, that evening, we were drafted into Romford because, it had been said, trouble was brewing. There was, however, no detailed briefing informing us what sort of trouble we might be expected to encounter, and Tony and I were in the CID office at Romford police station, prior to commencing our patrol. Two CID officers were in conversation.

'That Terry Dickens is about, tonight,' said one. 'I saw him in The Lamb.'

His companion nodded. 'Right little fucker he is. Terrible temper he's got. His brother's the same. One day, that pair'll kill someone.'

'I said to him, I said,' the first officer replied, '"Make one wrong move, and your feet won't touch." Know what he said? "Actually, I can do what I like," he said, "because I'm snouting for . . . "'

At that moment, he realized that I was listening and broke off the conversation.

'Who's Terry Dickens?' I asked.

The two CID officers looked at me askance. After all, I was only a scaly aid, and as such, beyond the pale.

'Piss off and find out for yourself,' was the dismissive reply.

Information, as you've probably guessed, was not necessarily freely disseminated in those days.

So Tony and I shrugged our shoulders and went out on patrol looking for trouble; and it wasn't too long before we found it. Outside a café was a large group of noisy youths, and matters were speedily getting out of hand. There were four main aggressors, and as we walked up, fighting had broken out and one of the antagonists, a short, stocky young tearaway, was not only threatening one of the crowd with an empty milk bottle but from the contorted look of fury on his face and his screaming, out-of-control language, it looked very much as if he was about to use it. Tony, demonstrating the fearlessness which he would later display to stunning effect when he served on the Flying Squad, grabbed hold of the lad's three companions, whilst I seized the bottle-waver, relieved him of the milk bottle and told him he was under arrest for possessing an offensive weapon. Right, folks, get ready for the coincidence contained in the title of this chapter.

Quite often, the very act of arresting someone has the effect of quietening them down, but my action had quite the opposite effect; in fact, his ire intensified.

'Don't you know who I am?!' he screamed. 'I'm Terry Dickens, that's who!'

Well, there *was* a coincidence; not that his rage subsided when he and his companions were placed in the police van. Time and again he screamed, 'Haven't you heard of me?' until he said it once too often, and I admitted that I had heard his name before, in connection with him touching up little girls in the local playground. His companions found this quite amusing, although for some unfathomable reason it failed to defuse the situation as far as Terry Dickens was concerned.

So that was Terry Dickens: aggressive, full of his own importance and the possessor of a temper which bordered on the psychotic.

During the Magistrates' Court hearing, during which his associates pleaded guilty and Dickens denied everything, his tantrums continued.

'Are you suggesting that the officer is mistaken?' asked the Beak frostily.

'No!' screamed Dickens. 'I'm saying he's telling lies!'

Finding the thoroughly disagreeable Terry guilty in record time, the magistrates remanded him in custody for sentence at the Crown Court, with a recommendation for Borstal Training, and Dickens, still shrieking defiance, was dragged off to the cells. His elder brother, Dennis, exploded with temper and went for me in court, before being hauled away by some of the conveniently placed jailers and court staff.

But interestingly, before Terry could be sentenced for my offence he appealed against conviction, and the appeal was heard at the Crown Court. Again I received a barrage of accusations, but now a witness for the defence was produced. It was the proprietress of the café in front of which the fracas had taken place. She had seen the whole thing, she said. She had seen Terry and his companions outside the premises. Then there had been some sort of altercation. This focused her attention on what was happening. Then she had seen me come along, pick up the milk bottle and 'plant' Terry with it.

Why, she was asked in cross-examination, had she not come forward at the Magistrates' Court? Because, she replied, nobody had asked her to. It was only when she read an account of the case in the local paper that she realized that a serious miscarriage of justice had occurred. And did she happen to know the appellant, one Terrence Michael Dickens, by any chance? She did. And was he a friend of hers?

The answer that she gave was pure genius.

No, she replied, he was not. In fact, she couldn't stand him. He and his mates were always turning up, inside and outside her café, causing trouble, and more than once, she said, she'd told them to clear off and had received several mouthfuls of abuse for her pains. But not on this occasion. Terry was guiltless; unlike the wicked police officer!

So what happened? Had the family bunged the café proprietress a few bob to commit perjury? Or had they just put the frighteners on her? Or was there a deeper, more corrupt reason? I later discovered exactly who Terry Dickens had been snouting for. Had this CID officer – a thoroughly disagreeable person and one who had no liking for me – put the idea in Terry's head? I never found out; but Terry got off with it.

Did the Dickens brothers go on to kill anybody, as the CID officer had gloomily prophesied? Well, the elder brother, Dennis, certainly did. A couple of years later, he had a blazing row with his girlfriend, jumped into his car and roared off home at near-lunatic speed. The pedestrian who was crossing the road in the built-up area didn't stand a chance as Dennis ploughed into him at more than 70mph. He struck the man so hard that he was knocked right over the top of the car and left a bloody handprint on the rear bumper. Dennis returned home, flounced upstairs and, still in a seething temper, threw himself into bed. It was there that the police found him, several hours later; it had not been a terribly complicated investigation – he had been traced by the front registration plate of his car which had snapped off on impact and was lying close to the lifeless body of the victim. Far from expressing penitence at the death of the unfortunate pedestrian, Dennis, woken from a deep sleep, characteristically screamed defiance at his tormentors and offered to fight them all. This offer was enthusiastically accepted by the local police officers, who had had more than enough of Dennis' shenanigans and proceeded to smash the living shit out of him. He was dragged downstairs, with the rest of the Dickens family shrieking abuse at the police and unsuccessfully attempting to free Dennis from their clutches. However, Terry was not amongst them.

A few weeks after his fortuitous acquittal, I had happened to coincidentally bump into Terry, one evening. He was by himself; so was I. Nobody else was about, so Terry did not have an audience. I had a few words with him. He appeared somewhat chastened, as a result. We parted company, and I never clapped eyes on him again, because he moved out of the area.

And when I say he moved out of the area, I mean *right* out of the area.

It was somewhere north of Carlisle, and for all I know, he's still there. The fact that Terry Dickens never again showed his face in East London is, I expect, just a coincidence.

CHAPTER 22

Smoke and Mirrors

There are a number of ingredients which go to make up a good detective: pluck, resolution, being well-informed, possessing a clear, investigative mind, having the determination never to give up, plus the ability to think ten, twenty jumps ahead in order to outwit the most committed criminal and his lawyer – usually, only a university degree separates the two of these. Then there is another component essential to the detective's make-up: guile.

Nowadays, this is absolutely prohibited. In the modern-day politically correct world of policing, where everybody is encouraged to be really, really nice to everybody else, the slightest suggestion that an officer might deploy craftiness, cunning or deviousness would make senior police officers shrilly demand that their staff officers rush out and purchase them a jumbo-sized pack of incontinence pads.

But you see, in days gone by, quite apart from any other police practices which would have caused the Archbishop of Canterbury's eyebrows to assume the shape of crescent moons, guile was a much prized and sought-after attribute. I have a number of stories to recount which illustrates this particular commodity; I shall start with a couple of benign examples.

As a uniform officer, very early in my career, I was called to a department store to arrest a weeping woman shoplifter, who had been detained by a store detective. As I escorted her into the charge room, a CID officer was walking by; he took one look at my prisoner, gasped and rushed off in the direction of the CID office. Within minutes, one of the detective sergeants entered the charge room and told me, 'All right, son, I'll deal with this.'

It transpired that the sobbing lady was the wife of a pub licensee, whose premises the CID were prone to visit regularly. There was, of course, no possibility of the charge being dropped – the inclusion of an interested third party, i.e. the store detective, saw to that – but an unfortunate situation could certainly be addressed. That was my total involvement in the case, just escorting the lady from store to station, before I was nudged to one side – but I happened to be attending the Magistrates' Court

with a completely different case when the licensee's wife appeared
and pleaded guilty to the charge of shoplifting. She did not have
a solicitor to offer mitigation for her one and only larcenous
outing; she simply did not need one. The detective sergeant gave
a brief outline of the theft which, he stated, had been carried out
'in a moment of madness'; and then came the outpouring of a
whole catalogue of illnesses, crushing money worries and deaths
in the family, which resulted in one of the magistrates wiping
her eye as the chairman of the bench discharged the weeping
landlady absolutely. This was an excellent result; an absolute
discharge did not count as a conviction.

Was it wrong of the detective sergeant to have seized hold
of the reins like that? Quite frankly, no, I don't think so. What
rewards (if any) he received for a performance that would not
have disgraced the stage of The Old Vic, I don't know, nor do I
particularly care. I do know that I received an education in how
court cases could be conducted. It also reminds me of something
that happened, years later, when I was a detective sergeant on the
Flying Squad. I was with Mick Geraghty, another Squad officer,
and we were about to leave Bethnal Green police station, which
was where Mick had previously worked. As we walked towards
the rear exit which led to the yard we passed the fingerprint room,
and Mick glanced in there.

'Jill!' he exclaimed.

There in the room was a thirty-something-year-old woman
having her fingerprints taken. She looked up at the sound of her
name, saw Mick and burst into tears.

'Oh, Mick!' she sobbed. 'They caught me bang to rights with
me fingers in the till – sorry, love!'

Jill, I later discovered, had been a barmaid in a pub which
Mick had regularly visited. Mick nodded; then, to the CID officer
who was taking Jill's fingerprints, he said, 'Can I have a word,
mate?'

The officer stepped out into the passageway, and although
Mick lowered his voice, it was still loud enough for Jill to hear
every word.

'Look, that lady in there is a friend of mine,' said Mick. 'When
you take her to court, I want you to make sure that she has a fair
deal, all right?'

The officer cracked on immediately to the unspoken meaning
of Mick's words.

'Sure, Mick, leave it to me – no problem.'

Just a few kind words which Jill probably thought she wasn't
supposed to hear, but Mick had exercised a little guile, and I

do know that thereafter she provided him with some top-level information.

Now Mick was just a junior officer, but having been tutored by the legendary Detective Sergeant Peter Holman MBE, QPM, he knew who was who and what was what. A case where cunning was required but was conspicuous by its absence came along at about the same time as Mick was reaping the rewards of his guile.

A top South London gangster decided to make an approach to the man in charge of all of the detectives at Scotland Yard, and the deal he proposed was this: he would prop up every South London armed robber in return for a blind eye being directed towards his own criminal activities. Unfortunately, the head of London's detectives was a deputy assistant commissioner who had spent practically all of his service in uniform and who had been hand-picked by Sir Robert Mark, following his pogroms of the 1970s.

'OUTRAGEOUS!' roared the DAC. 'HOW DARE YOU? GET OUT!'

What a pity. It was an opportunity missed. Because if the DAC had been someone possessing criminal investigative experience, plus a modicum of deviousness, instead of a head filled with goose feathers, he would have poured out two big glasses of scotch, pushed one over to the gangster, and said, 'Cheers, Joe – I reckon we've got a deal.'

He would then have appointed an astute officer, known for both his integrity and his ability to handle informants, to act as liaison with the gangster, to milk him dry of his information; and at the same time, the DAC would have set up a secret squad working round the clock to gather evidence by the use of phone-taps, probes, long-distance microphones, photography and live informants on the criminal activities of the gangster himself. Then, when the gangster had exhausted the list of armed robbers he was offering up, or when there was a sufficiency of evidence to nick him, whichever was more expedient, the net would be tightened. And once that had happened, I expect he would have been given the chance to become a Supergrass, so that even more top-level criminals could be caught. And if he refused, it wouldn't have surprised me in the slightest if the gangster's name hadn't been propped up to the grassed-up robbers as being the source of their downfall. That's the way to trap top London criminals and their associates – split them up, set one against the other, spread disinformation – although it did not, alas, happen on this occasion.

One of my cases which I prefer to forget about was of kidnapping and assault; it was a shitty mish-mash of a case involving two brothers and some of their chums who had given their victim a rough time over an unpaid debt – in fact, the victim went AWOL before giving evidence at the trial, and I spent a bit of time trying to find him, then nicking him. Precisely what I nicked him for, or where I kept him until the trial commenced, has now mercifully vanished into the mists of time, but I do remember one amusing aspect of the case.

I'd arrested the gang in ones and twos; one brother, Charlie, was in custody, the other was adrift. At the Magistrates' Court I asked for Charlie to be remanded in custody; whilst I was addressing the stipendiary magistrate, I happened to look in the public gallery. There I saw a young man who bore a marked resemblance to the youngster in the dock and I felt sure this must be the missing brother. By the time I'd finished making the application, the prisoner was remanded in custody and I ran round to the entrance for the public gallery, the look-alike had vanished. Bugger!

But a couple of weeks later, Sammy the Snout helpfully propped him up, and I arrested the brother in a typical low-life tenement in Tottenham. Sure enough, it was the same person I'd seen at court.

'You were at court a couple of weeks ago when Charlie was getting a lay-down, weren't you?' I said, casually.

'Yeah, I was, as it goes,' he admitted. 'So if you knew that, why didn't you nick me then?'

'You're a smart lad,' I replied. 'If I'd done that, you'd have known for sure it was Charlie who stuck you up, wouldn't you?'

'Did he?' muttered the brother, who really wasn't the sharpest knife in the drawer. '*Bastard!*'

Quite apart from sowing the seeds for a nice little internecine feud between the siblings, it also absolved Sammy the Snout from any suspicion.

Mind you, it also sowed a few seeds in my own mind; and I resolved that in future, when I had groups of prisoners, family or otherwise, in the dock at court and any of their associates or relatives were still wanted or were of interest, I'd have a 'plant' in the public gallery. Overall, this worked quite well, and I managed to amass quite a lot of useful intelligence, although I didn't fare so well on one occasion.

I had arrested a team for a lorry theft; again, one brother was in the dock, another was adrift. So I planted a young woman constable in plain clothes in the public gallery, where the uncle of the boys, plus some cronies, duly appeared. The following conversation took place.

'That Kirby – 'e's a dog, ain't 'e?'

That was the uncle; his companion agreed, without hesitation: 'Yer. A fuckin' dog.'

'Mind you,' the uncle continued, "e's well out of 'is class, taking us lot on.'

'Yer,' concurred his friend, 'but 'ow else could 'e 'ave got 'is promotion to DCI?'

Quite obviously, they had a higher regard for my promotional capabilities than my senior officers – but I do wish the WPC hadn't waited to impart this information to me until we were in the crowded CID office!

So that was the result of a bit of misguided zeal on my part. But the final story reveals that no matter how experienced a detective may be, no matter how much craftiness he's exhibited in the past, there's always someone who can still get one over on you – and when that person's a villain, acceptance of it is awfully hard!

I was dealing with a top-notch, dangerous gang of lorry thieves; the lad whom I'd arrested had very little form, but he was a hardened young villain and he came from a right family – his father had done time for manslaughter. Witnesses had been frightened, venal police officers had been approached (they had made tentative overtures to me and had been told to 'Fuck off') and it was clear that they'd stick at nothing to get the charges chucked.

I had a problem, and it was one of identification. I wanted to put up the prisoner to see if the witnesses could identify him; in fact, I was sure they would. The problem arose because of his distinctive appearance; he was short and stocky, with flaming red hair and a heavily freckled face. Where on earth was I going to get a line-up who bore a resemblance to him? It would have been easier if he had refused to take part; in that case, I would have simply confronted him with the witnesses, but he was too cute for that. He wanted an identification parade; in fact, he demanded one.

Just then, the telephone rang; it was the lad's father.

'Nah, look 'ere, Mr Kirby, my boy wants a proper ID parade; as I see it, that's 'is right. Why don't yer let 'im go on the escalator at Brixton station? Them blackies do it all the time – and if it's good enough for them, it's good enough for my lad!'

He had a point. The escalator at Brixton underground station had been used to great effect for identity parades. Because it had been so difficult to persuade black youths to come in off the streets of Brixton and participate in identification parades, somebody had come up with the brilliant idea of using the Underground station, just a short distance away from the nick. The way in which it worked was for the suspect to be at the foot of the 'up' escalator, guarded by police officers; the witnesses, together with the suspect's solicitor and the inspector in charge of the parade, were at the top. When a train arrived at the platform and disgorged its load, the suspect could join the throng of disembarked passengers on the escalator, taking any position he liked, and when he arrived at the top he might or might not be picked out. In fact, if a trainload of passengers got on to the escalator and the suspect didn't like the look of any of them, he could wait for the next batch. So the suspect would not be in amongst ten or so other participants as he would be in a line-up at the police station; here he would be amongst scores of them, and it was considered to be an exceptionally fair system for the suspect.

I'd mentally switched off from the father while I was mulling over the possibilities of such an identification parade, but he was still chuntering on, in much the same xenophobic vein.

''e's an Englishman, 'e is, 'e's got the same rights as them blackies . . .'

'All right, give it a rest,' I interrupted wearily. 'I'll get on to your brief and get it sorted out.'

'Thanks, Mr Kirby, you're a bleedin' gent, you are . . .' and it was then that I put the phone down on him, re-dialled and spoke first to the duty inspector at Brixton, then the solicitor.

So that was what happened in this case. I later found out what transpired. My prisoner was held at the bottom of the escalator. A trainload of passengers got on to the escalator. Suddenly, the escort received a call on the radio from the inspector at the top of the escalator.

'Right, you can come up; we've got a positive ID.'

'You can't have!' gasped the escort. 'The prisoner's still standing next to me!'

What I didn't know – what nobody knew – was that my prisoner had an identical twin; and the whole parade had been a set-up, with the twin brother inserting himself in amongst the trainload of passengers.

I took what was left of this sorry state of affairs to court on the remaining evidence but I wasn't particularly surprised when everybody involved was acquitted.

Some time later, it was a small consolation to hear that my prisoner had been sentenced to sixteen years' imprisonment for his participation in an armed hold-up; nevertheless, the wounds which I'd received for being well and truly outfoxed were still very raw!

CHAPTER 23

Murderers' Row

I'd like to tell you about my exploits as a lynx-eyed murder detective, how I solved murder after murder and got applauded for my expertise at the Old Bailey.

I'd like to but I can't, because it wouldn't be true.

Let me give you some facts about the grim reality of how murders were investigated at local police stations. If you were regarded as a good working detective and a murder occurred on your patch, the detective chief inspector would grab hold of you and snap up a couple of your equally well-regarded contemporaries for inclusion in his investigation. He would then phone round the surrounding stations and say to the detective inspector, 'Right – I want a DS and a couple of DCs.'

'Certainly,' the inspector would reply, and he would then collect three of his most worthless, work-shy officers and send them off to the murder squad, to cop obscene amounts of overtime and expenses. The other hard-working CID officers who remained would have to double their workload; and that, I'm afraid, is human nature.

Whenever a murder occurred, I was seldom at the station within its jurisdiction and consequently I copped the shit-end of the stick; and if I say that I served on many more than half-a-dozen murder squads in my career I'd be guilty of a gross exaggeration.

When I was serving with the Serious Crime Squad, we investigated the murder of a Soho prostitute and her maid, because the Maltese Syndicate were allegedly involved. Two men were very quickly arrested and just as quickly discharged.

Later, on the same squad, I received information that a German national who was affiliated to an Israeli murder gang was visiting the UK. I pulled him out of the disembarking passengers at Heathrow. *'Englischer politzei – Sie sind verhaftet!'* is not the most welcoming greeting to a visitor to dear old Blighty, but it ensured his detention at our Limehouse headquarters for a few days. When, as with the two members of the Maltese Syndicate, there was found to be an insufficiency of evidence to detain him any longer, he too was chucked out.

* * *

One murder investigation in which I was involved featured someone who turned out to be a double killer. It was in 1984 at King's Cross when a homeless person was stabbed to death by someone who had skewered him with a sword. Goodness, what a shitty investigation that was; with the exception of the police and the scientific forensic team, practically all of the witnesses were also homeless. Keeping track of their peripatetic lifestyle was a nightmare; getting them to remember what had happened was worse. Hugely cunning, they often demanded the price of a drink before they could recall an important piece of information, and when it was imparted it was difficult to assess whether or not it was genuine. At the end of a day's work most murder squad detectives would go to the pub for a drink; on this enquiry we often wondered if a trip to the local de-lousing centre would be more productive.

But finally I got a tip as to the killer's identity and his address, and it had me racing round to a flat in North Holloway. Donald Mackay was seated on his toilet when I kicked in his front door, and the sound of the door's fracture, plus my peremptory introduction as to who I was and the purpose of my visit, appeared to act as a catalyst to relieve pressure on his lower bowel more forcefully than was strictly desirable; the smell was atrocious.

However, that was nothing as compared with the stink that would now surround Mr Mackay.

★   ★   ★

Let me put a question to you. If a person carries a sword about with him and then stabs someone to death with it, would that suggest some sort of intent – some sort of premeditation – to you? Perhaps malice aforethought? Well, if it did, you could be forgiven for thinking so; and you won't be unduly surprised to discover that I was of that mindset, too.

But apparently, the prosecuting counsel at the Old Bailey was not; he accepted a plea to manslaughter so quickly it would've made you blink. He and I didn't get on; he'd prosecuted for me previously in a very important case and, in my opinion, had made a complete arse of things.

So in November 1984, Mackay (who had convictions, some of them for violence, going back to 1972) pleaded guilty to manslaughter and was sentenced to five years' imprisonment. After that, I went back to the Flying Squad, and on 15 September 1986 MacKay was released from prison and we never met up again. But that wasn't the end of his encounters with death.

In Victorian times, prostitutes were discreetly referred to as 'unfortunates', and on the evening of 17 February 1989 'unfortunate' completely fitted the description of the prostitute whom Mackay picked up. They returned to his noisome flat at Welby House, Hazelville Road, Holloway for what had initially been mutually agreed as 'straight sex' – but not, however, as far as Mackay was concerned. He marched naked into the room and placed a rope which had been fastened into a noose around her neck and tied her up. After sexually and physically abusing her for several hours, Mackay issued a series of threats: he would kill her, hang her from a hook placed in a door frame, put her body in a black plastic bag and dump it on Hampstead Heath. He then gagged the unfortunate woman, pulled the noose around her neck so tight that she lost consciousness and attempted to bugger her.

So terrified was the prostitute by Mackay's revolting behaviour that she voided both her bladder and her bowels, but a break in the proceedings came when Mackay, quite overcome by a combination of his exertions and drink, fell asleep.

The prostitute managed to escape and, by now hysterical, flagged down a motorist; the rope marks on her body were quite clearly visible when she was seen by the police, who promptly paid a visit to Welby House. There they found Mackay, still asleep, and something else as well. In a cupboard, concealed in two taped-up black bin liners, they found the decomposing body of 27-year-old Ann Petherick, another prostitute. She had been there for about six weeks.

Because of the body's state of decomposition, it was difficult to establish a precise cause of death, but her facial bones had been smashed in by three or four heavy blows, and it was probable that she had died from asphyxiation. She also had a broken bone in her foot and a bruise over one shoulder blade. Had she been subjected to the same sexual indignities as the other prostitute? Difficult to say.

Although at his trial at the Old Bailey Mackay denied everything, he was nevertheless found guilty. Describing him as 'a grave danger to the public and women in particular', Mr Justice Kennedy sentenced him to life imprisonment.

As can be imagined, there was wide press coverage at the time, with the headlines, all much of a muchness, describing Mackay thus: 'Bestial' murderer jailed for forty years.

In jailing him for life, the Judge (reported the press) made a recommendation that he serve at least thirty years, adding that the Home Secretary might regard him as being too dangerous ever to be released. For disposing of Ms Petherick's body there was another three-year sentence, and for the offences committed against the other prostitute – threats to kill, assault with intent to commit buggery, indecent assault and assault occasioning actual bodily harm – a further seven years' imprisonment.

All of which, even allowing for my dodgy arithmetic, adds up to forty years; and taking into consideration the circumstances of the case, plus Mackay's antecedents, many would agree with me that that sentence was not a day too long.

Certainly, Mrs Ida Petherick, the unfortunate girl's grieving mother, thought so. Her daughter's dreadful fate would haunt her for the rest of her life, but with her murderer banged up for at least forty years, with any luck she would never hear his name again.

Wrong.

*　*　*

As a Category 'A' prisoner – the highest category for the most dangerous of inmates – Mackay showed no remorse for his actions; indeed, he maintained his innocence.

It appeared that the trial Judge had not recommended a thirty-year minimum sentence – he had apparently only 'thought' that that time might elapse before Mackay might be safely released. In fact, he recommended that Mackay should serve perhaps eighteen, no, better make that nineteen years before being considered for release by the Parole Board. Oh, and the ten-year additional sentence? No, that was to be served concurrently, not consecutively.

Lord Chief Justice Lane recommended the minimum term should be sixteen years but he was known for frequently cutting prison sentences and was a member of the Prison Reform Trust. Instead, the Secretary of State fixed the minimum term at twenty years.

Therefore, Mackay asked the High Court to review the minimum term.

But in his judgement, Mr Justice Openshaw had to rely on Section 276 and Schedule 22 of the Criminal Justice Act 2003, which stated that when a Secretary of State fixes a minimum term, the High Court can only confirm or reduce it; it cannot increase it.

So that was that: twenty years to serve – minus, of course, the ten months and six days which Mackay had spent in custody prior to his trial.

Mrs Petherick was appalled when she discovered that the presumed sentence given to the man who had murdered her daughter had effectively been halved. Her husband, whose health had been dramatically affected by his daughter's death, had died a year prior to this devastating news at the early age of sixty-six. She was now alone.

Still, as Mr Justice Openshaw had remarked in his judgement, it did not mean that once Mackay had served twenty years he would automatically be released; that would not occur until the Parole Board was of the opinion that he no longer represented a risk to the public. So that was all right, then.

Except that it wasn't.

Still maintaining his innocence, Mackay demanded a judicial review, and in 2010 Mr Justice Bean upheld it, saying that he must have the opportunity to put his case to the Parole Board for the re-categorization of his prison status.

To nobody's surprise, the Parole Board accepted that a move to 'less secure conditions' – that, by the way, is Parole Board-speak for an open prison – would be 'a constructive move' for Mackay.

But I can't help thinking this. First, if Mackay had been prosecuted for murder in 1984 and had been convicted with a resultant life sentence, the life of one unfortunate young woman would have been spared and the terror and degradation of another avoided.

Next, two of the people that Mackay killed were, respectively, a vagrant and a prostitute. A third victim, who obviously thought she was going to meet the same fate as the other two, was also a prostitute.

What if the first victim had been a cabinet minister, strolling home across Hyde Park? Supposing victims two and three had been the wives of peers of the realm – or even the royal family?

In those circumstances, am I being just a tad cynical in believing that the authorities would have locked up Mackay, torn up his applications to the High Court and a judicial review in front of him and thrown away the key?

I don't think so.

★   ★   ★

Patricia Green was a respectable 32-year-old housewife who lived in a neat terraced house in Walthamstow. From the enquiries that were made it appeared that she hadn't an enemy in the world, but she must have had one – the person who in 1979 stabbed her to death in the hallway of that neat terraced house.

There appeared to be no motive; there had been no sexual molestation and nothing had been stolen. But she had been subjected to a frenzied attack, stabbed so many times that when someone commented that she'd received more perforations than a postage stamp he was not being in any way mocking or disrespectful – merely stating a fact.

The hallway was splattered with her blood, and the perpetrator must have also been soaked in it; yet nobody heard anything, nobody saw anything. Of the weapon used there was no trace; in fact, it would never be found.

Feelings amongst the murder squad – of which I was one – ran high. It was such a senseless, brutal murder.

'She could have been my sister,' said one of the officers.

'She could have been my wife,' intoned another grimly, and those feelings were shared by the rest of us.

We set to work with a will; there were about fifteen of us (including two Women Police Constables, Jan Naylor and Carole Ward), but try as we might, our enquiries resulted in dead ends.

I came up with a suspect – a violent young woman who appeared to be mentally unbalanced – but although I gave it my best shot I couldn't get any evidence to pin her down to the murder. I was convinced that she was the culprit and I was extremely concerned that I had to let her go. In fact, for years afterwards I was certain of her guilt, and it was not until I was well into my retirement that I happened to speak to my chum from the Flying Squad, Albert Patrick, who had carried out a cold-case review and had deduced who the murderer – now dead – actually was.

It wasn't my suspect at all. I felt rather cheated. I contacted Jan Naylor (in the interim period, she had become a good 'tec and later, a ReCIDivist) and asked her who she thought the murderer was; she came up with the same suspect as Albert had. In fact, she contacted Carole Ward – and *she* was of the same opinion. Now, I was more deflated than cheated.

'Well, it has to be said, Dick, you were very rarely wrong,' said Jan, which was rather comforting.

Less comforting was when Jan told me, 'Carole reminded me about the outstanding finger/palm print on the bottom of the front door which I'm sure came back to a police officer, after we all had elimination prints taken. I can't remember its owner being identified, though. Are you sure it wasn't yours? I'm joshing you!'

But with no forensic clues and no witnesses, this case became what was colloquially known as 'a sticker', and the usual pattern of a traditional murder squad investigation emerged; just plain slog, plenty of it – and as 1979 passed into 1980, a great many door-to-door enquiries were carried out in an ever-radiating area. Months afterwards, it became increasingly unlikely that anyone would recall anything pertinent to an offence which had occurred further and further away from their addresses; but with nothing else to go on, these were enquiries which had to be completed – see the occupants of each house, fill in questionnaires for all of them, tick them off the list and on to the next one.

But there was one person I couldn't speak to. I remember that he was a telephone engineer who worked unusual hours, and whenever I made an appointment to see him, it was always broken. Not his fault and not that he was in any way considered a suspect, or that he was trying to evade me, but I have to admit that what with the long hours involved and the sheer drudgery of the enquiries, I was getting a bit pissed off by these broken appointments.

However, one day I struck lucky and found my quarry at home. Introducing myself, I stepped into the hallway.

'Where shall we go – in here?' I said, pointing to the front room.

'No, don't go in there; I'm still decorating it,' replied the householder, whose name was Eric Small. 'Come into the back room.'

We sat down in the back room, I produced my clipboard and questionnaires, took out my pen and said, 'Well, Mr Small, I'm sure you know what this is all about, don't you?'

There was no doubt that he did, what with the heavy newspaper coverage plus, of course, the times I'd spoken to his wife to make appointments.

'Yes,' he replied, and after a pause he added sullenly, 'I can tell you my wife isn't impressed with all this, I can tell you *that.*'

Those of you who know me, who've read my books, may have come to the conclusion that I burn with a very short fuse. I don't entirely agree with those slanderous assertions, but Mr Small's answer did catch me amidships.

'WHAT?'

'It's my wife, you see. It's just that she's not at all happy about it.'

This is the conversation that followed. During much of it, given the volume of my voice and my disposition, Mr Small lowered his head and looked studiously at his shoes.

'Is that right?'

'Yes. Yes, it is.'

'Well, now. Isn't that just too fucking bad? Let me tell you something, shall I, pal? We've interviewed three thousand people during this enquiry and if necessary we're going to interview three fucking thousand more! We haven't got a result yet, but we're not going to give up. We're slogging our guts out, working thirteen fucking hours a day – do you know when I last had a day off? Well, do you?'

'Er, no. No, actually, I don't.'

'Well, for your information, pal, I can't fucking remember – that's how long it's been! For weeks I've been asking people the same fucking questions to get a result, so now I'll tell you something, old son. I'm absolutely mortified to hear that your missus isn't too impressed with the way things have been going. But give her my compliments and tell her from me that no matter now dissatisfied she is, we're going to carry on until we get a result – whether she's impressed or not! NOW – IS THAT CLEAR?'

'Yes, sir. It is.'

There was a moment of foot-shuffling before Mr Small cleared his throat.

'You see . . . what my wife isn't impressed with . . . is the fact that I haven't finished decorating the front room.'

CHAPTER 24

Dodgy Substances

Despite the seriousness of the drug problem, I have to admit that ruthlessly seeking out those involved in obtaining these pernicious substances never really grabbed my attention.

My expertise in and knowledge of such matters was nil; and the small number of arrests I made were mainly due, I think, to my stumbling over them. As an aid to CID I had a fight with someone I stopped in the street; why he'd put up such a struggle I had no idea until I got him to the nick, when he produced a phial of diamorphine which he'd stolen from his dentist's surgery the previous day.

'I don't know how you knew I'd done it,' he said, 'but you obviously did!'

And when three packets of cannabis and a jar containing sixty-nine sugar cubes impregnated with LSD were chucked out of the window of a high-rise block of flats, it wasn't me who caught them; I was still fruitlessly hammering on the flat's front door. One unusual arrest I made was for possessing opium; but it was a miniscule amount and hardly headline-making news.

Something that really pissed me off was when I was patrolling with another aid and, just by chance, we spotted a youngster doling out cannabis to two others in the street. They were nabbed, and it transpired that the extremely cocky dealer, who was just sixteen, had been supplying cannabis to quite a few of his schoolmates. He lived with his respectable parents in an affluent area; we took him home and when we went to search his room, pinned on the door was a notice which read 'F–CK OFF!' In place of the missing 'U' two rudely extended fingers had been drawn. I looked at the boy's father and raised my eyebrows; he simply, helplessly, shrugged his shoulders.

The matter was submitted to the Juvenile Bureau and I looked forward to summonses being issued so that hopefully, following his court appearance, three months in a detention centre would knock some of the cockiness out of this little shit.

When nothing happened, I sought out the elderly police constable dealing with the case at Juvenile Bureau. What a no-hoper he looked; he wore a green shirt and a paisley foulard tie, which were all the rage at that time, but these fashion accessories were complementing the post-war demob suit which he was still wearing.

I asked why I hadn't received the summonses and was furious and shocked to hear that the lad had received a caution.

'A caution?!' I shouted. 'What the hell for? That little bastard should be in court!'

He had the grace to look uncomfortable. 'Well, you see, his father's a bank manager . . .'

'A bank manager? So fucking WHAT!'

'And . . . and because he comes from a respectable family, we thought they could . . . you know . . . keep him on the straight and narrow . . . he's never been in trouble before . . . actually, it wasn't my decision . . . ' He trailed off.

'Keep him on the straight and narrow?' I echoed. 'Did you pay a visit to his room on your home visit? Did you see the sign on his door?'

The Juvenile Bureau officer simply studied his shoes before muttering, 'Well, it's done now', and then spotting my curled lip, he scurried away.

I only hope that whatever emolument he received for his helpfulness, it went towards updating his wardrobe.

That apart, I did think the whole matter of drugs was such a seedy business. There were rumours circulating that when some police officers made a seizure of a significant amount of drugs, a portion would be confiscated. The dealer would not be dismayed; a smaller amount of drugs could only result in a reduction of his sentence. But then the balance of the stash – or part of it – would be given to the informant as payment; and since the snout was inevitably a dealer himself, not only did it get one of the competition out of the way, it materially improved his own stock of drugs, plus of course the profits therefrom. The very thought of trading in the deadly stuff with some seedy dealer – being in fief with garbage like that, quite apart from the illegality of the operation – made me feel physically sick.

Just as bad was when cannabis which should have been destroyed following a seizure, wasn't; instead, it was recycled and sold on to a dealer by an unprincipled cop. This was done by a detective constable I knew; previously unaware of his venality, I had personally thought that he was quite a decent bloke. A judge at the Old Bailey disagreed with my character analysis of him and packed him off to quod for seven years.

Worse was when rogue cops searched a dealer's address and simply stole his profits, working on the assumption that he could hardly complain to the police. One particular officer, thinking that betrayal might be a possibility, allegedly told the dealer, 'One word out of you and I'll come back and murder your kids!'

But to be fair, there were officers who staffed the Yard's Drugs Squad, plus those ad hoc drugs units on division, who did an excellent job, honestly carried out, to curtail these pernicious activities.

I'd have been happy to have passed on to them the information that, from time to time during my career, was imparted to me, if it was of any use – 'The word is, Mr K, there's a kilo coming in – I'll keep me ear to the ground!' But despite the snout's diligent eavesdropping, whatever 'the kilo' consisted of – cannabis, heroin or sawdust – it never materialized.

Which brings me on to the organization Release, formed in 1967 and given charitable status in 1972 after being reviewed by the Rowntree Foundation (who fund research into solving poverty in the United Kingdom) and supported from the 1970s by a Home Office grant.

Briefly, their remit was to assist drug offenders to get bail and to instruct solicitors, and a 24-hour helpline was made available for them to do so. Their efforts were applauded and supported by Beatles George Harrison (who donated £5,000) and John Lennon; so on the face of things, it was a laudable organization for those who contravened the parameters of the Dangerous Drugs Act, 1971 and wanted fair treatment for their transgressions.

'Fair treatment' became a little questionable when, in the late 1970s at Acton, two kilos of cannabis resin were seized; and since this amount was far in excess of that for personal use, the person concerned was charged with possession with intent to supply. Opting for trial by jury, the man pleaded not guilty at the Crown Court, and Release provided someone said to be an expert defence witness. He gave a fascinating peroration to the jury, describing the different types of resin and their sources in the producing countries, adding that this was something, of course, that the Metropolitan Police Forensic Science Laboratory failed to touch on.

He then blithely added that it was becoming quite common to purchase in bulk for one's personal use and, indeed, Release were seeing more and more of this trend . . . however, when he was asked to describe the level of investment in this particular quantity, there was a sharp intake of breath from the jury as he was obliged to admit it was in the region of £2,500. That was a hefty lump of dough well over forty years ago – of course, it still is – and the jury took very little time in finding the defendant well and truly guilty.

My one and only encounter with Release was about the same time as the Acton episode. I was running a 'Q'-Car and received information as to the whereabouts of a person wanted for drugs offences. He had been charged with possessing cannabis, had failed to appear at court and a warrant for his arrest had been issued. This, of course, was typical 'Q'-Car fare: a quick in-and-out arrest with the minimum of fuss.

I arrested him in a seedy squat, where others of his ilk were staying. It was an extremely peaceful arrest; I told him who I was and why he was being arrested.

'Oh, right', he said. 'I forgot', and with that I took him to the police station, which was no more than a ten-minute drive away. Taking him into the charge room, I informed the station officer of the details of the charge, whereupon he told me that a phone call had been received for me from a detective superintendent from CIB2 – the Police Complaints Department.

When I phoned that officer, he informed me that a complaint had been lodged against me in respect of this arrest by Release. I asked for details of my malefactions and he told me there weren't any.

'Just forget about it,' he said. 'Release are always doing this – as soon as an addict is arrested, they make a complaint. It's so that if the person arrested does decide to make a complaint later on, they can say that they facilitated it by making the complaint on his behalf at the earliest possible opportunity.'

Helpfully, he added, 'It's all a load of bollocks' – and these were sentiments with which I thoroughly concurred.

CHAPTER 25

A Little Bit of Blarney

I think that running a crime squad with its collection of young hopefuls, eager to become as famous – and as successful – as Fabian of the Yard, was very similar to an exacting physical workout in the gym.

There were the potential no-hopers: lazy, wanting to just drift along, happy to participate in whatever case came up and reap any plaudits that might arise from it, before slipping back into indolence. They were useful for developing my back and shoulder muscles as I pushed them forwards, but not for long. They were also given a short sharp warning: 'Shape up or ship out!'

Then there were those responsible for honing my biceps to perfection as I held them back: wild, impetuous young men and women, eager to get to grips with the underworld but going about it in a rather reckless fashion.

And then there were some who could be referred to as 'naturals': those who needed little advice or supervision, who knew what they were doing and where they were going. One officer who fitted the mould was Police Constable 334 'NH' Ian Chiverton. From the outset, 'Chiv' (as he'll be referred to in this narrative) made it quite clear that he wished to be a career CID officer. Did I have much to do with his career? Well, probably not. Of course, I expect I chamfered off the odd rough edge or two (as I did with other hopefuls' personalities), but Chiv needed little tutoring when it came to feeling collars. By the time I left the 'N' Division Crime Squad in 1985 to return to the Flying Squad, Chiv was well on the way to securing his goal. Posted to Holborn police station in 1986 as a detective constable, he passed the examination for sergeant in the top hundred. This meant an opportunity for accelerated promotion, plus a return to uniform duties. In what he later referred to as 'a tumbleweed moment', Chiv informed the interviewers of his career intention; it cost him four years' seniority, because he did not become a detective sergeant until 1991.

But whilst Chiv had been serving at Holborn, there had been a conspiracy to rob at the Sir John Soane's Museum, Lincoln's Inn Fields. On 9 February 1987 a number of men, led by 26-year-old

Dennis Bergin – he also liked to be known as Dennis Regan – who was armed with a sawn-off shotgun, decided to relieve the museum of two paintings by J.M.W. Turner, another by Canaletto and the eight canvases which made up William Hogarth's series of 'A Rake's Progress'.

But police – their numbers included Chiv – had been alerted and staked out the museum; and when Bergin burst in, roaring threats as he brandished his firearm, he was shot dead. The others fled, and 22-year-old Dereck Smith was shot in the shoulder, which failed to stop him changing jackets and running off. Chiv gave chase, jumped on Smith and arrested him. Five men (including Bergin's 24-year-old brother, George) appeared handcuffed at Clerkenwell Magistrates' Court – a sixth man, later interviewed – ahem! – was released, but whenever a piece of gun-toting slime is shot by police, there is the usual hysterical outcry. This occasion was no different.

Sorrowfully referred to by 'Mad Frankie' Fraser as 'Poor Dennis', Bergin's shooting raised the ire of Labour MP for Holborn, Frank Dobson, who bellowed that he was 'shocked', adding that 'police are loafing around with guns far too much.'

Walter Easey, the police policy advisor to the Association of London Authorities for whom the police were a favourite target, roared, 'Arming gun-crazy cops and telling them to shoot on sight is no solution to a democratic society', and Islington Council's Trevor Jones accused the police of being 'trigger-happy'.

Everyone appeared to forget that Bergin, a career criminal about to commit a multi-million pound robbery, had been screaming threats at police as he wielded a loaded sawn-off shotgun – even though it was later alleged at the inquest that the weapon couldn't be fired. But there you are; the dangerous prime mover was dead, his associates went off to collect sixty-six years' imprisonment and there was a memento of the incident: a bullet hole in the entrance to the museum.

By 1988 Chiv's new boss at Holborn was Detective Chief Inspector Steve McCusker – we'd worked together on the Serious Crime Squad and had been commended by the commissioner, the trial Judge at the Old Bailey and the Director of Public Prosecutions for our input into 'The Hungarian Circle' investigation – and Steve was a very reliable officer who was able to impart both good and bad – perhaps not so bad – news to Chiv.

Through no fault of his own, Chiv was one of several Crime Squad officers who, after I left 'N' Division, had become involved in a serious complaint, the investigation of which had dragged on for over three years.

So there were two matters that Steve McCusker wished to bring to Chiv's attention.

'Ian, I've got some good news and some bad news; what do you want first?'

'Well, I'll take a seat, Boss', replied Chiv, 'and have the bad news first.'

Referring to the complaint, McCusker said, 'You've been recommended for dismissal.'

As Chiv's mouth dropped open, seeing his career as a detective in tatters, McCusker continued, 'But don't worry. The outgoing CIB Commander[1] has altered it to "words of advice", based on your exemplary career. You have to attend North-West Headquarters for words of advice from the Deputy Assistant Commissioner in respect of a complaint arising from the arrest of someone committing an armed robbery at an off-licence.'

Once Chiv's heartbeat had returned to normal, he asked, 'And the good news, Boss?'

'You've been recommended for a DAC's commendation for bravery and professionalism in arresting one of the robbers at St John Soane's museum.'

Chiv was married with a 3-year-old son and another child on the way, and with nine years service under his belt, he now arrived at Vine Street police station in London's West End as a detective constable.

There were probably another dozen, older detectives in the CID office; it could be that they regarded Chiv as being 'a bit flash' and wanted to know, 'Who's this boy detective?'

They soon found out, as I did. A soupçon of impetuosity had crept into Chiv's persona.

★   ★   ★

Roelant Savery was a well-thought-of painter; and when he was thirty-four years of age, in 1610, he painted *Peasants Dancing outside a Bohemian Inn*. Measuring 47cm x 61cm and valued at £350,000, it was purchased by Willem, Baron van Dedem in London on 21 May 1977, but for some unaccountable reason it was being displayed in the window of an antique dealer in Old Bond Street.

---

1 This was Perry Richard Nove CBE, QPM, who had just left the Met to become Commissioner of the City of London Police

Someone took a liking to it, because one afternoon in 1989 there was a smash and grab at the shop and the painting vanished. There was no evidence from CCTV, no witnesses, no marks at the scene – just a missing painting and an entry in Vine Street's crime book – and the case was allocated to Chiv.

A loss adjuster named Mark Robert Lennox Dalrymple was appointed and he liaised with Chiv. They agreed that a circulation should be made through *Trace Magazine*, which dealt with art and antiques, offering a reward of £15,000 for the painting's return.

Loss adjuster and 'tec discussed the possibility of carrying out a sting operation, which would require an undercover officer from the Yard's SO10 Department; suitable equipment was fitted to Dalrymple's telephone, and an introduction effected between him and a UC officer.

But when the bait was taken from the entry in *Trace Magazine* and a telephone call was made, the caller – with a marked Irish accent and wishing to be known as Liam – refused to speak to anyone other than Mark Dalrymple. Therefore a deal was set up; the French, who are a very practical people and also have a name for everything, refer to such an arrangement as *récompense proportionelle*.

It was decided to hand over £15,000 in £20 notes as an act of good faith in exchange for the very distinctive circular frame which encased the painting, after which Liam would turn up with the actual canvas.

Not knowing Liam's true identity or his address, this seemed to me a very unhappy state of affairs; in those circumstances would I have gone ahead with it? Probably not, and if I had, it would have been with profound misgivings.

'A risky strategy,' admitted Chiv to me, 'but nothing ventured, nothing gained . . . and we were told the painting's owner would pay any compensation.'

'I never saw this in print,' he added, 'but I just wanted to progress the job!'

Chiv collected the money from the Yard's imprest (special fund) and noted the serial numbers of the notes; the decision had been made not to dye the currency or fit a tracking device into the bag.

As Chiv related these arrangements to me, I found my original reservations about the scenario becoming graver, although more was to come.

Liam duly arrived at the Sandys Row office of the loss adjusters and handed over the painting's frame; in return he received the bag containing £15,000. And as Chiv sat and waited in a back office, Liam left, considerably better off than when he had arrived.

Mind you, Liam was not having it all his own way; the Yard's machinery was now in operation.

★ ★ ★

At the end of the 4th floor, Victoria Block, at the Yard, was the 'Confi Section', where telephone interceptions were noted and disseminated to interested parties. Next door to it was a room known as 'Central 500', which was part of C11 (or the Criminal Intelligence Department). Central 500 was now active; it was used in cases such as kidnapping and extortion and it had a huge range of equipment, including CCTV screens, plus very up-to-date radio communications. The officer in charge was referred to as 'Gold'; in this case, it was Detective Superintendent John Beadle, whom I recalled as a very active Flying Squad detective sergeant. With the information that had been received about Liam, it was decided to mount an armed operation involving three agencies: the Regional Crime Squad (RCS), the C11 Surveillance team and – because the loss adjuster's office was situated within the boundaries of the City of London police force – officers from there as well.

The officer in charge was Detective Sergeant Jim Dickie from No. 9 RCS. He told me:

> Attempts were made to source a SFO (Specialist Firearms Officers) team, but none were available due to other jobs. The number of SFOs in those days was much smaller than today. Back then, only one or two of the C11 team were armed for self-protection. The same for the RCS team. I was an AFO (Authorized Firearms Officer); there would have been one or two others. A request was made to the City of London for an SFO team, which was placed on standby. Then the fun started, getting up at silly o'clock and deploying on the suspect. We were given the run-around. He was clearly surveillance aware and knew South London very well.

But before Liam left the loss adjuster's office he had been told to photograph the painting next to a copy of that day's newspaper, as proof that it was in his possession. To me, that would have made good sense, had the money not already been paid over to him. Well, there you have it.

Jim Dickie was driving his own car, a 2-litre Ford Sierra which had been fitted with a Home Office National RCS set – the City of London inspector who accompanied Jim could use this communicate with his colleagues in their cars – as well as having a Met main set tuned to Channel 7 in order to keep in contact with Central 500.

Liam was followed to the Rotherhithe area of Surrey Quays and was seen to enter a block of flats. The surveillance team deployed around the block, with one of them going to the rear.

He later returned, telling the others, 'He's on the fifth floor, seventh window on the right.'

This was pretty amazing stuff, and he was asked, 'How can you be sure?'

'Saw the flash of the camera when he took the photo, didn't I?' he laconically replied, and he was right – but the surveillance team would have expected nothing less from a former member of 14 Intelligence and Security Company.[2]

Liam stayed in the flat for most of the afternoon, before leaving and being seen digging in the ground near his address – but the surveillance team were too far away to observe exactly what was happening. From there he went to Bermondsey and then, in those crowded streets, he was lost to view . . .

But eventually the painting was recovered by the C11 team, and as Liam went to the loss adjusters he was arrested on the pavement outside by Jim Dickie and the City of London inspector and charged with handling stolen goods. In the fullness of time, Liam appeared before an especially benevolent judge at Southwark Crown Court who placed him on probation for two years; but the most rigorous of searches had failed to discover the whereabouts of the money . . .

★   ★   ★

Gerry O'Donoghue was Chiv's detective chief inspector at Vine Street. A compassionate Guv'nor and a keen boxing fan, who commiserated with Chiv when in the finals of the Lafone Cup he lost his bout and his chance of winning as a light-heavyweight, he had nevertheless pointed out to Chiv, 'Ian, if you lose that fifteen grand you'll be writing reports for the rest of your service' – and as Chiv told me, 'He meant it!'

Chiv had always exhibited perspicacity in large quantities; he did so now. Liam had a telephone in his flat, and Chiv checked out the calls he had made on the day that he was followed

---

2 Known as '14th Int', this secret unit of the British Army kept clandestine tabs on Northern Ireland's terrorist groups and was sometimes responsible for sowing a little dissention in their ranks as well.

there, plus one day either side. Two calls had been made to the Bermondsey area, and they were investigated.

What he discovered was an address in an old Greater London Council block of flats in Bermondsey, and Chiv knocked on the door.

Chiv was a Londoner, although he had recently spent a considerable amount of time with those two stalwarts from the Emerald Isle, Steve McCusker and Gerry O'Donoghue. He had assimilated their accents and now, addressing the 70-year-old lady who answered his knock, he spoke to her thus: 'I'm heer fer Liam. He tole me to colleckt a packidge.'

It was not the most convincing of brogues, but Chiv hoped that in the event of his authenticity being challenged, he might pass himself off as one of the 180 inhabitants of Inisbofin, a tiny island off the west coast of Ireland, or perhaps Clare Island whose population was even smaller; there might be a disparity between those accents and the ones used in Wicklow or Limerick.

But Chiv's bona fides were accepted without reservation, and the presence of the woman police constable in full uniform, who was tucked out of the way at the end of the balcony in case the flat's occupant screamed the place down, was superfluous. Ushering Chiv into the living room, the lady handed him the plastic bag left with her by Liam for safekeeping. It was later discovered that it contained £14,980; Liam had removed one of the £20 notes to check its authenticity.

After that, matters went swimmingly. The delighted owner of the painting (which in September 2002 he donated to a museum in The Hague) demanded Chiv's attendance at the prestigious Buck's Club, as well as taking Chiv, Gerry O'Donoghue, Mark Dalrymple and their wives to a swanky fish restaurant in Jermyn Street. The loss adjusters pointed two cases of 12-year-old Johnnie Walker in the direction of the surveillance team.

Chiv never returned to uniform and completed his career as the detective superintendent at the Detective Training School – now renamed the Crime Academy. It was a win-win situation; Chiv had realized his career dream, and the instructors and the pupils benefitted from his wide-ranging experience of how proper coppering should be carried out.

CHAPTER 26

The Old Pals' Club

For all my faults – and my detractors will say they're many – one of my virtues is that I am reliable. If I say I'll do something, I'll adhere to the promise; but if something unforeseen crops up, I'll let the interested party know at the earliest opportunity that I can't fulfil my pledge, and say why.

I don't therefore have any time for people who are unreliable, but someone who doesn't fit that bill is fellow ReCIDivist, Mike Bucknole.

If Mike says, 'I'll get that done by the weekend', you can rest assured that, as the sweep-second hand of your watch passes twelve and Sunday vanishes to become Monday, whatever it is that Mike has promised to undertake, it's been done.

Mike had a tremendous career, running successful Crime Squads on 'S' & 'Q' Divisions as well as with the Regional Crime Squad and the Flying Squad. It was whilst he was serving on the Flying Squad with the legendary Ray Wood that they received information about two armed robbers whose arrest, Mike was convinced, would result in one of the biggest breakthroughs into the activities of South London robbery teams.

Since Mike and Ray were working in North London and the two villains lived in Kent, the head of the Flying Squad – a person with rather limited vision – was reluctant to permit the officers to go swanning around the Garden of England; but Mike was insistent that he was right. He and Ray went ahead and arrested three, not two armed robbers; all of them turned supergrass, and between the three of them they confessed to a total of 315 offences and named 198 criminals who had committed a total of 640 major crimes.

It was Mike's insistence on 'getting things done' that stood him in good stead when he was called in to help investigate a very grisly murder.

★　★　★

In the 1970s there was a sudden upsurge in the number of gay clubs in London. The first was Fangs, situated underneath a Paddington hotel, which opened in 1975. The next year, it was followed by Bang in Charing Cross Road, Shane's in West Hampstead and The Catacombs in Earl's Court. When The Embassy Club opened in Old Bond Street in 1978 it was described as 'like being in a Hollywood movie with everyone wanting to be the star'.

Gays, lesbians, cross-dressers and those who were 'not too sure' about their sexuality flocked to London to visit these clubs, of which the latest in that era was Heaven, which opened in 1979. It was situated underneath the railway arches at Charing Cross station, and soberly dressed businessmen entered the establishment, soon to reappear in flowing garments more suited to the whims and desires of the rest of the habitués. It had its detractors – the *News of the World* dubbed Heaven as being 'more like hell' – but the nightclub prospered. With a capacity of 1,800, it was set on two main floors where, it proclaimed, 'Bitches become Witches' and a band worryingly named 'Throbbing Gristle' performed, as did a number of popular singers, including Cher. It was packed to bursting point, and in those confined surroundings the clientele could excitedly and passionately indulge in jolly social intercourse.

But two floors down, intercourse of a different variety was being discussed; in the area known as Hell, rent boys plied their trade and were greedily snapped up by those of a similar persuasion to themselves for a little homosexual fun. One person desirous of such company was a clerical administrator to the transport division of the Department of the Environment named George Francis Clune, who met up with a certain David Oren.

Born in South Shields, 26-year-old Oren's criminal activities had been of interest to the authorities for the previous ten years, and he had spent three years of his life in the Reeperbahn district of Hamburg. At 930 metres in length, it's not really accurate to refer to the Reeperbahn as *Die sündigste Meile* ('The most sinful mile'), because it's only half that length; but without doubt, at one time, with bars and brothels which catered for both sexes, it had the reputation of being the sleaziest, most depraved area of Hamburg's St Pauli district.

Whether the unfortunate Mr Clune was ever apprised of his companion's unimpeachable Teutonic references will never be known; but having taken David Oren back to his flat at Highfield Avenue in the leafy suburb of Golders Green in mid-March 1981, that was the end of George Clune.

Initially, his disappearance was treated by police as a missing person enquiry; two of his work colleagues were concerned because he had been absent from the office for six days.

It was not until 24 March that police broke into George Clune's flat, to find his partially-clothed and lifeless body concealed under his bed. It was – if you'll excuse a rather sweeping generalization – a typical queer's murder.

The attack had been frenzied. It was estimated that Clune had died 3–6 days earlier, and the cause of death was asphyxia; he had been manually strangled (the perpetrator using his left hand), fracturing the hyoid bone in his throat, but there was much more. The deep ligature mark on his throat had probably been caused by a TV aerial wire which had been found draped over his body. There were extensive head injuries, fractures to the nose and mouth and multiple bruising to the body, the result of kicks and punches. He had been stabbed (two bloodstained knives were found), and there were burn marks on Clune's back. These had been caused by an electric iron; they had been administered after death.

Clune's credit cards, cash and valuables were missing, and of Oren there was no sign, but he had left his calling card in innumerable blood-stained fingerprints everywhere, including on the two knives and the iron.

Mike Bucknole was the detective sergeant in charge of the 'S' Division Crime Squad; he was co-opted onto the murder investigation team.

Much of Mike's time was spent at Heaven, in an effort to trace Oren and his associates.

'I had a couple of snouts to help me . . . well, not actual snouts, more like helpers,' he told me. 'I repaid them with a box of chocs.'

My eyebrows were superciliously raised. 'Helpers?' I queried.

'They were both as straight as a die!' snapped Mike, taking umbrage at my implied question, but he refused to expand on precisely how his helpers acquired their information.

Sources of information were sacrosanct to a detective, and even forty years after the event, Mike adhered to his principles. However, there was no doubt it was impressive intelligence which, before the days of police computers, had to be fed into the murder squad's index cards before being cross-referenced. It was in this fashion that Mike discovered Oren's past addresses, including his association with Hamburg's 'sinful mile'.

Within a few days information was received from one of Clune's credit card companies that a transaction had been made using one of the stolen cards. A ticket had been purchased for a ferry crossing from Harwich to the Hook of Holland. Could it be that Oren was going on to Hamburg? mused Mike. Why not a direct sailing to Hamburg? Because Harwich ferries didn't sail to

Hamburg, that's why, and now Mike was certain that Hamburg would be Oren's ultimate destination. However, that was a hunch – admittedly a good one – but nothing more.

So – what to do? Mike's solution was immediately apparent. Initiate 'The Old Pal's Act', that's what. And to those who utilized that splendid piece of freemasonry between coppers everywhere – as I did, on a regular basis – what follows will bring a nostalgic smile to your faces. For today's cops who never have (and now never will) availed themselves of that wonderful lump of extra-curricular policing, stand by to be educated. But before I do so, I have to point out the official way of dealing with enquiries in respect of police forces other than those situated in the United Kingdom.

★ ★ ★

In 1923, the International Criminal Police Organization (Interpol) was set up in Rue Paul Valéry, Paris, its aim being to provide international assistance to police forces battling crime all over the civilized world. Its present budget of €142 million is funded mainly by the 194 member countries. However, one of Interpol's presidents was recently found guilty of corruption and then another was arrested for bribery; during his enforced absence, the Russian vice-president took over the reins. It was later revealed that he was irregularly issuing arrest notices to target critics of the Russian government. It may be felt from these revelations that Interpol was a bit of a dog's breakfast; and if you were to come to that conclusion, I would not seek to dissuade you.

Because, you see, long before those peccadilloes were disclosed, working cops had a healthy contempt for Interpol; officers posted to their branch at Scotland Yard spent their days shuffling paper. Requests were made, received, docketed and dealt with whenever. Using their services, I once made a request for the ownership details of a car registered in Milan. It took four months to get a reply. It appeared to many that Interpol was a sort of palliative centre inhabited by the sick, the lame and the dying. Despite the frantic efforts of ITV in their frankly imbecilic television series, *Interpol Calling!* which droned on for thirty-nine mind-rotting episodes to reassure viewers that with Inspector Paul Duval (the actor Charles Korvin) on the case, 'international criminals are on the run', the fact was that not only did Interpol detectives not make arrests, they were seldom fired with enthusiasm.

So should Interpol be troubled with Mike Bucknole's hunch? Well – no. Better not.

Many of us detectives of that era had spent time working with police forces in Europe; we had also greeted their representatives when they came to the UK to carry out their enquiries. Friendships developed, we were welcomed into each other's homes, and Mrs Kirby was frankly astonished at the great hubbub of languages from the Dutch, German, Swiss and French visitors around her dining table. And therefore, when assistance was required, it took the simple expedient of lifting up a telephone to speak to Hans, Walter or Jean-Louis and 'get things done'.

So, invoking The Old Pal's Act, Mike telephoned Horst Bergmann, a member of Cologne's *Kriminalpolizei* with whom he had successfully worked, both at home and abroad, in cases involving currency, drugs and not a few stolen Mercedes. Bergmann's judgement could be trusted implicitly.

'To go through Interpol procedures would take many days of negotiation through the Home Office, countless reports and bureaucracy in both countries,' Mike explained to me, although really he was preaching to the converted. 'We decided, in the interests of expediency to bite the bullet, take the consequences of upsetting "the paper tigers" – and go for it.'

Mike's reasoning was absolutely right. Every minute that ticked by meant a dangerous criminal was still on the loose; and that was how David Oren came to be circulated as being wanted for murder on the German police system.

The very next day, Mike intended to visit Heaven late into the night in order to trace Oren's associates, so at 10 o'clock in the morning he was still at home. He suddenly received an emotionally charged telephone call from the murder squad's office manager:

'Where the fuck are you? The German Old Bill keep phoning the office and won't speak to anyone but you!'

Arriving at the office, Mike dialled the number of the headquarters of criminal investigations at Oldenburg in north-west Germany.

The officer in charge told him, 'Commander Bucknole? We have your prisoner for murder in custody here. He was caught by a patrol officer crossing the border between the Netherlands and Germany. Will you come and get him?'

Well, that was a turn-up for the books! Horst, knowing of the possible implications, had told Oldenburg not to speak to anybody but Mike and had impressed upon them his suddenly elevated rank of 'commander'.

With Oren in custody, steps had to be taken to get him back; and the first step was for Mike to inform his officer in charge, Detective Chief Superintendent Reg Dixon. This was not a happy thought.

*   *   *

Reg Dixon was a career detective with a terrific reputation, having served on the Flying Squad and the Regional Crime Squad. As a detective inspector, he had been part of the Wembley Robbery Squad who had utilized the services of one Derek Creighton Smalls (known to his fast-diminishing number of friends as 'Bertie') to become a prolific supergrass. Promoted to chief inspector, Reg was highly commended by the commissioner for his daring work as an undercover officer which resulted in the arrest of four dangerous armed criminals. I knew Reg as a detective superintendent on the Serious Crime Squad, but not for long; he was whisked away to assist on a silver bullion robbery enquiry which was being investigated by his chums on the Flying Squad.

But apart from having a well-deserved reputation as a thief-taker, Reg also had a head for the practicalities of police work. When a chief inspector was told to investigate a scurrilous complaint made against a team of Flying Squad officers, he cried, 'I can't carry out this investigation, sir – I know one of the officers – he's a friend of mine!'

Reg's response was, 'All the more fucking reason for you to fucking well do it then!'

He possessed an explosive temper, and if his sentences contained fewer than two expletives, his subordinates worried in case Reg had suddenly found God! The only person I ever met who could beat Reg for profanity was Terry Crawley of 21 SAS, who was known as 'Fuckin' 'ell Tell'; he and Reg would have got on like a house on fire!

So Mike expected an ear-bashing from Reg, who did not disappoint him – but the focus of his invective-laden tirade was not that Mike had driven a horse and cart through the regulations. In fact, he thought that Mike's actions were praiseworthy; his annoyance stemmed from the fact that Mike hadn't informed him sooner!

Sensing approval of his actions, Mike informed Reg that he spoke fluent German, had carried out many successful operations in Germany and fully understood German police expectations. Reg Dixon gave permission for Mike and Detective Chief Inspector

Roger Thomas to travel to Germany, but with a steely adieu: 'OK, Bucknole, but this had better finish in a good result!' However, this was typical Reg Dixon *faux* irascibility; in his later report to the Director of Public Prosecutions he described Mike as being 'the stalwart of any investigation'.

Mike acquired a *Commission Rogatoire* (a letter requesting help and judicial assistance for the British police from the German authorities) and prior to their flight taking off, he delayed matters by taking a mysterious trip to the Yard and Lambeth stores to collect some unknown although essential items for the investigation.

Some fifteen minutes after take-off, Mike asked DCI Thomas if they were indeed en route to Hamburg and unlikely to turn back, and having had it confirmed that was the case, Mike confessed that the German version of the *Commission Rogatoire* had been typed by his German neighbour, which was just as well because he spoke not one word of the language. However, he added to his very annoyed chief inspector, more in hope than expectation, that all the German police spoke perfect English.

Met by the Oldenburg officers, DCI Thomas stated that he wished to be taken to the prison holding Oren, so that he could interview him immediately. No, replied one of the officers, first you must meet our boss at headquarters so that he can instruct your investigations. He then surreptitiously winked at Mike, who smiled back at him – he knew exactly what was going on. Taken to the top floor of the police headquarters, the two English officers entered a room to find some forty uniform and plain clothes officers inside.

Amidst rapturous applause, their chief cried, 'Welcome to our respected guests from New Scotland Yard!'

As they were directed to tables groaning under the weight of beer and buffet, Mike revealed the reason for the second part of his duplicitous trip prior to take-off and presented the Oldenburg police with a Metropolitan Police helmet, as well as badges and shields from the Metropolitan Police Athletic Association.

'I looked at Roger, who smiled and winked,' said Mike, 'so I knew I was safe from his wrath.'

In Oren's property a key and ticket for a left-luggage locker at Amsterdam Centraal railway station was found, and since items in those lockers are only kept for a short period of time, Roger Thomas left the following day to retrieve the contents; they turned out to be a holdall containing Oren's bloodstained clothing and a credit card belonging to the dead man.

In the meantime (although Thomas was furious when he found out), German regulations demanded that the prisoner should be interviewed without delay. The interview was conducted in both English and German (since Oren spoke the language fluently), with a full written transcript being recorded and translated. Mike obtained a written statement which amounted to a full confession from Oren, although, 'When speaking to him,' Mike told me, 'I found him to be cold and without any emotion or sentiment at all.'

Evidentially, the interview would not affect the investigation or the procedure in the English courts, so blood and forensic samples were obtained, and Thomas flew back with the samples in order to formulate the documentation necessary for Oren's extradition. Mike – with Reg Dixon's approval ('but don't make a fucking holiday of it!') – took the Red Line Hamburg–Altona Deutsche Bahn Express, travelling the 268 miles south to Cologne in order to personally thank Horst Bergmann for his utterly invaluable input into the case.

There were four other unsolved homosexual murders at that time, and their modus operandi bore a marked similarity to that of the unfortunate Mr Clune. Since Oren had known at least one of the victims, Mike and DCI Thomas questioned him, but Oren strenuously denied any involvement with the murders and, there being no corroborative evidence, the matter was dropped.

Oren was extradited some three weeks later and on 2 June 1982 he was eventually convicted at the Old Bailey for that grisly murder and sentenced to life imprisonment, with a recommendation that he serve not less than fifteen years. Commendations were awarded, one to WPC 442'S' Jenny Hounsell, a young, inexperienced officer who was first on the scene, who meticulously recorded every detail and thereafter carried out house-to-house enquires which were extremely helpful. Mike, too, was commended by the commissioner for exhibiting dedication and detective ability, although as he told me, 'No mention was ever made on paper of us circumventing Interpol protocol!'

But in recounting this tale to me, Mike voiced sentiments – shared by many of our generation of CID officers – which I commend to you now:

> In my humble opinion, the police in the UK and New Scotland Yard in particular at this time were held at home and abroad as a role model for excellence. Our system of CID training schools, experienced detectives showing youngsters how to promote and generate informants, how to cultivate good public relations by personally mixing with and speaking to people was paramount to their trust in us. The advent of advanced

computer communication, internet systems and social media-generated images has destroyed personal public interaction and the perception of the police role. Relying purely on technology, in my view, has degraded the excellence recognized both by the UK public and internationally, too. My reference to the German police reaction to our presence in Oldenburg by spontaneous applause upon our arrival was an example of their approval of our methods and work.

CHAPTER 27

The End of the Golden Age

When the death of that golden era came, I think it arrived at more or less the same time for my contemporaries as it did for me. I did my best to make it die as hard as possible, but disillusionment had already started in the mid-1980s with the arrival of the Police & Criminal Evidence Act, as well as the Crown Prosecution Service.

On the day before my departure for what would become an 18-month tenure in Northern Ireland, I was presented with my Long Service and Good Conduct Medal by Sir Peter Imbert, that much-admired Commissioner of Police, one who'd rolled his sleeves up and been a working detective during his 40-year career. By the time I returned to the mainland his place had been taken by Paul Condon, who could accurately be described as the first of the politically correct commissioners. On the eve of his departure from Kent Police, where he had been the chief constable, the Met apparently received a message from Condon's erstwhile force: 'For what you are about to receive, God help you.'

We can leave Condon for now; he'll resurface later. During my time in Northern Ireland I gave thought to the continuance of my career. By now I had served five years of my second tour with the Flying Squad, and although I had been placed on 'overhold' whilst I was in Ulster, it was because I had also been appointed a 'core officer', to serve a further five years following my return in order to instruct newcomers on the workings of the Flying Squad. But did I really want this? Certainly, I had enjoyed my time on the Squad, but now I was feeling perhaps a little jaded. There came the possibility of being part of a team investigating war crimes in Germany and Russia which sparked my interest, but that fell through. I enjoyed the type of work against terrorists that I was presently tasked with; could I find a slot with C13, the Anti-Terrorist Squad, upon my return? I was recommended for it, but no, afraid not. The Commander of that branch was someone with whom I'd had a fearful row some seven or eight years previously; I'd seen him several times since, and he'd made it quite clear that he'd neither forgiven nor forgotten me.

Then there appeared an application in *Police Orders* for detective constables and sergeants to join No. 9 Regional Crime Squad (RCS). Now, *this* was something right up my street. I'd been pencilled in to join the RCS just prior to being claimed once more by the Flying Squad; I knew a lot of the officers and, what was more, I knew the way they worked, because as a Serious Crime Squad officer, when I travelled all over the country to carry out enquiries or arrests, I had always liaised with the local RCS. They were a tough, well-informed bunch, and I admired them a lot.

So in went my application for the RCS, which was strongly supported by my senior officers – only to have it bounced.

This was due purely to the pasty-faced inhabitants of Personnel Department at the Yard, not police officers but civilians who'd never encountered an angry man in their lives. This was their response:

> Detective Sergeant Kirby will be aware (or he should be) that one cannot transfer in the same rank from one Specialist Operations Department to another. Furthermore, by consulting his record, over the past ten years of his service, eight of them have been spent on Specialist Operations and therefore, when he completes his present tenure in Northern Ireland, he will be transferred to divisional duties.

Well, it didn't matter what attributes I might be able to bring to the RCS or as a 'core officer' to the Flying Squad, I didn't fit the criteria of the workings of the establishment – the custodians of Scotland Yard had spoken!

Since I hadn't had a home posting for twenty years, that was what I asked for and that was what I got. It was just a few miles away from my home address; but as I discovered, that was the only good thing about it.

* * *

I had been pretty well sheltered from working in a CID office since 1975; since that time I'd been a Serious Crime Squad officer, and apart from that, plus two tours on the Flying Squad, I'd worked 'Q'-Cars and mostly run Crime Squads in which I was in charge of young uniform hopefuls wanting to become CID officers.

Now, sixteen years later, I discovered that things had changed considerably. Condon, the new commissioner, believed that every officer should be a Jack and Jill of all trades, and in swapping around people who were quite happy and competent in their respective jobs he managed to ensure that they became masters and mistresses of none. This was particularly the case with the CID, and the result was that the majority of the junior ranks had little idea of the workings of the Department, since many of their detective sergeants had a paucity of experience, having been brought in directly from the uniform department.

As a detective sergeant, I was given a team of detective constables and 'trainee investigators' (aids, to you and me) and I was to be a sort of administrator – someone to allocate crimes for them to investigate, ensure they kept their enquiries up to date, keep an eye on their expenses and an even sharper eye on their overtime. Points were awarded to each investigation, so that if low points were given to a high-value burglary for them to investigate one day, and a high number to identify the culprit in a bike theft the next day, they would be told to concentrate on the bike theft. All of these tasks were to be carried out with me safely ensconced behind a desk.

Of course, I couldn't work that way; I'd always led from the front, so if a blackmail or a sizeable theft was reported, I'd investigate it myself and take one of the junior ranks along to show them how it was done, which departments to call out, who to go to for technical assistance.

There seemed to be little enthusiasm amongst the sergeants, and few of them took pride in their work; the uniform made a good arrest of a little team who had smashed into a wall of a bank and ripped out the cash-dispensing machine. Everything was there: prisoners, the vehicle used and a scene chock-a-block with forensic evidence. But the detective sergeant who dealt with the investigation seemed apathetic; it appeared that any get-up-and-go that he might have possessed had got up and gone. Consequently, the prisoners had laughed at him when he tried to interview them, and when he quickly wrapped up the investigation (keeping well within the constraints of the overtime budget), I heard him say, 'Well, that's all I can do – if the CPS want to chuck it out, that's up to them.'

I was present when a detective sergeant was furiously castigated by a barrister who was prosecuting one of his cases because of the sergeant's utter incompetence. Aspects of the case which should have been routinely dealt with as a matter of course simply hadn't been covered. It was an embarrassing spectacle; but the barrister was absolutely right.

I saw one of the Trainee Investigators heading for the exit; he was moving in such a surreptitious manner that I called out to him, 'Oi! Where're you off to?'

'Oh, I've got a snout to meet, Sarge,' he replied and edged ever closer to the exit.

'Right, come over here,' I said, and the following conversation ensued.

'This snout of yours – is he registered?

'It's not a "he", it's a "she".'

'Is *she* registered, then?'

'Well . . . no.'

'OK – sit down and we'll get her registered.'

'Well . . . she's not really a snout, as such . . . actually she's my cousin.'

'Your *cousin*?'

'Not actually my cousin, so to speak . . . actually she's a girl I knew at school.'

'Right, now listen up. The next time you want to go off for an afternoon's shagging, you do it in your own time, understand? Now, get back to your desk and get on with a little police work – and if you haven't enough to occupy you, I can get you plenty more!'

I'd had my eye on him for some time; I'd come to the conclusion that he was a bit too smart for his own good, and I was right.

I heard a little later that he'd met up with an officer who was known to both of us.

'That fucking Kirby!' moaned the trainee investigator. 'He needs to get into the twentieth century!'

The officer, with whom I'd been involved in some ticklish situations, told him, 'When Dick Kirby speaks to you, you need to listen!'

It appears he didn't; after I'd left that office I heard that the young man had got involved in a very dodgy bit of business. I seem to recall it involved the opening of a bank account in a false name to facilitate a lady depositing money of dubious provenance, and I was very surprised that he didn't get his collar felt. However, when a small black cloud arrived over the nick, he left under it.

*   *   *

I collected an allegation of rape; except that it wasn't. A young woman had previously been the subject of a similar allegation. The man involved had been tried for that offence and had been acquitted. Now she stated that the same man had attacked her again and raped her – but by the time I arrived at her parents' address with a woman detective, she'd changed her mind, the rape had been reduced to an indecent assault and then to an assault with no indecency involved at all; he'd just punched her in the back. But all this information had been shrilly imparted to us, and matters were not helped by the woman detective, who had unreservedly accepted the young woman's fluctuating versions of events, excitedly informing her, 'Don't worry! This time, 'e'll get a sentence! 'E will – I swear it!'

Quickly replacing her with a less emotional and a more experienced female investigator, I arranged for the girl's back to be photographed and also examined by a Force Medical Examiner, while I interviewed a friend who was with her at the time of the alleged incident and who fully backed up her story. The man named as the perpetrator of the outrage was quickly traced and interviewed; but his alibi for the time of the incident appeared copper-bottomed and watertight. He was miles away at the time, and a number of reputable citizens confirmed his whereabouts.

Now if that man whom the girl and her witness had named as the perpetrator was innocent (and it seemed to me certain that he was), had there been an assault at all? I looked at the photograph; there were scratches not bruises on her back, and when I spoke to the examining doctor, he told me that he had no doubt that those scratches had been self-inflicted by the girl rubbing her back against a brick wall. And after I re-interviewed the alleged witness to the offence and wished to know if he fancied a trip to the Old Bailey, as a defendant rather than as a witness, he confessed that the whole thing had been a put-up job in order to incriminate the guiltless man. When the doctor's (and her erstwhile witness's) evidence was placed before the girl, she also admitted that the whole matter had been pure invention because 'she wanted to get her own back after the last time'.

After the girl pleaded guilty to the offence of attempting to pervert the course of public justice, the Judge at the Old Bailey placed her on probation and had some complimentary remarks to make about the investigation which had prevented an innocent man from being prosecuted. I mentioned that to the detective inspector in the office.

'Huh! Nobody ever put me up for a commendation,' he said, 'so I'm not going to do it for anyone, either!'

The civilian staff at the station were an eye-opener; then again, I'd been over-indulged in the past. The Flying Squad divisional office had been run by Joy Guest, an attractive, well-dressed woman married to a police officer. Hugely admired, she was a professional to her fingertips and performed her duties seamlessly; everything was in its place, nothing was too much trouble; the administration of the Flying Squad at the Yard and the four area offices worked like clockwork under her control.

The vision that greeted my eyes at this police station took the form of a junior clerk, dressed in matador pants, entering the CID office in her bare feet with an armful of files. She attempted to address the detective chief inspector, but with extreme difficulty since her speech was impaired by a Mars bar protruding from her mouth. It was rather like listening to Eliza Doolittle endeavouring, with a mouthful of marbles, to display her enhanced pronunciation to Professor Higgins.

It was the sort of place that I wanted to spend as little time in as possible. A lifeline – of a sort – came my way when I was sent for by a very senior officer, who was in an advanced state of panic.

I was told that a woman police officer had become unwisely involved with a local character with whom she'd had a child. Her partner had a car dealer's business and had accompanied her to various police functions, where he had met and socialized with a great many police officers, some of whom might well have then included the car dealer in their own social circle.

The woman officer and the dealer had had a tempestuous relationship; he had beaten her up on more than one occasion and now he had gone on the run, threatening to kill her and 'blow the whistle' on the local police.

I was informed that I was the only person who could successfully undertake this investigation (oh really!) and I was told that I could have whatever resources I needed: unlimited manpower, overtime and technical support were no problem at all.

Having made it clear that for the moment all I required was time and my usual guile and experience, I got to work; what I didn't need was a stream of extremely perturbed uniform and CID officers telling me out of the corner of their mouths that they hoped 'I'd sort things out' – precisely what it was that needed to be sorted out I never did discover. I managed to avoid any more similar entreaties; it was like being in the exercise yard at Brixton prison in the 1930s, where speaking out of the corner of the mouth was how the inmates tried to circumvent the 'no talking' rule.

Meanwhile, I spoke to the woman officer and, after a series of interviews, I gradually gained the impression that whatever misfortunes had befallen this couple, it appeared to be a case of 'six of one and half a dozen of the other'.

Nevertheless, it was undeniable that he had assaulted her, had threatened to kill her and was allegedly in possession of a firearm with which to carry out the dirty deed.

Where was the dealer? Thanks to the expertise of a constable who had formerly been a member of the Special Air Service Regiment and who carried out a clandestine nocturnal foray, it was quickly established that he was not at his address or his yard, so I did what I always did in those circumstances – put myself in the suspect's shoes. Where would I go? Who would I see? Who could help me? I compiled a list of names, addresses and telephone numbers and went through them one by one.

It wasn't too long before I discovered he had just left an address in south-west England and that in all probability he would return to London. I sat down with a large map, noted the time he'd left the area, guessed his average speed and the likeliest route he would take. I then had his home address staked out, contacted all of the constabularies he would probably pass through on his way to London, provided them with the dealer's name, description and details of his vehicle, stressed caution because he was likely to be armed, got a cup of coffee, sat down and waited.

The call came through late at night; the dealer had been stopped on a rolling roadblock by armed police in Dorset.

I stood up and yawned; it had been a long day.

'Bring him in and lock him up,' I said. 'I'm going home to get some kip; I'll see him in the morning.'

The following morning, freshly shaved and showered, in a smart suit with a good breakfast inside me, I arrived to interview the prisoner. It was a good psychological ploy, because the dealer was scruffy, unshaven and had just consumed a typical Metropolitan Police fried breakfast; he was therefore at a distinct disadvantage.

He was a very large gentleman with a ferocious temper and leapt to his feet as I opened the cell door; but remember, I had been raised on a diet of vicious armed robbers and more recently some of the toughest terrorists in Ulster, so I was unlikely to be fazed by a bellowing, blustering wife- (or rather, partner-) beater.

So I just stood there alone, not interrupting, saying nothing, whilst the prisoner screamed and roared and raved, mainly about the police officers he was going to take down with him. And after about ten minutes he ran out of steam and stood there panting, which is when I said to him, 'Right. Now, you listen to me, mister . . .'

Actually, I can't recall the discourse that followed, but I do know that it was sufficient for the bully to burst into tears, make a full and detailed confession to the assault and plead guilty in court. And the gun? The allegations of police misconduct? There wasn't one and there weren't any. He'd used those words to add lustre to his bluster and apologized for doing so.

In a very short space of time, unaided and without having to trouble any of the technical resources offered to me, I had managed – using as little of the overtime budget as necessary – to wrap up a very messy, sensitive case involving an assaulted woman member of the police, as well as to establish that undisclosed allegations of police malpractice were completely unsubstantiated.

Putting the finishing touches to my closing report to the senior officer who had assured me that 'I was the only officer who could deal with the case', I submitted it and received not one work of thanks. I didn't expect any. In fact, the matter was never referred to, again.

* * *

Now – let's pause for a moment. I've just read over what I've written in this chapter, and if you believe it's a vainglorious account of me purporting to be a one-man crime-buster – while it's understandable for you to think that – it's not true; and if that's the impression that was conveyed to you, I apologize.

It's not that I'm saying I was that good; it's just that standards had dropped so dramatically. What I was doing in this CID office was what my contemporaries and I had been doing for years. We were seasoned CID officers who had been taught by professionals; but now the workforce was riddled with officers who, thanks to piss-poor management and a chronic lack of leadership, were often totally unsuited to the work they were given. They had not been brought up with the commitment which had been instilled in us.

On the reverse side of the coin, there was a cadre of young men and women who were really switched on and who did display utter commitment to their work – in fact, at least two of them reached very high ranks – but they were in the minority.

But there was also the uniformed inspector who had suddenly been created a detective inspector. He was utterly clueless; he arrived in his office at 7.00am so that he could leave at 3.00pm – 'I like to get a bit of work done in the allotment before the light goes'! he said. As a uniformed inspector, when he finished his shift, whatever was left over was passed on to his successor on the following shift. But what he didn't realize was that in the CID you didn't keep regular hours and what you got you kept!

I received a telephone call from a detective chief inspector on No. 9 Regional Crime Squad who asked me if I fancied joining his unit.

'I'd love to, Guv'nor,' I replied, 'But I've already tried it and my application was blocked by personnel.'

'Dick,' he replied, using the tone of voice that kindly adults use when addressing a dim-witted child, 'when I want someone, I get 'em – understand? Leave it to me; have a good Christmas and I'll get back to you in the New Year.'

I arrested a bogus doctor – an American – and when it was discovered that in the space of two months out of 210 elderly patients in his care 40 had died, I was conscripted on to the No. 2 Area Major Investigation Team to assist in the enquiry.[1] Christmas came and went and I'd heard nothing, so I phoned up the DCI on the Regional.

'Sorry, Dick,' he apologized. 'It got blocked by personnel!'

The bogus doctor enquiry took me over four of the USA's southern states, but when I returned I had to escape from this lacklustre nick and I applied to join the newly formed National Criminal Intelligence Service (NCIS) as a Regional Intelligence Officer; and since this was a Home Office appointment instead of one emanating from Specialist Operations, personnel department didn't get a look-in and I was accepted.

It didn't last. I fell out with an acting detective inspector who was issuing more and more absurd and contradictory orders; what I didn't know – none of us did – was that he was suffering from the first stages of vascular dementia.

With that, the troublesome time I'd spent in Northern Ireland, the strains of being continuously 'up the sharp end' of policing for a quarter of a century and my disillusionment in the short time I'd spent at my last CID office finally caught up with me. I collapsed with chest pains at my desk at the Yard and was carted off to the Westminster Hospital, where it was initially thought – by me as well – that I'd suffered a heart attack. In fact, it was stress – and one of the doctors who examined me came to the conclusion that, to use an expression conferred upon many Victorian policemen, I was 'worn out'.

So for those reasons – plus the injuries I'd sustained in a car collision on the M25 – eleven months later, I was medically discharged from the police. For me, the Golden Age of policing

---

1 For further details of this investigation, see *The Real Sweeney*, Robinson Books, 2005

was over; in fact, by now – thanks to poor performances, the unsuitability of the personnel in senior ranks, the Police and Criminal Evidence Act and the CPS (dubbed 'Couldn't Prosecute Satan') which had dragged investigations and prosecutions to a snail's pace – the gold was rather tarnished.

Epilogue

In the days leading up to my retirement – and since then, as well – I reminisced about some of the cases in which I'd been involved. There were the big ones: the multi-million pound 'Hungarian Circle' investigation which had taken me to Germany and Switzerland, and the running of the Metropolitan Police's one and only 'double-supergrass'. But there were the quirky ones as well: the arrest of the Scotland Yard employee who had screwed the Flying Squad commander's safe, not once but several times; the robber who threatened to detonate dynamite in a building society unless he got some cash – the staff handed over the money, failing to appreciate that had the robber's (imaginary) dynamite exploded, he would have been the first of the casualties. Then there were the cigar boxes filled with plasticine into which were pressed impressions of keys for safety deposit boxes; the owner was one of London's top key men – in fact, since Leonard Wilde aka 'Johnny the Boche' was by then serving twenty years for his part in the Bank of America robbery, my prisoner was *the* top key man – and when he was interviewed, his legal representative was a former Flying Squad officer. I hope he was proud of himself.

What was rather disquieting were the cases which were important but where I couldn't remember the details. I arrested a fellow for possessing explosives, and I know that at Crown Court he pleaded not guilty but was convicted. But who he was, where he lived, how I came to arrest him, what evidence I gave and what the explosives were or whether he had detonated any of them, I simply can't remember.

There was a gang of robbers who used young prostitutes to lure their victims in. I was convinced that not only was Julie Hillman heavily involved in the investigation but also that she was commended for her work – but if she was, she couldn't remember it. The only aspect of the case that I can recall is when I walked into Snaresbrook Crown Court to give evidence in the case. The Judge, who had previously been a barrister with whom I had crossed swords in a bitterly contested robbery trial, cried out, 'Good heavens, members of the jury – it's Detective Sergeant Kirby!

Now we'll see some fireworks!' In fact, we did; and although the gang were convicted and sent to prison and I was given a glowing commendation by the Judge, any other aspects of the case have now vanished in the mists of time – a bit worrying, that.

There were recollections of violence in London's East End . . . the Glaswegian hard man who had broken a little girl's nose after she disturbed him drinking. At the end of a police cells' passageway he was told, 'If you can get past me, you'll be free to go.' One might think this a charitable offer, but not to the Gorbals Gladiator. Without a word, he stepped into a vacant cell and shut the door.

Or being called to a dump of a council flat, where the violent husband had treated his wife as a punchbag once too often. On this occasion he called upon his battered spouse for assistance, screaming, 'Don't leave me alone with him!'

I plundered the Yard's Informants' Fund on a regular basis to supplement the income of 'Rosie the Grass'. She left several husbands in her wake – her first received a long term of imprisonment after Rosie discovered he was screwing houses instead of her – and a string of discarded boyfriends as she rapidly tired of them. Collating their misdeeds, she'd say, 'Come and pick this bastard up, Dick; he's getting on my bleedin' nerves.' And this was the odd thing; none of her erstwhile lovers ever tumbled to the fact that Rosie was their betrayer. Even when she acted as a participating informant,[1] when her involvement might have been in excess of what was regarded as being proportionate, her boyfriends still didn't associate Rosie's presence with their arrest. In fact, following his sentence, one of the abandoned Lotharios arrived back at Rosie's hovel in the hope that he would be welcomed back once more into the embrace of her chubby arms. He was doomed to disappointment. Whatever fulfilment he had once brought to Rosie's loins was by now ancient history, and he was summarily dismissed.

There was so much more: the hair-raising car rides, the punch-ups and the companionship of the best men and women in what was then the world's greatest police force.

Killers, kidnappers, gangsters and grasses . . .

I had started and finished my career on a low note; but what adventures my contemporaries and I had in between.

---

1 A participating informant was permitted to take part in a crime, providing they took a minor role such as a lookout or getaway driver, in order to frustrate the crime and catch the main offenders. The guidelines were unfortunately not always rigidly adhered to.